POSTAL SAVINGS AND FISCAL INVESTMENT
IN JAPAN

Postal Savings and Fiscal Investment in Japan

The PSS and the FILP

THOMAS F. CARGILL

and

NAOYUKI YOSHINO

OXFORD

UNIVERSITY PRESS

*This book has been printed digitally and produced in a standard specification
in order to ensure its continuing availability*

OXFORD
UNIVERSITY PRESS

Great Clarendon Street, Oxford OX2 6DP

Oxford University Press is a department of the University of Oxford.
It furthers the University's objective of excellence in research, scholarship,
and education by publishing worldwide in

Oxford New York

Auckland Cape Town Dar es Salaam Hong Kong Karachi
Kuala Lumpur Madrid Melbourne Mexico City Nairobi
New Delhi Shanghai Taipei Toronto

With offices in

Argentina Austria Brazil Chile Czech Republic France Greece
Guatemala Hungary Italy Japan South Korea Poland Portugal
Singapore Switzerland Thailand Turkey Ukraine Vietnam

Oxford is a registered trade mark of Oxford University Press
in the UK and in certain other countries

Published in the United States
by Oxford University Press Inc., New York

ISBN 978-0-19-925734-8

Contents

Figures

Tables

Preface

Japan has experienced over a decade of economic and financial distress. Despite signs of a weak recovery in 2000, the economy was in recession by the end of 2001. The 1990s were characterized by stagnant or declining real GDP, gradual decline in the price level, insolvent financial institutions, nonperforming loans estimated to be 10 percent of GDP, and a series of policy failures on the part of the central bank and regulatory authorities. Japan has made significant attitudinal and institutional changes, especially near the end of the 1990s, but has yet to reverse the economic and financial distress of the past decade. The continued distress has been explained by several factors: the willingness of the Bank of Japan in the late 1990s to permit a gradual decline in the price level, by the failure of the Ministry of Finance and the Financial Services Agency to impose penalties on private banks and their borrowers to resolve the nonperforming loan problem, and the general unwillingness of policymakers to depart from the essential elements of the preliberalization financial regime that emphasized mutual support, nontransparency, and limited failures of financial institutions and markets. The explanation is most likely a combination of these and other factors.

There is no doubt Japan is at a turning point. Economic, political, and technological forces require modernization of the financial system if Japan wishes to remain a dynamic component of the world economy. In addition, Japan's population is projected to start declining within the next decade and the dependency ratio (number of nonworking to working population) is projected to increase significantly placing further pressure on raising the rate of return on the high level of Japanese saving.

This book reviews the role of government financial intermediation in Japan's postwar economy. Government financial intermediation is institutionalized by the Postal Savings System (PSS) and the Fiscal Investment and Loan Program (FILP), two institutions that have received little attention outside of Japan. Despite the lack of familiarity with these institutions by outside observers, they are the most visible manifestation of the old regime that characterized Japan's economy before liberalization became official policy in the late 1970s. The continued growth of these institutions through the 1990s provides the most visible manifestation of the unwillingness and/or difficulty of modernizing Japan's financial system. Reform has begun, however, and one can identify the emergence of new policies and recommendations for further change that has the potential to provide the basis for a modern, open, and competitive financial system. It would not be an exaggeration to suggest that how Japan reforms the PSS and the FILP will provide a leading indicator of whether Japan will finally modernize its economy and its financial system.

This book is the outcome of a collaboration between the authors that commenced in 1996 involving meetings in Tokyo; New York; Santa Cruz, California; and Reno, Nevada. The book has been supported by a grant from the Japan–US Friendship Commission (1997 and 1998) and funds provided by the Center of Excellence Project at Keio University. The Center of Excellence Project is supported by a grant from the Ministry of Science and Education. The Center of Excellence Project, titled the Asian Financial Crisis and its Macroeconomic Response, is a five-years project (1 April 1999 through 31 March 2004), focusing on macroeconomic, regulatory, foreign direct investment, and historical perspectives of the Asian Financial Crisis of 1997 and 1998. This book forms part of the regulatory component of the project.

Cargill and Yoshino both express appreciation to the Japan–US Friendship Commission, the Ministry of Science and Education, and Keio University for supporting their efforts in producing this book. They would also like to express appreciation to Takeo Hoshi, Yuri Okina, and two reviewers for Oxford University Press that significantly improved the manuscript. The authors, however, assume all responsibility for the views expressed in the book or any remaining errors. Appreciation is also expressed for Margaret Dalrymple, Theresa Moser, and Dave Kelly for help at various stages to improve the readability of the book. Cargill would also like to express appreciation to the Bank of Japan for providing visiting research opportunities in 1997, the Pacific Asian Management Institute of the College of Business Administration, University of Hawaii, for providing an opportunity to make presentations on the Japanese economy, and the East–West Center and the Federal Reserve Bank of San Francisco for providing visiting scholar positions to work on the project. Yoshino would also like to express appreciation to Ryutaro Komiya, Keimei Kaizuka, Masaaki Honma, Hiromitsu Ishi, Seiritsu Ogura, and Keimei Wakasugi for encouraging his research in government financial intermediation.

The authors are professors of economics at the University of Nevada, Reno and Keio University, Tokyo, respectively.

1

The Transition of Finance, Postal Savings, and Government Financial Intermediation

1.1. INTRODUCTION

The Postal Savings System (PSS) and the Fiscal Investment and Loan Program (FILP) are major components of the Japanese economy measured by their size relative to both the economy and the financial system, and together they support a pervasive system of government financial intermediation. The PSS and the FILP also play an important role in Japanese politics, since they are an integral part of the budgeting process. Although extensively discussed and debated within Japan, the PSS and FILP are not familiar to many outside observers. In fact, it would not be an exaggeration to say that, in general, the PSS and FILP are among the least-understood elements of postwar Japanese finance. The outside public became aware of some aspects of Japan's extensive system of government financial intermediation when Junichiro Koizumi was elected prime minister by the Diet on 26 April 2001. Koizumi won a popular mandate to reform the Liberal Democratic Party (LDP) and lead the country out of a decade of economic and financial distress. His mandate was reaffirmed in July 2001 when the LDP won a majority of the seats in the Upper House of Representatives. One of Koizumi's campaign promises was to privatize the PSS, and widespread news accounts of his reform package, which included the privatization proposal, probably represent the first time in postwar Japan that the outside community became aware of the PSS.

Koizumi's plan to privatize the PSS, if successful, would be the most significant institutional change in Japanese finance since the early 1950s. News accounts of Koizumi's program and his popular support at the time he assumed power, however, grossly understated the difficult task ahead. By summer 2002, Koizumi had encountered intense resistance to his proposal to privatize the PSS and eliminate a number of the FILP entities, including several government banks, that obtained funds from the PSS. It appeared unlikely he would achieve the promised reforms. The difficulty of such significant change in the PSS and FILP is not surprising when one considers the role these institutions have and continue to play in Japanese finance. The PSS and FILP are based on the administrative and credit-allocation role of the government in the flow of funds that characterized the old or preliberalization financial regime, and despite over two decades of financial liberalization, the PSS and FILP are larger and more pervasive at the start of the new century than at any time in the postwar period.

Reform of the PSS and FILP, however, commenced in 1998, and many of the changes became effective on 1 April 2001. Although incomplete, the reforms have the potential to significantly alter the role of government financial intermediation in Japan; however, those who formerly benefited from the PSS and FILP can still limit the effectiveness of the reforms and end up with a system not much different from what existed previously. This is an outcome one cannot dismiss, given Japan's past record of incomplete financial liberalization. Nonetheless, serious reform has commenced, and Prime Minister Koizumi had for the first time provided political leadership to a program of reform. Even the most ardent supporters of PSS and FILP reform, however, recognize the difficulty of significantly reforming these institutions, nor do they believe that reform of the PSS and FILP is the most urgent item on Japan's agenda for reversing over a decade of economic and financial distress. Nonetheless, Japan needs to address the issues raised by the PSS and FILP if recovery and stable economic growth are to be achieved. To understand the motivation for reform, we need to discuss the role of the PSS and FILP in Japan's financial system and the issues raised by that role. A knowledge of the PSS and FILP is therefore a necessary part of understanding postwar Japanese finance and assessing the ability of Japan to establish a modern financial system that will be on a par with the financial systems of the United Kingdom and the United States as envisaged by the November 1996 "Big Bang" announcement, which remains the operating guideline for financial liberalization.

This chapter places reform of the PSS and FILP in the context of the broader transition of the Japanese economy and financial system, provides an institutional outline of the FILP system, discusses the reforms that commenced in 1998, discusses the underlying motivation for reform, discusses the political changes initiated by Koizumi and how they impact reform, and outlines the remainder of the book.

1.2. THE TRANSITION OF THE JAPANESE ECONOMY AND FINANCIAL SYSTEM: OVERVIEW

Economic, financial, and political events in Japan during the past several decades have been remarkable. Table 1.1 presents selected macroeconomic performance measures for much of the postwar period. The 1975–85 period is the high point of Japanese economic, financial, and political stability in the postwar period. Economic and financial development from 1950 to 1975 was impressive, with

Table 1.1. *Indicators of macroeconomic performance in Japan, 1955–2000*

Fiscal year	WPI growth	CPI growth	HPM growth	M2CD growth	Nominal GNP growth	Real GDP growth	$/yen exchange rate	Nikkei 225 stock price	Land price, six large cities	Interbank rate call rate	Discount rate	Unemployment rate	Individual savings rate
1955							360	391	0.7	6.77	6.78	2.60	11.9
1956		5.1	0.94		12.1	6.4	360	520	0.9	7.44	7.31	2.20	12.9
1957		6.31	8.62		14.5	7.5	360	523	1.1	11.39	8.32	1.90	12.6
1958	2.33	0	11.62		7.0	7.3	360	619	1.3	9.04	7.57	2.20	12.3
1959	0.23	5.94	3.82		17.2	11.2	360	890	1.7	8.38	7.06	2.00	13.7
1960	1.14	6.9	11.89	22.91	19.9	12.2	360	1,248	2.7	8.31	7.01	1.50	14.5
1961	-1.69	8.47	16.31	17.11	20.9	11.7	360	1,547	4	8.46	7.01	1.40	15.9
1962	2.17	2.97	22.87	24.60	10.6	7.5	360	1,417	4.9	8.64	7.01	1.30	15.6
1963	0.00	6.86	16.37	20.61	17.4	10.4	360	1,385	5.7	7.56	5.89	1.20	14.9
1964	0.22	5.74	17.25	15.72	15.8	9.5	360	1,253	6.4	10.07	6.49	1.10	15.4
1965	1.29	4.47	15.61	18.49	11.1	6.2	360	1,268	6.6	6.33	5.56	1.30	15.8
1966	2.98	5.81	12.46	15.74	17.6	11.0	360	1,472	6.8	5.87	5.48	1.30	15.0
1967	1.86	5.49	13.98	14.93	17.0	11.0	360	1,380	7.4	6.85	5.77	1.20	14.1
1968	0.81	4.93	16.40	15.41	18.3	12.4	360	1,663	8.3	7.79	5.97	1.10	16.9
1969	3.02	5.74	16.18	18.20	18.4	12.0	360	2,099	9.7	7.95	6.08	1.10	17.1
1970	2.15	6.91	17.99	18.00	15.8	8.2	360	2,148	11.4	8.02	6.09	1.20	17.7
1971	-0.76	5.98	18.58	24.04	10.2	5.0	335	2,569	12.9	5.87	5.23	1.30	17.8
1972	4.05	5.38	15.95	23.18	16.6	9.1	297	4,304	16	4.74	4.37	1.30	18.2
1973	21.67	15.92	18.17	26.53	20.9	5.1	274	4,591	20.3	8.88	6.94	1.30	20.4
1974	20.09	20.93	26.92	22.69	18.4	-0.5	293	4,178	19.8	12.74	9	1.50	23.2
1975	2.28	10.2	20.25	11.92	10.2	4.0	290	4,375	19.1	9.23	7.36	1.90	22.8
1976	6.07	9.59	13.59	13.10	12.4	3.8	292	4,760	19.5	6.93	6.47	2.00	23.2
1977	1.99	6.94	11.08	15.11	11.0	4.5	257	5,061	20	5.14	4.59	2.10	21.8
1978	-0.57	3.81	9.11	11.38	9.9	5.4	201	5,776	21.2	4.28	3.5	2.20	20.8
1979	8.76	4.76	9.81	11.75	8.0	5.1	230	6,421	23.8	7.04	5.5	2.00	18.2

Table 1.1. *(Cont.)*

Fiscal year	WPI growth	CPI growth	HPM growth	M2CD growth	Nominal GNP growth	Real GDP growth	$/yen exchange rate	Nikkei 225 stock price	Land price, six large cities	Interbank rate call rate	Discount rate	Unemployment rate	Individual savings rate
1980	12.50	7.52	11.65	11.85	8.9	2.6	217	6,999	26.1	10.76	8.1	2.10	17.9
1981	0.20	4.1	7.01	8.90	6.2	2.8	220	7,599	27.9	6.96	6.02	2.20	18.4
1982	0.30	2.55	3.99	9.20	4.9	3.2	235	7,531	29.4	6.94	5.5	2.50	16.7
1983	−0.70	1.92	6.85	7.40	4.6	2.4	232	9,323	30.9	6.28	5.32	2.70	16.1
1984	0.30	2.11	5.40	7.80	6.9	4.0	251	11,061	33	9.06	5	2.70	15.8
1985	−1.70	1.95	4.08	8.40	6.6	4.2	201	12,935	36.8	4.56	4.89	2.60	15.6
1986	−5.20	0	6.12	8.70	4.5	3.2	160	18,032	45.5	4.28	3.27	2.80	15.6
1987	−1.70	0.46	7.40	10.40	5.0	5.1	122	24,195	59.7	3.39	2.5	2.80	13.8
1988	−0.60	0.79	10.31	11.20	7.1	6.3	126	28,865	72.8	4.13	2.5	2.40	13.0
1989	2.70	2.81	10.77	9.90	7.5	4.9	143	34,968	93.7	4.38	3.53	2.20	12.9
1990	1.30	3.17	11.09	11.70	8.1	5.5	136	26,872	104.1	6.66	5.69	2.10	11.3
1991	0.40	2.9	1.94	3.60	5.3	2.5	125	23,350	92.5	8.34	5.31	2.10	12.7
1992	−1.00	1.5	2.24	0.60	1.8	0.4	125	17,189	71.4	5.56	3.29	2.20	12.8
1993	−1.80	1.2	3.66	1.10	0.9	0.4	112	19,641	63.2	3.91	2.11	2.50	12.1
1994	−1.40	0.5	4.85	2.10	1.0	1.1	99	19,509	54.7	2.44	1.75	2.90	10.9
1995	−1.00	−0.3	5.28	3.00	2.0	2.5	103	19,868	48.6	2.28	1	3.20	10.1
1996	−1.50	0.4	9.03	3.30	2.6	3.4	116	19,361	44.9	0.44	0.5	3.40	8.9
1997	1.00	2	8.20	3.10	1.0	0.2	130	15,259	42.6	0.47	0.5	3.40	9.9
1998	−2.10	0.2	9.20	4.00	−1.1	−0.6	115	13,842	39.5	0.32	0.5	4.10	10.8
1999	−1.00	−0.5	6.00	3.60	−0.2	1.9	102	18,934	36.1	0.05	0.5	4.70	8.7
2000	−0.10	−0.6	7.40	2.10	−0.3	1.7	114	13,786	35.0	0.2	0.5	4.70	8.9

Sources: National Income Account Statistics, Economic Planning Agency, various issues; Bank of Japan, Economic Statistics, Annual various issues; Bank of Japan, *Handbook of Main Statistics*, Ju 01; Kinyu (Finance) Federation of Bankers Association; *House and Loan Monthly Magazine*, The Government Housing Loan Corporation.

the exception of the early 1970s when Japan experienced oil-price shocks, the so-called Nixon shock[1], high rates of inflation, and the collapse of the fixed exchange-rate system. Economic stability was achieved by 1975, however, and a decade of impressive development ensued during which Japan emerged as a major industrial power and achieved a level of economic and financial development that attracted world attention. During this period, Japan managed a transition toward more open and competitive economic and financial institutions while at the same time achieving a high degree of macroeconomic stability in the face of oil-price shocks in 1979 and 1980. This performance stood in contrast to the financial disruptions and macroeconomic instability experienced by most other developed countries, such as the United States. Japan's economic institutions, especially its financial system, were increasingly viewed as a model by policymakers in both developed and developing countries.

In the late 1980s, however, Japan experienced a period of equity and land-price inflation in the context of rapid real GDP growth and price stability, now referred to as Japan's "bubble economy" period. Asset-price inflation exposed the economy to serious risk, and the eventual asset-price collapse set the stage for a decade of economic and financial distress that now can be referred to as Japan's "lost decade" in terms of economic and financial development. Economic growth for the first two-thirds of the 1990s was essentially zero, negative starting in the fourth quarter of 1997 through 1998, and again negative starting in 2000. After almost a decade of dealing with troubled financial institutions, many of Japan's financial institutions in 2000 were either market insolvent or close to market insolvent. The government was required to resort to extraordinary means to deal with troubled financial institutions and nonperforming loans, even to the extent of nationalizing two large banks—the Long Term Credit Bank and the Nippon Credit Bank—in 1998, which were subsequently sold to the private sector in 1999.

The "collapse of the bubble economy" was initiated by the Bank of Japan's decision to raise the discount rate in May 1989 because of concerns about CPI and WPI inflation and, especially, about asset inflation in the equity and real-estate markets. The subsequent collapse of equity and land prices revealed fundamental weaknesses in Japan's economic and financial institutions, and a series of policy failures on the part of the Ministry of Finance, Bank of Japan, and government in general generated stagnant or declining real GDP, a gradual decline in the price level, and near-collapse of the financial system.

Four causes of the prolonged economic and financial distress can be identified. First, failure to resolve the nonperforming loan problem and the close relationship

---

[1] The Nixon shock refers to the decision in 1971 by President Nixon to abandon the fixed exchange rate system by abolishing the gold standard without first informing the Japanese government. The sudden and unexpected appreciation of the yen adversely impacted the Japanese economy.

between equity prices and bank capital deteriorated bank balance sheets and generated a bank credit crunch, especially after 1997 when Hokkaido Takushoku Bank and Yamaichi Securities Company failed in November 1997. This outcome is generally attributed to the fact that Japan had pursued an incomplete and flawed financial liberalization process that exposed the system to shocks such as a sudden collapse of asset prices. Second, the Bank of Japan made a series of policy mistakes. The Bank accommodated asset inflation after 1986, thereby ensuring that a soft landing would be difficult to achieve; then, once asset prices collapsed after 1990, the Bank waited too long to shift to easy monetary policy. After 1997, the Bank initiated an insufficiently aggressive policy and permitted a slow and gradual decline in the price level. Third, fiscal policymakers also made a series of policy mistakes. The decision to raise the consumption tax in 1997 is generally regarded as one of the causes of the sharp decline in economic growth in the fourth quarter of 1997, and subsequent fiscal actions were insufficient and/or directed to unproductive uses to stimulate the economy. Fourth, the Asian Financial Crisis that started in the summer of 1997 in Thailand and spread to Indonesia and South Korea by the end of the year did not cause Japan's economic and financial distress nor did Japan's depressed economy cause the Asian Financial Crisis; however, the extreme economic and financial distress in East Asia in 1997 and 1998 did adversely affect Japan through various financial and trade channels.

The economic and financial distress of the 1990s provided clear evidence that Japan needed to reform its economic and financial institutions. An official policy of liberalization had been in place since the late 1970s, but the 1990s revealed that Japan had not yet achieved the degree of liberalization required to modernize the economic and financial system. By the late 1990s, it became evident to the majority of policymakers that a new economic and financial regime would be required to support economic and financial development in the new century.

The economic and financial distress of the 1990s also had far-reaching political consequences. The longstanding dominance of the LDP ended in August 1993 when it lost the majority of the Lower House. Although the party regained power in the Lower House in October 1996, the LDP was more fractionalized than previously. Dissatisfaction with the failure of the LDP to resolve the continuing economic and financial distress and a series of scandals at the Ministry of Finance and the Bank of Japan, however, led to the LDP's loss in the Upper House elections in July 1998, and as a result, Prime Minister Ryutaro Hashimoto resigned. Prime Minister Keizo Obuchi, Hashimoto's successor, brought some stability; however, health considerations led to his replacement by Prime Minister Yoshiro Mori. Mori failed to provide effective leadership, and by early 2001 he had less than a 10-percent popularity rating. In April 2001, Koizumi became the new prime minister and leader of the LDP, promising radical reform to reverse Japan's stagnant and declining economic growth. Overall, by the end of the decade, Japan's stable political structure no longer existed. Japanese politics became more fractionalized, thereby increasing the potential for closer interaction between economic and political institutions.

Japan's economic and financial distress in the 1990s is unprecedented among the industrial economies in the postwar period. The distress followed a postwar record of stability and growth impressive by any standard, and it has been deep and widespread, reaching crisis proportions in late 1997 when Japan came close to a deflationary spiral and the financial system was on the verge of insolvency. Japan's macroeconomic performance brought comparisons with the 1930s and regenerated debates about monetary policy, deflation, and liquidity traps that had been absent for the previous four decades.[2]

In response, institutional and attitudinal reform has been unprecedented in postwar Japan. The "new" Bank of Japan was established in 1997 with enhanced legal independence from the Ministry of Finance, in contrast to the "old" Bank of Japan, which formerly operated under the direction of the Ministry of Finance. The "new" financial regulatory and supervisory regime was established in the second half of the 1990s by a series of institutional changes. The role of the Ministry of Finance was reduced, the Deposit Insurance Corporation was restructured and expanded, the Financial Supervisory Agency and Financial Reconstruction Commission were established,[3] and new guidelines, referred to as Prompt Corrective Action, were adopted for dealing with troubled financial institutions. The "new" financial regulatory and supervisory regime emphasizes transparency, prompt action to resolve the problems of troubled financial institutions, and a willingness to impose penalties on troubled financial institutions, in contrast to the "old" regime that emphasized nontransparency, mutual support, and a policy that did not permit the failure of financial institutions and markets. The "new" attitude emphasizes market principles and accepts risk and bankruptcy as a normal part of the economic process, as opposed to the "old" attitude that emphasized the minimization of risk and bankruptcy.

These changes are designed to establish a fundamentally different monetary and financial regime than what previously existed in postwar Japan. In the new regime, market forces rather than government direction will play the dominant role in the allocation of credit. In the new regime, an acceptance of risk and bankruptcy, rather than mutual support and minimizing risk and bankruptcy,

---

[2] Comparisons between Bank of Japan Policy in the 1990s and policies followed in the 1930s by Japan, Sweden, and the United States are presented in Cargill (2001). Mikitani and Posen (2000) compare Japan's economic and financial distress with that experienced by the United States in the 1980s.

[3] The Financial Supervisory Agency and the Financial Reconstruction Commission were combined into a new institution named the Financial Services Agency, effective 6 January 2001.

will be a normal part of the economic development process. As part of the reform effort, attention was finally directly toward the PSS and the FILP, starting in 1998. The PSS and FILP had previously avoided any meaningful reform, despite their incompatibility with a modern market-oriented financial system.

1.3. THE PSS AND THE FILP

The transition from the old to the new financial regime has resulted in fundamental changes[4] in Japan's private financial institutions, financial regulatory institutions, and the Bank of Japan. The PSS and FILP, however, have largely avoided being part of the financial transition toward more open and competitive markets. The PSS and FILP are special features of Japanese finance and, although frequently discussed within Japan, they have received little attention outside of Japan.[5] Private banks and some academics frequently voiced criticism of the PSS and FILP because, in their view, these institutions unfairly competed with private banks and were incompatible with financial liberalization; however, these criticisms received little support from regulatory authorities (with, perhaps, the exception of the Bank of Japan), the public, or the business sector.

The PSS and FILP in many ways represent an essential and large element of the old financial regime currently in transition. As such, the way that reform of the PSS and FILP evolves in the coming years will provide insight into whether Japan can achieve a modern financial system and break with the past. Reform of the PSS and the FILP will represent a major challenge for regulatory authorities for two reasons. First, the PSS and FILP until 1998 for all practical purposes avoided any reform, and second, these institutions represent a major and pervasive part of the old financial regime with widespread public and political support.

The reforms initiated in 1998 are potentially significant and have already generated sufficient institutional change to the degree that we can distinguish between the "old" and "new" FILP system. The New FILP system started on 1 April 2001.

1.3.1. *The Old PSS and FILP*

The PSS was established in 1875 as part of the postal services system and has since then been a prominent feature of Japanese finance. The role of the PSS in

---

[4] These changes are discussed in Blomstrom *et al.* (2001); Cargill *et al.* (1997, 1998, 2000); Hoshi and Kashyap (2001), and Hoshi and Patrick (2000).

[5] There are a limited number of discussions of Japan's PSS and FILP in English. The following is a selected list of references: Alexander (2000); Anderson (1990); Calder (1990); Cargill (1993); Cargill *et al.* (1997, 2000); Cargill and Royama (1988); Cargill and Yoshino (1998, 2000, 2001); *Economist* (1998); Elixman (1992); Kuwayama (2000); Ministry of Finance (2000); Ogura and Yoshino (1998); Okina (2000); Patrick (1967); Sakakibara (1991); Strom (1997); Suzuki (1987); United Nations (1993) and Yoshino (1993).

Japan's financial system in the 1990s is as large, if not larger, than it has ever been since its establishment. The PSS is Japan's largest financial institution, holding 34 percent of household deposits. The PSS also sells life insurance and accounts for about 30 percent of the life-insurance market. The financial resources of the PSS, measured in terms of deposits of 255 trillion yen as of 31 March 2000, or 2.32 trillion dollars (110 yen to the dollar), make it larger than any other private or public financial institution in the world.

The quantitative size of the PSS, however, does not fully convey the role of the PSS in Japan, nor can the PSS be fully appreciated without considering its role in the larger FILP. The FILP is an integral component of the old financial regime, which assigned an important role to government regulation and administration of the flow of funds to support industrial policy, compensate unproductive enterprises or sectors left behind in the economic development process, and minimize risk and bankruptcy. The PSS is the most important component of the FILP, which together represent a set of multidimensional and complex policies for transferring funds from the public to designated sectors of the economy.

The FILP is not so much an institution or government agency as it is a process of decision making concurrent with the formulation of the national budget that directs financial resources under the government's control to targeted sectors of the economy. The PSS, the related institutions, and the decision-making process of allocating government financial intermediation are collectively referred to as the FILP system.

Table 1.2 illustrates the flow of funds through the FILP system for amounts outstanding as of 31 March 2000, which is the end of the fiscal year in Japan. The process started with household postal deposits of 255 trillion yen, national welfare and pension premium payments of 140 trillion yen, other premium payments of 48 trillion yen, and life-insurance premium payments of 112 trillion yen. The first three items total 443 trillion yen and were deposited directly into the Trust Fund Bureau of the Ministry of Finance. The life-insurance premiums of 112 trillion yen were transferred to the Postal Life Insurance Reserve Fund.

The Trust Fund Bureau purchased 115 trillion yen of government bonds, leaving 328 trillion yen to fund the FILP. The Postal Life Insurance Reserve Fund retained 62 trillion yen for its own portfolio management and transferred 60 trillion yen to the Postal Life Insurance Fund, which in turn was used to fund the FILP. The Trust Fund Bureau and Postal Life Insurance Fund together provided 388 trillion yen to be distributed through the FILP system; however, the FILP also received funds from other sources. The FILP received an additional 26 trillion yen from purchases of government bonds by private financial institutions (22 trillion yen) and the Industrial Investment Special Account Fund (4 trillion yen), which increased total FILP funding to 414 trillion yen. The 414 trillion yen were then distributed to a total of forty-eight FILP-financed entities consisting of special accounts,

Table 1.2. *Outline of the old PSS and the FILP system, fiscal 2000 (in trillion yen)*

	Trillion yen
Households provide funds to the FILP system in the form of	
Postal deposits	255
National welfare and pension premiums	140
Other premiums	48
Postal life-insurance premiums	112
Total household-provided funds	555
Distributed to the following accounts	
Trust Fund Bureau of the Ministry of Finance	443
Postal deposits	255
National welfare and pension premiums	140
Other premiums	48
Postal Life Insurance Reserve Fund	112
Postal life insurance premiums	112

Distribution of Trust Fund Bureau and the Postal Life Insurance Reserve Fund

Of the 443 trillion yen received by the Trust Fund Bureau, the Trust Fund uses 115 trillion yen to purchase government bonds, etc., and the remaining 328 trillion yen are provided to the FILP (FILP-financed entities). Of the 112 trillion yen provided to the Postal Life Insurance Reserve Fund, 60 trillion yen are provided to the Postal Life Insurance Fund, which in turn are provided to the FILP (FILP-financed entities).

The sources of funding of the FILP for FILP-financed entities are	
Trust Fund Bureau	328
Postal Life-Insurance Fund	60
Industrial Investment Special Account Fund	3
Government Bonds purchased by private financial institutions	22
Total FILP funding	414
Distribution of FILP funding to FILP-financed entities	
Government banks or financial institutions (8)	145
Government Housing Loan Corporation	
Japan Finance Corporation for Small Business	
Development Bank of Japan	
National Life Finance Corporation	
Agriculture, Forestry, and Fisheries Finance Corporation of Japan	
Japan Finance Corporation for Municipal Enterprises	
Okinawa Development Finance Corporation	
Japan Bank for International Cooperation	
Quasi-government corporations (27)	110
Urban Development Corporation	
Pension Welfare Service Public Corporation	

Table 1.2. *(Cont.)*

	Trillion yen
Japan Environment Corporation	
Teito Rapid Transit Authority	
Japan Regional Development Corporation	
Japan Sewage Works Agency	
Social Welfare and Medical Service Corporation	
Organization for Pharmaceutical Safety and Research	
Promotion and Mutual Aid Corporation for Private Schools of Japan	
Japan Scholarship Foundation	
Japan Green Resources Corporation	
Bio-oriented Technology Research Advancement Institution	
Japan Highway Public Corporation	
Metropolitan Expressway Public Corporation	
Hanshin Expressway Public Corporation	
Honshu-Shikoku Bridge Authority	
Japan Railway Construction Public Corporation	
New Tokyo International Airport Authority	
Corporation for Advanced Transport and Technology	
Water Resources Development Public Corporation	
Fund for the Promotion and Development of the Amami Islands	
Metal Mining Agency of Japan	
Japan National Oil Corporation	
Japan Science and Technology Corporation	
Information-Technology Promotion Agency, Japan	
Japan Key Technology Center	
Postal Life Insurance Welfare Corporation	
Special accounts (7)	73
Lending Urban Development Funds	
Consolidation of Specific National Property	
National Hospital	
National School	
Government-Operated Land Improvement Project	
Airport Development	
Postal Savings Special Account	
Local governments	83
Special firms (5)	3
Kansai International Airport Co., Ltd	
Central Japan International Airport Co., Ltd.	
Electric Power Development Co., Ltd	
Shoko Chukin Bank	
Organization for Promoting Urban Development	

Source: Ministry of Finance (2000, pp. 6, 40–1).

government financial institutions, government corporations and enterprises, special firms, and local governments (counted as one entity).

Not all of the forty-eight FILP-financed entities indicated in Table 1.2 received funds from the Trust Fund Bureau in fiscal 2000. Some of the entities are financed by non-Trust Fund Bureau funds, such as postal life-insurance funds or funds from the special account for industrial investment. In some cases, the entities had FILP loans outstanding and did not receive new FILP funds. Of the eight FILP-financed government banks, seven received funding from the Trust Fund. Of the twenty-seven FILP-financed quasi-government corporations, twenty received funding from the Trust Fund. The local governments, the seven special accounts, and one of the five special firms received funds from the Trust Fund. Special firms are those in which the government has no equity interest but which are supported by public funding.

Before 1987, all postal deposits were transferred to the Trust Fund Bureau; however, starting in 1987 the Ministry of Posts and Telecommunications[6] was permitted to manage a percentage of postal funds that varied from year to year but which gradually increased to about 20 percent in fiscal 2000. As of 31 March 2000, the portfolio managed by the Ministry of Posts and Telecommunications was 58.9 trillion yen and consisted of government bonds (47.3 percent), local government bonds (15.9 percent), public institution bonds (4.5 percent), private bonds and bank debentures (6.2 percent), and foreign bonds (7.9 percent). The remaining 18.1 percent were invested with private financial institutions.

There are four important issues regarding the FILP system as outlined. First, the FILP budget, like the PSS, is large by any reasonable standard; for example, Figure 1.1 illustrates the FILP budget in flow terms as a percentage of GNP from 1953 to 1998. In 1998, the FILP budget represented 10.9 percent of GNP. Also note that the FILP budget continued to increase relative to the economy over time despite an official policy of financial liberalization that commenced in the 1970s.

Second, the PSS is the most important contributor to the FILP system. In 2000, postal deposits accounted for 62 percent of the amount budgeted for FILP-financed entities and represented 58 percent of the Trust Fund Bureau Account. As the FILP budget has increased relative to GNP, postal deposits continued to increase relative to total deposits, as illustrated in Figure 1.2. Likewise, postal life insurance became an increasingly important source of funds to the FILP and, like postal deposits, postal life insurance has increased relative to total life-insurance sales (Figure 1.3). The relative growth of postal

---

[6] As of 6 January 2001, the Ministry of Posts and Telecommunications was reorganized and renamed the Ministry of Public Management, Home Affairs, Posts, and Telecommunications. This was part of the general reorganization of the Japanese cabinet and bureaucracy initiated in the late 1990s. The Ministry of Finance was renamed the Ministry of the Treasury in Japanese to reflect the reduced role it plays in financial regulation and supervision; however, the English name remains unchanged.

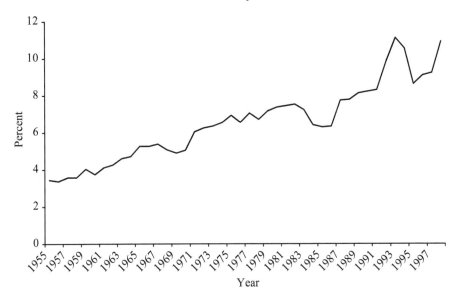

Figure 1.1. *FILP budget as percentage of GNP, 1955–1998.*

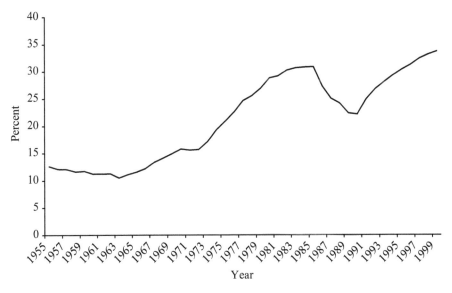

Figure 1.2. *Postal savings as percentage of total deposits, 1955–1999.*

deposits and postal life insurance, like the relative growth of the FILP budget to GNP, are contradictions to an official policy of financial liberalization.

Third, the FILP system is wide ranging in terms of projects and activities funded. It supports transportation, education, electricity, housing, roads, bridges,

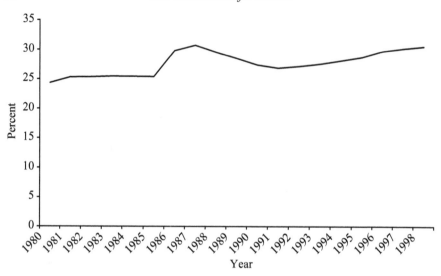

Figure 1.3. *Postal life insurance as percentage of total life insurance, 1980–1998.*

and small and medium-sized businesses. As a result, the FILP system is pervasive in the Japanese economy with few aspects of economic life in Japan not under some influence of the FILP system.

Fourth, the FILP budget is determined in tandem with the national budget (discussed in more detail in Chapter 2); consequently, the FILP system plays an important role in Japan's political institutions, since the distribution of the funds plays a key role in maintaining and enhancing political power.

1.3.2. *The New PSS and FILP*

The outline in Table 1.2 is a reasonable description through 31 March 2001, of Japan's FILP system; however, the reforms commenced in 1998 fundamentally changed the flow of funds through the FILP system starting 1 April 2001. As part of the June 1998 Laws to Reform Central Government Ministries and Agencies, the formal relationship between the PSS and the FILP changed. Starting 1 April 2001, postal deposits, postal life-insurance premiums, national welfare and pension premiums, and so on, were no longer provided to special accounts or government banks through the Trust Fund Bureau. FILP-financed entities previously dependent on the Trust Fund Bureau must now raise their own funds in the form of (a) FILP-agency bonds without a government guarantee, (b) FILP-agency bonds with a government guarantee, or (c) FILP bonds issued by the Ministry of Finance, which essentially represent general government debt to be treated equally with Japan Government Bonds (JGBs).

As part of an effort to require FILP entities to raise funds in the private market and achieve a greater degree of transparency, thirty-three FILP entities that previously obtained funding from the Trust Fund Bureau will be required after fiscal 2001 to disclose a policy or subsidy cost analysis consisting of estimates of the present value of future subsidies of each FILP entity. The thirty-three FILP entities subject to the new regulations (Table 5.1, page 155) were selected for immediate attention because they account for the major part of lending by the Trust Fund Bureau. This disclosure is designed to bring about the greater transparency needed to raise capital in the private market. In fiscal 2001, twenty FILP entities planned to raise a small part of their funding (1.1 trillion yen) through nonguaranteed agency bonds. In early 2001, four entities issued agency bonds that received high ratings by Moody's, S&P, and Rating and Investment Information, Inc. The agency bonds issued by the Government Housing Loan Corporation (mortgage-backed securities), Japan Highway Public Corporation, New Tokyo International Airport Authority, and Water Resource Development Public Corporation have been rated at Aa2 (Moody's) or better, largely because they are viewed as having the implicit guarantee of the government.

In fiscal year 2001, 43.9 trillion yen of FILP bonds were issued by the Ministry of Finance, with the majority issued at five- and ten-year maturities. These FILP bonds are government debt used to finance Trust Fund distributions to various entities. The FILP bonds are indistinguishable from construction and deficit-financing bonds. At the time bonds are sold, the Ministry of Finance indicates amounts that represent FILP bonds, construction bonds, and deficit-financing bonds; however, there is no further designation, and all three types of bonds are regarded as general government debt or JGBs.

Thus in fiscal 2001, nonguaranteed agency bonds represented only a small fraction of the total funding by the Trust Fund Bureau. The intent of the reforms, however, is to increase the agency bond offerings to provide the major source of financing for FILP entities.

The new process of funding FILP entities through general FILP bonds or agency bonds will be officially referred to in the budget as the Public Funding Mechanism; however, the term FILP will continue to be used to describe the process of allocating funds. In this new system, the PSS is not required to transfer funds to the Ministry of Finance and for all practical purposes has become a stand-alone government bank. In June 2000, the Ministry of Public Management, Home Affairs, Posts, and Telecommunications (formerly the Ministry of Posts and Telecommunications) announced a strategy to manage postal deposits. The portfolio "in principle" should consist of 80 percent in "safe" assets (government bonds, etc.), 5 percent in foreign bonds, 5 percent in foreign equities, 5 percent in domestic equities, and the remaining 5 percent in money-market instruments. The plan to hold 80 percent of postal deposits in

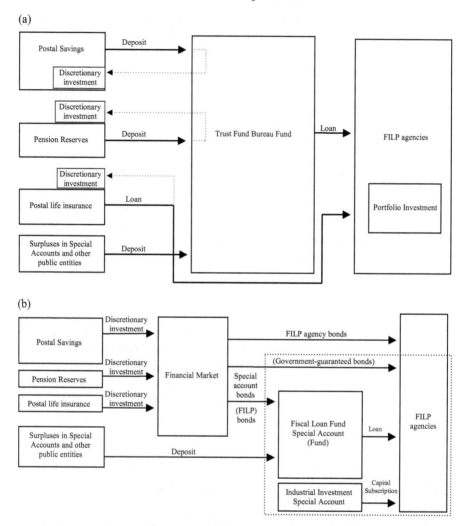

Figure 1. 4. *(a) Pre 1 April 2001 and (b) post 31 March 2001 FILP system.*

Notes: 1. In addition to the above, the FILP also includes loans to local governments from the Postal savings and the Postal Life Insurance Fund. 2. Special account bonds refer to government bonds issued on the Fiscal Loan Fund Special Account (i.e., "FILP bonds").

Source: Ministry of Finance (2000, p. 27) and modified by the authors.

government bonds and other safe assets essentially turns a major part of the PSS into a "narrow" bank. On 1 April 2003, the PSS will become a separate public corporation collecting funds through postal deposits and allocating those funds according to its own portfolio decision-making process.

Figure 1.4 contrasts the old with the new PSS and FILP systems. Under the old system, postal savings and pension reserves were transferred to the Trust

Fund Bureau of the Ministry of Finance, though some of the funds were retained for discretionary management. The Trust Fund Bureau in turn distributed the funds to the various FILP entities. Under the new system, these funds are placed directly into the financial market through the purchase of FILP agency bonds (guaranteed and nonguaranteed) issued by the FILP-entities and the purchase of FILP bonds issued by the Ministry of Finance. The Trust Fund Bureau will cease to exist. The FILP entities will henceforth obtain funding from the financial system or directly from the Fiscal Loan Fund Special Account (Fund) in the form of loans. The Fund will be supported primarily by FILP bonds.

The reforms of the PSS and FILP are potentially important; however, the fact remains that the PSS and the FILP have avoided meaningful reform for over two decades of official financial liberalization policy in Japan. As a result, there is reason to be cautious about whether this is real reform. Even if these turn out to be significant reforms, the PSS remains as a government bank. However, as a prerequisite to offering an assessment of the 1998 reforms and subsequent administrative decisions, it will be useful to first discuss the role of the PSS and the FILP in Japan's policy of financial liberalization during the past two decades.

1.4. THE PSS, THE FILP SYSTEM, AND FINANCIAL LIBERALIZATION: 1976–1989

Japan initiated a policy of financial liberalization in 1976 when the Ministry of Finance officially recognized the *gensaki* market, a market in repurchase agreements based on government bonds that had been unofficially in operation since the mid-1960s. The transition appeared to progress smoothly for the next ten years as a large number of incremental changes were made that increased the role of competitive forces (Cargill and Royama, 1988, 1992; Feldman, 1986). Although the structural changes made during this period were substantial when compared to the financial system in 1975, the financial supervision and regulatory framework remained wedded to the old financial regime.[7] This is especially true of the PSS and the FILP system.

The PSS and FILP resisted meaningful reform during the first decade of financial liberalization through 1985, and despite an official policy of liberalization, the PSS and FILP increased their relative role in the economy (Figures 1.1–1.3). The large and increasing role of the PSS and FILP system was at odds with the official policy of liberalization; however, this was not a major concern to regulatory authorities for three reasons.

First, financial liberalization was not enthusiastically pursued in Japan despite an official policy of liberalization. Some significant accomplishments

---

[7] The old financial regime is summarized by Cargill (1999), which in turn draws from a number of well-known studies cited in that work.

occurred through the 1980s, but financial liberalization can be characterized more as rhetoric than as substance. Despite interest-rate liberalization, development of money and capital markets, and internationalization of the yen, the Japanese financial system remained dependent on a bank-finance model with pervasive deposit guarantees, nontransparency, and a mutual-support system designed to limit risk and bankruptcy.[8] As a result, there was little enthusiasm on the part of regulatory authorities to reform either the PSS or the FILP system, which together represented a major and widely supported role of government in the financial intermediation process.

Second, financial liberalization in Japan was mainly a response to internal and external pressure in which various groups saw liberalization as a way to reestablish lost markets (domestic banks), expand markets (foreign financial institutions and domestic securities companies), enhance profit via portfolio management (domestic corporations), or deal with trade-balance issues (mainly the United States). Only the domestic banks expressed concern with the FILP system, along with some academics, and, on occasion, the Bank of Japan. Their complaints, however, found no support among regulatory authorities, politicians, or the public; hence, there was no internal pressure for reform, and the fact that the FILP system was not directly associated with trade-imbalance disputes with the United States and was often not well understood outside of Japan meant that there was little external pressure for reform from the United States.

Third, the slow and incremental approach to financial liberalization through the 1980s appeared successful in terms of balancing the desire to adhere to the old financial regime while giving in to pressure to liberalize specific components of the financial system. That is, judged by Japan's macroeconomic performance, the gradual and incremental approach to liberalization appeared successful.

Japan avoided financial disruptions like the collapse of the S&L industry in the United States in the 1980s or the inflation and disinflation experienced by most industrial countries in the wake of the oil-price increases in 1979 and 1980. As a result, Japanese regulatory authorities saw little benefit to reforming the PSS or the FILP or to departing from the slow liberalization process that for all practical purposes left unchanged many of the core elements of the Japanese financial system. This reluctance to change in the presence of new circumstance is a characteristic of Japanese society in general and has often been identified as a separate set of factors from economic considerations that account for the slow pace of financial liberalization in Japan.

Much of the financial policy success during this period was attributable to Bank of Japan policy (Cargill, 1986, 1990; Cargill and Hutchison, 1988). The Bank of Japan from 1975 to 1985 achieved a record of economic stability that brought

---

[8] Lincoln (2001) provides an interesting discussion of the reasons reform has been so slow in Japan.

world attention to Japanese monetary policy and led some observers to regard the Bank of Japan as a "model central bank." In hindsight, the macroeconomic stability established by the Bank of Japan covered up fundamental weaknesses created by adherence to elements of the old financial regime, while at the same time liberalization policies were increasing the role of market forces in the Japanese financial system. It was only a matter of time before a problem would arise.

1.5. FINANCIAL DISTRESS IN THE 1990s, THE PSS, AND THE FILP

The economic and financial distress of the 1990s originated during the second half of the 1980s when increasing equity and land prices generated the bubble economy. Banks and other financial institutions, long protected by extensive deposit guarantees and limited competition, expanded credit without sufficient regard to economic fundamentals, thereby generating a speculative bubble in land and equity prices. Bank of Japan policy contributed to the credit expansion and subsequent asset inflation by pursuing easy monetary policy in an effort to restrain appreciation of the yen to offset the negative effect of an appreciating yen on economic growth (Cargill *et al.*, 1997; Ueda, 2000; Yoshino and Yoshimora, 1995). Regulations introduced in 1988 allowing unrealized capital gains on bank holdings of equities to count as Tier II capital in satisfying BIS capital requirements ensured a close relationship between increasing equity prices and bank lending.

The collapse of asset prices, initiated by Bank of Japan policy to raise interest rates starting May 1989, deteriorated bank balance sheets, increased nonperforming loans, and reduced spending. The resulting economic and financial distress, however, was not unique to Japan. Many countries experienced financial distress and banking problems in the late 1980s and early 1990s (*Economist*, 1997; Borio *et al.*, 1994; Hutchison and McDill, 1999; Lindgren *et al.*, 1996). Japan's economic and financial distress, however, was deeper and longer lasting than that experienced by any other industrial country and continued through the end of 2002.

Part of the distress can be traced to an unwillingness on the part of government policymakers to depart from attitudes and policies embedded in the old financial regime that had served Japan so well for so many years, and part can be traced to inappropriate fiscal and monetary policies. The collapse of asset prices in 1990 and 1991 exposed the fundamental weaknesses of the old regime and especially weaknesses in the government's ability to manage the resulting financial distress. The slow and inadequate government response can be traced to attitudes embedded in the old financial regime that preferred policies of delay, forgiveness, and forbearance covered up by a general lack of transparency in the financial system.

The policy was also based on the belief that asset deflation would not be long lasting, and thus forgiveness and forbearance were viewed as short-run solutions. Nonetheless, the emphasis of the old regime on limiting risk and bankruptcy in a nontransparent manner ensured that forgiveness and forbearance would be the preferred policy even in the longer run. As a result, Japan's economy stagnated in the first half of the 1990s with essentially zero real GDP growth, the financial system deteriorated as nonperforming loans accumulated, a number of small depository institutions failed, and the resources of the Deposit Insurance Corporation were exhausted by 1994.

The financial distress in the first half of the 1990s raised new concerns about the PSS and ultimately the entire FILP system. It became increasingly clear that the PSS complicated Japan's government deposit-guarantee system in the context of financial liberalization, in general, and financial distress, in particular. The disintermediation of private-bank deposits to the PSS exposed private banks to liquidity risk. Disintermediation resulted from an explicit government guarantee of postal deposits up to 10 million yen, household concern about the condition of the banking system, and concern over the failure of several small banks and credit cooperatives in the first half of the 1990s.

The PSS in the early part of the 1990s encouraged this disintermediation by informing the public that postal deposits were safer than bank deposits. The Deposit Insurance Corporation, established in 1971, insures private bank deposits up to 10 million yen and while postal deposits are limited to 10 million yen, the public does not view the two guarantees as equivalent. The public understands that postal deposits are the same as general government debt; however, the public has no experience with insurance-type government guarantees. What experience they do have is negative. Japan's limited deposit-insurance system failed in the early 1990s. Thus, the claim that postal deposits are safer than private bank deposits appeared credible as, for the first time in postwar Japan, small depository institutions failed and the Deposit Insurance Corporation became market insolvent by 1994, as was Japan's smaller deposit-insurance agency for small financial institutions (Cargill *et al.*, 1996). In 1993, however, post offices were officially directed to stop advertising the problems of private banks and to stop appealing to depositors' fears about the stability of the banking system as a means to attract deposits to the PSS. In 1994, an agreement was reached between the regulatory authorities that the PSS would set deposit rates "close to" private-bank deposit rates[9] in an effort to reduce disintermediation. The majority of

---

[9] The 1994 agreement specified two conditions depending on whether interest rates were increasing or decreasing. Increasing interest rates: in this case, the postal rate (*teigaku* deposit) is "normally" set at 0.95 of the bank rate. Decreasing interest rates: in this case, the postal rate (*teigaku* deposit) is "normally" set at 0.5 percent less than the ten-year government bond rate; however, the postal rate can range from 0.5 to 1.0 percent less than the government bond rate.

postal deposits (about 80 percent) are in the form of *teigaku* deposits. These are ten-year time-deposits with an option to withdraw the funds after six months without penalty. The 1994 agreement did not eliminate the potential for disintermediation. The *teigaku* time-deposit was superior to any deposit offered by private institutions because of its favorable interest-rate risk feature and postal deposits were viewed as a direct obligation of the government, whereas private-bank deposits were viewed as private-bank obligations insured only by an agency of the government.

The general situation deteriorated in 1995 and forced the government to depart from its passive policies of the early 1990s. The *jusen* or housing-loan industry was declared insolvent and liquidated, the Deposit Insurance Corporation was reorganized and recapitalized, the Resolution and Collection Bank was established to assume the assets of failed credit cooperatives, and the government announced a complete guarantee of all private-bank deposits, to expire on 1 April 2001. The economy appeared to improve in late 1995, and recovery in 1996 appeared to be at hand. Although land prices continued to fall, equity prices slowly improved in 1996.

The direct action of the government in dealing with the financial distress in 1995 and 1996, combined with the apparent economic recovery, generated a sense of cautious optimism that Japan had turned the corner. The Hashimoto government regained control of the Lower House in October 1996 on a pledge to reform and deregulate the economy. Prime Minister Hashimoto in November 1996 announced the Big Bang financial reform, so-named after similar reforms were announced in Great Britain a decade earlier. The Big Bang was intended as a plan of action to make Japan's financial system fair, open, transparent, and competitive by 2001.

The objective of the Big Bang proposal was nothing less than to render Japan's financial system equal to any financial system in the world in terms of efficiency and stability. The new financial regime envisaged by the Big Bang announcement differed significantly from the old regime, and many observers doubted whether Japan was ready to embark on such an ambitious agenda that would fundamentally change the structure of the financial and real sector. Financial reform had been on the table for almost two decades at the time of the Big Bang announcement. Japanese regulatory authorities during this period had found it difficult to depart from the essential elements of the old regime for two reasons. First, the old regime had provided Japan's financial infrastructure for over a hundred years and especially had contributed to Japan's postwar economic successes. The financial regime served as a base model for other Asian economies in the postwar period, and thus the "Asian miracle" added further credibility to the Japanese financial regime's ability to support rapid and sustained economic growth. Second, transition to the new financial regime involved many winners but also created many losers who had benefited from the old regime. The slow and incomplete pace of liberalization in Japan can partly be explained by the fact that those who have benefited the most from the old financial regime are still in power and at the same time are likely to experience the greatest loss. The winners, however, are widely dispersed, not always clearly identified, and—most important—lack political power.

One would have thought that the PSS and FILP would be part of the Big Bang announcement, given their prominent role in the financial system and their clear conflict with the type of market-oriented financial system envisaged by the Big Bang announcement. Their omission from the announcement suggested an official reluctance to deal with one of the most important and complex constraints interfering with financial modernization. In fact, during this period the PSS was being held up by Japan as a model for other Asian countries (*Kanabayashi*, 1997).

In the spring of 1997, a flurry of legislation was passed to begin implementation of the Big Bang objectives. The Bank of Japan Law was revised to give the Bank of Japan legal independence from the Ministry of Finance. The Financial Supervisory Agency was established to consolidate regulatory and supervisory responsibility over the financial system and thereby to reduce the role of the Ministry of Finance. Foreign-exchange laws were completely liberalized so that a special license was no longer needed to conduct foreign-exchange transactions.

There were no proposals in the Big Bang announcement, however, to deal with the PSS or the FILP, other than some minor comments regarding accounting for government corporations (Cargill *et al.*, 1998). Like the elephant in the room for all to see, however, everyone in Japan knew that these institutions would soon be on the agenda for structural reform. The PSS and the FILP, in fact, had increased their relative importance in the financial system during the past two decades despite an official policy of liberalization, and it was not until 1994 that the PSS was subjected to any significant reform.[10] In 1994, the PSS and the Ministry of Finance reached an agreement that the PSS would set competitive interest rates on time deposits in order to reduce the disintermediation of funds from private banks. There were no reforms of the FILP system.

Financial distress and economic recovery in 1996 and 1997 turned to financial panic and economic decline in late 1997. The failures of Hokkaido Takushoku Bank and Yamaichi Securities Company in November 1997, combined with the financial and economic distress spreading through much of Asia in the summer of 1997, shocked observers both within and outside of Japan. In response, in

---

[10] Tax reform in 1986 reduced a significant advantage of postal over bank deposits. However, this reform was not specifically directed at the PSS. It will be discussed in Chapter 2.

early 1998 the government committed 30 trillion yen in public funds raised by bond sales to protect depositors and recapitalize banks. By October 1998, a total of 60 trillion yen in public funds was committed to deal with the troubled financial system. The Long Term Credit Bank and the Nippon Credit Bank were nationalized in late 1998, and new institutions were set up to liquidate the loans of failed institutions. More aggressive policies were adopted to deal with the financial crisis, such as forcing banks to be more transparent about the extent of their nonperforming loans and requiring them to produce realistic resolution plans as a precondition to receiving public injections of capital. However, negative real GDP growth in 1998 and low growth in 1999 and 2000, combined with fiscal and monetary policy failures, complicated the situation.

At this point, policymakers in Japan realized that adherence to policies of delay, forbearance, forgiveness, and nontransparency had failed. These policies rooted in the old financial regime had prolonged and intensified the financial distress. After 1997, policymakers could no longer claim that financial distress was confined to the smaller and less important part of the financial system. The failure of Hokkaido Takushoku Bank and Yamaichi Securities Company indicated that financial distress had spread to the very core of Japan's financial system. Only significant structural reform, accompanied by large amounts of public funding, could solve the problem. By early 1998, there was general consensus that serious public funding would be needed to recapitalize the banking system and resolve the nonperforming loan problem. This was a significant turning point. Regulatory authorities by 1998 realized that only an extensive institutional redesign of Japan's financial institutions would provide the basis for achieving the goals of the 1996 Big Bang proposal, which remains the operating outline for financial reform in Japan. At this point, policymakers were willing to consider reform of the PSS and FILP.

1.6. PRODUCTIVITY, AGING, AND THE FILP SYSTEM

The economic and financial distress of the 1990s and the recognition that the old financial regime could no longer be sustained provided the incentive, for the first time in the postwar period, for regulatory authorities seriously to consider reforming the PSS and the FILP. However, another and more long-term issue began to emerge in the 1990s that provided additional incentive to consider reform. Japan's population growth is slowing dramatically, and population is projected to decline significantly by 2050.[11] Table 1.3 presents Ministry of Welfare[12] population estimates through 2050. Not only is population projected

---

[11] Takayama (1998) presents a comprehensive overview of Japan's population changes.

[12] The Ministry of Welfare as of January 2001 is now the Ministry of Health, Labor, and Welfare.

Table 1.3. *Population and aging in Japan, 2000–2050*

Year	Population (millions)	Persons 65 or older
2000	126,919	16.7
2005	127,684	19.6
2010	127,623	22.0
2020	124,133	26.9
2030	117,149	28.0
2040	108,964	31.0
2050	100,496	32.3

Source: Ministry of Welfare.

to decline starting in the first decade of the twenty-first century, but the percentage of persons aged 65 and older is projected to increase significantly. Japan's population is expected to age faster than the population of any other industrial country. These demographic changes require that savings be channeled to the most productive uses possible in order to increase productivity if Japan is to maintain the current standard of living for its population.

Japan has one of the highest and most stable savings rates in the world, although the household-sector savings rate declined after 1975 from the high levels in the previous decade (Table 1.1). Many would argue that much of this saving has not been utilized productively because of an inefficient financial system and, more specifically, because of the large amount of funds allocated by government financial intermediation for domestic purposes. Many observers argue that the rate of return on FILP-financed activities is low and in some cases negative. Japan will pay a high price in terms of reduced productivity if institutions are not soon changed to channel funds to higher rate-of-return uses.

Feldman (1996) provides a simple framework to emphasize this point. Based on a production function identity that expresses output as the product of productivity (output per worker) and the number of workers, the standard of living measured as output per capita can be expressed as:

$$Y/P = [\Sigma s_j(Y_j/L_j)](1-u)(W/A)(1-d) \qquad (1.1)$$

where Y represents output, P represents population, s_j represents the allocation of working labor in the jth sector, (Y_j/L_j) represents labor productivity in the jth sector, Y_j represents output in the jth sector, L_j represents working labor in the jth sector, W represents the labor force, A represents the working-age population, d represents the dependency ratio (non-working age population to population), and u represents the unemployment rate. Feldman and others emphasize the fact that Japan faces a difficult future given projected demographic trends. The increase in the dependency ratio, d, will reduce the standard of living, other things held constant. The only way this can be offset is if labor productivity is increased, the unemployment rate is lowered, or the participation rate is increased. Greater participation can be obtained by opening up more opportunities for females, postponing retirement age by changing the seniority wage system through more merit-based pay after a certain age, or allowing more immigration. There are constraints on how much offset can be expected from a decline in the unemployment rate or an increase in the participation rate. The unemployment rate may decline in the near future assuming Japan returns to positive and sustained growth. The participation rate will increase because of increasing participation of females in the labor force; however, postponing retirement through adjustments in the seniority wage system or allowing greater immigration is more difficult to achieve. Few observers believe the participation rate other than through greater female participation will significantly increase. Despite the anticipated improvement in the participation rate and the unemployment rate however, they will be insufficient by themselves to offset the effect on the standard of living by the increase in the dependency ratio. The major issue is labor productivity, and it is this factor that raises concern about the role of government financial intermediation.

Thus, aside from the efforts to reform Japan's financial system that emerged from the economic and financial distress of the 1990s, the near-term demographic changes provide an additional incentive to modernize the financial system to ensure that Japan's high savings are put to the most productive uses.

1.7. CONTINUED GROWTH OF THE PSS AND ENHANCED ROLE OF POSTAL DEPOSITS IN JAPAN'S PAYMENTS SYSTEM

PSS officials have shown little inclination to slow their growing role in the financial system, and its scheduled public corporation status in 2003 provides the PSS with incentive to establish itself as a government provider of financial services. Okina (2000) provides a detailed documentation of the new services offered by the PSS and the increasing willingness of private financial institutions to enter into formal relationships with the PSS to handle transactions between individuals and between individuals and businesses. In 1985, the PSS established cash dispensers (CDs) and automatic-teller machines (ATMs) outside the premises of the post office. In 1989, automated transfer service accounts were established linked to ordinary savings accounts and remittance functions. In the 1990s, the postal savings network was opened to private financial institutions with 1,823 members as of year-end 1999; it also established international remittance services and began discussions with private institutions to establish Internet banking services, inter-institutional remittance services, and debit cards. Whereas the majority of these relationships are being established with

Table 1.4. *Applications for CD and ATM tie-ups from private financial institutions, 31 December 1999*

Type of institutions	Number of institutions	Major applicants
City banks	3	Daiwa, Tokai, Asahi
Trust banks	7	Sumitomo, Mitsui, Chuo, Yasuda, Toyo, Mitsubishi, Orix
Foreign banks	3	CityBank, Bank of Brazil, Banco do Estado de São Paulo S.A. (Banespa)
Regional banks	16	Hokuetsu, Musashino, Okinawa, Ryukyu, Tokyo Tomin, etc.
Regional banks II	50	Niigata Chuo, Chubu, Tokyo Sowa, Kagawa, etc.
Long-term credit banks	3	Long-Term Credit Bank of Japan (now Shinsei Bank), Industrial Bank of Japan, Nippon Credit Bank
Shoko chukin banks	1	
Shinkin banks	316	
Labor credit associations	41	
Credit cooperatives	145	
Credit federations of agricultural cooperatives	29	
Agricultural cooperatives	1,000	
Credit federations of fishery cooperatives	1	
Fisheries cooperatives	115	
Securities companies	15	Daiwa, Nomura, Nikko, etc.
Security-investment trust companies	3	
Life-insurance companies	12	
Non-life-insurance companies	4	
Charge companies	52	
Bank-affiliated card companies	7	
Total	1,823	

Note: Each private financial institution holds postal savings accounts and makes payments using cash and checks.

Source: Okina (2000, p. 16).

smaller depository institutions (regional banks, credit cooperatives, and other cooperatives), the PSS is also establishing relationships with several city banks, trust banks, long-term credit banks, securities companies, and life-insurance companies. Table 1.4 lists the CD and ATM tie-ups between the PSS and various private financial institutions as of 31 December 1999. The PSS is also in the process of establishing payment services not only with private financial institutions, but with nonfinancial business firms such as NTT Data and All Nippon Airways.

These developments are problematical, aside from the increased competition with private financial institutions. The increased role of the PSS in the payments system provides a strong argument that the PSS should be formally incorporated into the official settlement system operated by the Bank of Japan. This will be necessary to improve efficiency in the settlement of outstanding balances and, more important, to ensure that the Bank of Japan has oversight over the settlement process to maintain financial stability. At the same time, incorporation of the PSS into the formal Bank of Japan settlement system enhances the economic and political power of the PSS. Private financial institutions, especially banks, have been vocal critics of the PSS; however, the various relationships being established between the PSS and private financial institutions will either turn private financial institutions into reluctant supporters of the PSS or, at a minimum, into silent critics of the PSS.

These developments suggest that the window of opportunity to deal with the PSS problem and to modernize Japan's financial system is not large.

1.8. CONSENSUS FOR REFORM

Thus, by the late 1990s there was sufficient consensus that reform of the PSS and the FILP be placed on the reform agenda. To recapitulate, four factors generated the consensus. First, financial distress in the first part of the 1990s revealed the potential instability that the PSS presented to the financial system by encouraging disintermediation of funds from private banks to the PSS and by complicating the government deposit-guarantee system. Second, political consensus was growing that Japan needed a major overhaul of its economic institutions. The PSS and FILP together were the elephant in the room that had been ignored, and the elephant could no longer be ignored if Japan wanted to achieve a credible financial reform process. Third, the projected decline in population and increase in the dependency ratio (nonworking-age population as a percentage of the population) will lower the standard of living under current conditions. Increasing labor productivity through higher yield investment is the only practical offset to a decline in the standard of living that will occur under current conditions. Fourth, the increasing role of the PSS in the payments system and the potential that the PSS will become an important part of the payment system imply that reform will encounter increasing resistance as time progresses.

In 1993, post offices were officially directed to cease appealing to the fears of the public to attract deposits. In 1994, the regulatory authorities agreed that the PSS would set deposit rates "close to" private-bank deposit rates in an effort to reduce disintermediation. These were not trivial reforms, but the most significant reform commenced in June 1998.

1.9. **THE FIRST SERIOUS EFFORT TO REFORM THE PSS AND THE FILP: 1998**

As a reflection of this greater willingness to depart from the old regime and of an emerging consensus that reform of the PSS and FILP could no longer be avoided, the PSS and the FILP were targeted for reform in 1998. The PSS or FILP were not regarded as a fundamental cause of the financial distress, and in fact the FILP played a counter-cyclical role by offsetting part of the private-bank credit crunch in the last part of the 1990s. However, the time had arrived for serious reform of the PSS and the FILP to transform the financial system into the one envisaged by the Big Bang announcement. Regulatory authorities recognized that unless meaningful reform of the PSS and FILP were attempted, Japan would be unable to make a creditable case to the international community that serious reform was in progress. Concerns about enhancing the productivity of the economy in the face of projected population changes provided further incentive to reform the PSS and FILP.

As part of the Laws to Reform Central Government Ministries and Agencies passed in June 1998, the structure of government budgeting was fundamentally changed. The process of reform initiated by the June 1998 legislation has the potential of significantly redesigning the role of government financial intermediation in Japan. This legislation was developed by the Ministry of Finance, which has responsibility for the Trust Fund Bureau and the FILP system; however, responsibility for the PSS resided with the Ministry of Posts and Telecommunications, so the June 1998 legislation only dealt with the FILP.

The June 1998 legislation and subsequent administrative decisions do not solve the PSS problem, nor do they address the larger role of government financial intermediation. The legislation essentially restructured government intermediation and set up a framework to make the sources and uses of funds more market sensitive. In fact, a cynic could argue that the changes are in form only, and not in substance, by pointing out that the PSS will now merely purchase bonds issued by FILP entities and/or bonds issued by the Ministry of Finance earmarked to fund entities previously financed by the FILP.

It is possible to view the changes in a positive manner, however, and to regard them as a meaningful step in the right direction, with the potential to modernize an important part of the Japanese financial system. These changes bring the issue of government financial intermediation to the forefront of policy discussion and establishes a framework that has the potential to generate additional fundamental reforms consistent with the Big Bang proposals. At a minimum, the reforms will provide more transparency to government financial intermediation and will render government financial intermediation more market sensitive, since many of the entities previously funded by the FILP will be required to rely partly on funds obtained in the capital market at market-determined rates. To assist in their greater reliance on market sources of funds, thirty-three FILP-financed entities that previously obtained funds from the Trust Fund Bureau are now required to provide public disclosure of a detailed analysis of the present value of their operations. With respect to the PSS, the closer link between uses and sources of funds in the PSS may also make it more difficult for the PSS to continue offering *teigaku* deposits.

Liberalization has been a major agenda item in Japan for over two decades, and although some progress has been achieved, essential elements of the old financial regime remained in place until the late 1990s. There were indications, however, in the late 1990s that Japanese regulatory authorities were in the process of making fundamental changes in the financial regime in a variety of areas. It would not be an exaggeration to view Japan's solution to the problems created by the PSS and FILP system as a fair indicator of whether the goals of the Big Bang will be realized. The PSS and FILP have been an integral part of the old regime, and reform of these key elements of the old regime will indicate just how willing Japan is to move to a new, more open, and competitive financial regime. Japan is indeed at the crossroads, and a review of the issues, politics, and economics of the PSS and FILP is needed for any assessment of the future of the Japanese financial system.

1.10. KOIZUMI AND THE PSS

On 26 April 2001, Junichiro Koizumi became Japan's new prime minister after winning a popular mandate on 24 April 2001, at the local LDP chapter level, to reform the ruling LDP and lead the country out of a decade of economic and financial distress. Koizumi is known as a radical and a maverick because of his position on privatizing the PSS as well as other positions on reforming Japan's depressed economy. He advocated a far more aggressive approach to resolving the nonperforming loan problem than had been attempted to date, by forcing banks to write off bad loans; he had criticized Japan's inefficient pension system; and he advocated the popular election of prime ministers. Prime Minister Koizumi came from the traditional LDP; however, his reform proposals, his grass-roots rather than party-boss support, and his resounding victory over the far more traditional LDP candidate, Ryutaro Hashimoto, who served as prime minister from late 1996 to July 1998, set him apart from the typical LDP politician. Hence, radical and maverick are well-deserved characterizations of Koizumi.

Prime Minister Koizumi must contend with the economic, financial, and political instability that have characterized Japan since the collapse of asset prices in the early 1990s, and his proposal to privatize the PSS would be the most significant structural change in Japan's financial system undertaken in the postwar period. The immediate problem as of late 2001 is to resolve the nonperforming loan problem and to adopt a more aggressive monetary policy to reverse the downward movement in the price level, but in terms of the long-run modernization of Japan's financial system to support sustained growth and deal with projected demographic trends, reform of the PSS and the FILP has high priority.

The reforms of 1998 and subsequent administrative decisions were significant steps toward modernizing Japan's financial system, but they lacked political leadership and were incomplete since they left the PSS as a government bank. Koizumi provides and adds a new dimension to the debate. Despite the significance of the 1998 reforms, the PSS remains a government bank, and liberalization of the PSS and FILP must ultimately entail privatizing the PSS as well as rendering the majority of FILP-funded entities dependent on market sources of funds.

The reality is that Koizumi, or any political leader advocating privatization of the PSS and further reform of the FILP, faces a daunting process. It is not by accident that the PSS and FILP have avoided reform. Cargill and Yoshino (2001) listed several reasons why change would be difficult. First, they provide significant advantages to the participants. The *teigaku* time-deposit, which represents about 80 percent of postal deposits held by the public, provides a no-penalty option to withdraw funds after six months to take advantage of interest-rate movements; hence, the *teigaku* deposit offers a higher effective interest rate than any time-deposit offered by private banks. Post offices are more convenient than private banks, as their numbers exceeded those of private-bank branches in every prefecture for much of the postwar period. The PSS shows no interest in restraining growth and, in fact, has expanded its services and formed CD and ATM relationships with private financial institutions; for example, buses from Narita Airport to Tokyo advertise the availability of Visa services for cardholders at local post offices. According to Okina (2000), postal offices are devoting much effort to becoming "financial convenience stores." Funds obtained through the FILP are subsidized—a benefit to many borrowers who would have been unable to obtain funding from the private-banking system. Second, the FILP as part of the budgeting process is an instrument to maintain and enhance the political standing of the LDP. The PSS is also an important support system for the LDP and allows the LDP to reach virtually every area of Japan. Postal officials frequently play a role in the election process at the local level, since they in turn can depend on the LDP to support the PSS. According to *Strom* (2001), there is evidence that local postal authorities attempted to influence the April 2001 grass-roots voting in favor of

Hashimoto, the LDP-designate to replace Mori. Third, the size and pervasiveness of the PSS and FILP render reform a difficult process even under the most favorable conditions, so policymakers are willing to put PSS and FILP reform on the back burner. Fourth, the PSS and FILP are immensely popular in Japan, criticized only by a few academics, private banks, and, on occasion, the Bank of Japan. The FILP increased its popularity in the 1990s as funds allocated to business and housing grew more rapidly than other FILP uses of funds, which mitigated the credit crunch at private banks. Fifth, financial liberalization has been mainly a response to internal and external pressure from various groups who saw liberalization as a way to reestablish lost markets (domestic banks), expand markets (foreign financial institutions and domestic securities companies), enhance profit via portfolio management (domestic corporations), or deal with trade-balance issues (mainly the United States). Their agenda did not focus on government financial intermediation. Thus, reform of the PSS and FILP is primarily an internally generated process and, until Koizumi, it lacked any political leadership. Sixth, the increasing role of postal deposits and the increasing relationship between the PSS and private financial institutions emphasized by Okina (2000) makes radical reform of the PSS more difficult and shortens the window of opportunity for reform. The increased role of the PSS in the payments system requires that it become a formal component of the Bank of Japan settlement process; however, this will only strengthen the economic and political influence of the PSS.

Koziumi's popularity masked the difficult road ahead for reforming the PSS and FILP. After 16 months, Koizumi had achieved no measurable success. Upon taking office in April 2001, Koizumi set up an advisory committee to recommend changes in Japan's postal system and introduced legislation during the Spring 2002 session of the Diet to begin the privatization process. This followed a December 2001 announcement by Koziumi to begin dismantling several government banks, including the large and popular Government Home Loan Corporation. Koizumi, however, met stiff opposition and has been unable to garnish any broad public support for change. By late 2002, it became clear that Koizumi was unable to achieve reform beyond what had been accomplished in 1998.

The opposition came from two groups. First, the LDP strongly opposes any change since it relies on the postal system to maintain power by mobilizing votes at the local level and relies on the postal system as part of the *amakudari* or "descending from heaven" reward system in which after leaving office, one is rewarded by retiring to a position in the postal system. Second, the regulatory agencies that deal with the PSS oppose any change since it would involve a reduction in regulatory power as well as eliminate an important part of the *amakudari* system for government bureaucrats. There was no group in favor of reform to offset these opposing groups. Small businesses and the household sector benefited from expanded FILP lending for small business and housing in the 1990s. Household holdings of postal deposits return reasonable real rates of interest given the decline in the price level, and postal deposits are viewed as safer than private bank deposits given the changes in deposit insurance made 1 April 2002 and planned for 1 April 2003. Private banks, for reasons stated above, are becoming less vocal critics.

Even if politicians were willing to dismantle a major part of the FILP program, they may be constrained by an unwillingness to reveal to the public the magnitude of the nonperforming loan problem in the FILP. In Chapter 4, this book suggests the existence of a nonperforming loan problem on the books of the government banks that has not been revealed. Doi and Hoshi (2002), however, provide a far more extensive analysis of the potential for nonperforming loans in the FILP system. They estimate that as much as 75 percent of the outstanding loans to FILP recipients are nonperforming representing about 16 percent of GDP. Even with a large margin of error, Doi and Hoshi's estimate of nonperforming loans in the FILP system is a serious policy issue that has not even been addressed in Japan, let alone admitted.

1.11. OUTLINE OF THE REST OF THE BOOK

The remainder of the book is composed of the following four chapters. In Chapter 2, we discuss the historical evolution of the PSS and FILP, with emphasis placed on developments in the postwar period. Flow of funds and related statistical measures indicate that the PSS and FILP have been a major feature of Japanese finance and, despite an official policy of liberalization since 1976, the PSS and FILP increased their role in the economy. Chapter 3 develops a formal flow-of-funds model of the PSS and FILP to provide a representation of how the PSS and FILP interact with other elements of the financial regime. Comparative static results are derived to shed light on important policy issues that have been raised in the past with regard to the PSS and FILP, as well as to evaluate the 1998 reform effort. Chapter 4 presents empirical evidence on various aspects of the PSS and FILP in postwar finance and attempts to evaluate their impact on Japan's flow of funds and economy from several perspectives. Chapter 5 summarizes the main points of the study, reviews the report of the Asset Management Council of the Trust Fund Bureau that led to the June 1998 legislation, evaluates the reform process, and offers some recommendations for further reform.

2

The Postal Savings System and the Fiscal Investment and Loan Program in the Japanese Financial System

2.1. INTRODUCTION

In this chapter, we consider the role of the PSS and FILP in Japan's financial system from three perspectives. The chapter first quantifies the role of the PSS and the FILP in Japanese finance by reviewing selected flow-of-funds statistics[1] for each institution and identifying trends with an emphasis on the postwar period. This review will reveal the longstanding importance of the PSS and the FILP in Japan's financial system and the continued growth of government intermediation after 1975, despite an official policy of financial liberalization. The chapter then reviews the relationship between the PSS and the FILP, the role of the PSS and FILP in Japan's flow of funds, the sectors most dependent on FILP lending, trends in FILP lending, and the relationship between the PSS, FILP institutions, and the national budget. This discussion will show that the PSS and the FILP are a large part of the financial system; more important, the discussion will show that government financial intermediation is a pervasive element of the relationship between the government and the economy and, as such, has established a set of relationships between politicians at both the national and local levels, many sectors of the economy, and the general public that renders reform difficult at best. Not only have the PSS and the FILP conferred benefits on various sectors of the economy and the public, they have become important instruments used by politicians to maintain and enhance their power. The chapter then discusses the evolution of the Japanese financial

[1] The flow-of-funds statistics are prepared by the Bank of Japan, and many of the statistics can be obtained from the Bank of Japan's Website. The Bank of Japan flow-of-funds statistics, however, have recently been revised, and the revisions are carried back for only a few years. To illustrate, securities are now valued at market, whereas in the past they were valued at historical cost. The personal sector, which included very small businesses, is now called the individual sector, which excludes business firms. Numerous other definitional changes have occurred that in some cases make historical comparison questionable. The statistics relating to the PSS and the FILP in most cases are obtained directly from the Ministry of Posts and Telecommunications and the Ministry of Finance and are not plagued with the same problems. In order to minimize confusion, we make limited use of Bank of Japan flow-of-funds statistics, and then only where they can be reasonably compared over time.

system from the start of industrialization in 1868 and the role played by the PSS and FILP. The PSS and FILP were not isolated elements of Japanese finance but integral to an overall approach to finance that had a limited set of objectives and depended on a limited set of circumstances. These conditions were not sustainable and began to unravel in the 1970s in the face of new economic, political, and technological forces. As a result, Japanese finance has been in transition from a state-directed to a more market-directed orientation; however, the transition through the early 1990s left unchanged many of the core elements of the old financial regime. The economic and financial distress of the 1990s accelerated the transition and revealed the problems of the previous incomplete liberalization policy. By the end of the 1990s, major institutional and attitudinal changes were occurring in Japan, including an effort to reform the PSS and FILP. The projected demographic changes in Japan also provided an incentive to reform the PSS and the FILP.

2.2. POSTAL DEPOSITS IN HISTORICAL PERSPECTIVE

The PSS was established in 1875 to support a broad economic and financial policy to industrialize and centralize government control over the economy with the objective of achieving economic and military parity with the West, and eventually of surpassing the West. As part of the industrialization process initiated by the Meiji Restoration in 1868, Japan sought assistance from the outside on how to proceed in setting up a financial system. Japan established a national banking system in 1872 based on the US national banking system, and in 1882 the government established the Bank of Japan based on several European central banks. In the process of establishing a nationwide postal system, Japan was influenced by the UK system of postal deposits and, in 1875, established a system of post offices that also accepted deposits. In 1916, post offices were authorized to sell life insurance. Japan's PSS is among the oldest such system among the industrial countries (Table 2.1).

The PSS from the start was an important component of Japanese finance. Figure 2.1 and Table 2.2 illustrate this point by presenting the ratio of postal deposits to total deposits, defined as the sum of all private-bank deposits and postal deposits over the period from fiscal year-end 1888 (31 March 1889) to 1999 (31 March 2000). The ratio of postal to total deposits is a useful measure of the relative role of the PSS in Japan's financial system over time. Until the liberalization efforts of the 1980s, direct money and capital markets played essentially no role in postwar Japanese finance, and even after 1975, when money and capital markets began to develop as part of the liberalization process, bank finance continued to dominate the Japanese financial system.

Table 2.1. *Initiation of PSS in developed countries*

Country	Date
Austria	1883
Belgium	1870
Canada	1868[*]
Denmark	1991
Finland	1887
France	1881
Germany	1939
Greece	1902
Ireland	1923
Italy	1876
Japan	**1875**
Netherlands	1881
New Zealand	1867
Norway	1950
Spain	1916
Sweden	1884
United Kingdom	1861
United States	1910[†]

Source: Elixman (1992); Kuwayama (2000).

[*]Abolished in 1968.

[†]Abolished in 1966.

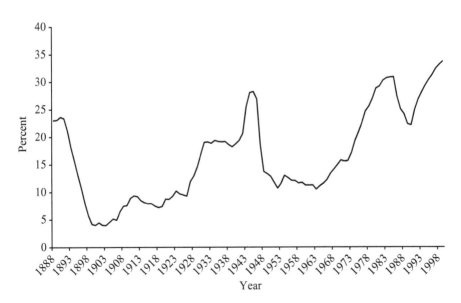

Figure 2.1. *Postal deposits as percentage of total deposits, 1888–1999.*

Table 2.2. *Postal and private-bank deposits in Japan, 1875–1999*

Fiscal year	Postal deposits fiscal year-end outstandings (1,000 yen to 1910, 1 million yen to 1945, 100 million yen to 1999)	Growth rate of postal deposits	*Teigaku* deposits (1 million yen to 1945, 100 million yen to present)	*Teigaku* as a percentage of total postal deposits	Private-bank deposits (1 million yen to 1945, 100 million from 1946 to 1999)	Growth rate of bank deposits	Postal deposits as a percentage of total deposits
1875	15						
1876	41	173.33					
1877	100	143.90					
1878	286	186.00					
1879	494	72.73					
1880	662	34.01					
1881	821	24.02					
1882	1,058	28.87					
1883	2,298	117.20					
1884	5,260	128.89					
1885	9,050	72.05					
1886	15,462	70.85					
1887	18,213	17.79					
1888	19,758	8.48			66		23.04
1889	20,441	3.46			68	3.03	23.11
1890	19,514	−4.54			63	−7.35	23.65
1891	20,149	3.25			66	4.76	23.39
1892	22,826	13.29			85	28.79	21.17
1893	24,815	8.71			112	31.76	18.14
1894	24,962	0.59			134	19.64	15.70
1895	27,748	11.16			184	37.31	13.10

1896	28,078	1.19	235	27.72	10.67
1897	26,335	−6.21	305	29.79	7.95
1898	22,492	−14.59	371	21.64	5.72
1899	23,335	3.75	536	44.47	4.17
1900	24,015	2.91	576	7.46	4.00
1901	27,009	12.47	579	0.52	4.46
1902	28,804	6.65	692	19.52	4.00
1903	31,471	9.26	759	9.68	3.98
1904	38,779	23.22	811	6.85	4.56
1905	52,836	36.25	974	20.10	5.15
1906	72,266	36.77	1,395	43.22	4.93
1907	91,531	26.66	1,325	−5.02	6.46
1908	105,330	15.08	1,304	−1.58	7.47
1909	123,379	17.14	1,506	15.49	7.57
1910	161,026	30.51	1,649	9.50	8.90
1911	183	13.65	1,776	7.70	9.34
1912	197	7.65	1,941	9.29	9.21
1913	195	−1.02	2,110	8.71	8.46
1914	195	0.00	2,212	4.83	8.10
1915	221	13.33	2,569	16.14	7.92
1916	298	34.84	3,464	34.84	7.92
1917	416	39.60	5,146	48.56	7.48
1918	562	35.10	7,236	40.61	7.21
1919	698	24.20	8,734	20.70	7.40
1920	847	21.35	8,829	1.09	8.75
1921	906	6.97	9,494	7.53	8.71
1922	976	7.73	9,551	0.60	9.27
1923	1,102	12.91	9,692	1.48	10.21
1924	1,100	−0.18	10,232	5.57	9.71
1925	1,136	3.27	10,821	5.76	9.50

Table 2.2. (*Cont.*)

Fiscal year	Postal deposits fiscal year-end outstandings (1,000 yen to 1910, 1 million yen to 1945, 100 million yen to 1999)	Growth rate of postal deposits	Teigaku deposits (1 million yen to 1945, 100 million yen to present)	Teigaku as a percentage of total postal deposits	Private-bank deposits (1 million yen to 1945, 100 million from 1946 to 1999)	Growth rate of bank deposits	Postal deposits as a percentage of total deposits
1926	1,156	1.76			11,272	4.17	9.30
1927	1,523	31.75			11,247	−0.22	11.93
1928	1,742	14.38			11,691	3.95	12.97
1929	2,051	17.74			11,972	2.40	14.63
1930	2,337	13.94			11,546	−3.56	16.83
1931	2,609	11.64			11,093	−3.92	19.04
1932	2,704	3.64			11,455	3.26	19.10
1933	2,801	3.59			12,049	5.19	18.86
1934	3,064	9.39			12,755	5.86	19.37
1935	3,232	5.48			13,626	6.83	19.17
1936	3,482	7.74			14,726	8.07	19.12
1937	3,891	11.75			16,405	11.40	19.17
1938	4,738	21.77			20,716	26.28	18.61
1939	6,153	29.86			27,626	33.36	18.22
1940	7,915	28.64			34,284	24.10	18.76
1941	9,975	26.03			41,518	21.10	19.37
1942	13,044	30.77			50,041	20.53	20.68
1943	18,973	45.45	3,180	16.76	55,328	10.57	25.54
1944	30,375	60.10	6,179	20.34	77,926	40.84	28.05
1945	47,151	55.23	9,919	21.04	119,829	53.77	28.24
1946	533	13.04	100	18.76	1,448	20.84	26.91
1947	535	0.38	97	18.13	2,343	61.81	18.59
1948	805	50.47	177	21.99	5,053	115.66	13.74
1949	1,220	51.55	92	7.54	7,920	56.74	13.35

Year							
1950	1,547	26.80	323	20.88	10,485	32.39	12.86
1951	2,008	29.80	532	26.49	15,063	43.66	11.76
1952	2,667	32.82	817	30.63	22,238	47.63	10.71
1953	3,550	33.11	1,202	33.86	27,076	21.76	11.59
1954	4,551	28.20	1,670	36.70	30,366	12.15	13.03
1955	5,382	18.26	2,113	39.26	37,243	22.65	12.63
1956	6,569	22.05	2,769	42.15	47,642	27.92	12.12
1957	7,566	15.18	3,398	44.91	55,048	15.55	12.08
1958	8,538	12.85	4,055	47.49	64,840	17.79	11.64
1959	9,866	15.55	4,890	49.56	74,136	14.34	11.74
1960	11,230	13.83	5,659	50.39	88,722	19.67	11.24
1961	13,105	16.70	6,478	49.43	103,324	16.46	11.26
1962	15,392	17.45	7,763	50.44	121,187	17.29	11.27
1963	18,373	19.37	9,536	51.90	156,481	29.12	10.51
1964	22,297	21.36	12,102	54.28	178,462	14.05	11.11
1965	27,025	21.20	15,450	57.17	206,531	15.73	11.57
1966	33,099	22.47	19,870	60.03	237,900	15.19	12.21
1967	41,093	24.15	25,747	62.65	266,671	12.09	13.35
1968	51,027	24.17	33,136	64.94	310,123	16.29	14.13
1969	63,165	23.79	42,433	67.18	359,789	16.01	14.93
1970	77,439	22.60	54,306	70.13	413,088	14.81	15.79
1971	96,541	24.67	70,421	72.94	522,757	26.55	15.59
1972	122,932	27.34	92,783	75.48	660,378	26.33	15.69
1973	153,765	25.08	117,758	76.58	744,172	12.69	17.12
1974	194,278	26.35	150,124	77.27	810,996	8.98	19.33
1975	245,661	26.45	196,488	79.98	929,213	14.58	20.91
1976	305,248	24.26	253,001	82.88	1,046,484	12.62	22.58
1977	377,264	23.59	319,316	84.64	1,152,386	10.12	24.66
1978	449,962	19.27	382,715	85.05	1,310,489	13.72	25.56
1979	519,118	15.37	442,480	85.24	1,407,448	7.40	26.95
1980	619,543	19.35	544,697	87.92	1,529,783	8.69	28.82

Table 2.2. (Cont.)

Fiscal year	Postal deposits fiscal year-end outstandings (1,000 yen to 1910, 1 million yen to 1945, 100 million yen to 1999)	Growth rate of postal deposits	Teigaku deposits (1 million yen to 1945, 100 million yen to present)	Teigaku as a percentage of total postal deposits	Private-bank deposits (1 million yen to 1945, 100 million yen from 1946 to 1999)	Growth rate of bank deposits	Postal deposits as a percentage of total deposits
1981	695,676	12.29	615,289	88.44	1,687,445	10.31	29.19
1982	781,026	12.27	694,985	88.98	1,799,957	6.67	30.26
1983	862,982	10.49	773,377	89.62	1,948,955	8.28	30.69
1984	940,420	8.97	840,511	89.38	2,110,313	8.28	30.83
1985	1,029,979	9.52	928,555	90.15	2,306,019	9.27	30.87
1986	1,103,951	7.18	996,260	90.24	2,936,055	27.32	27.33
1987	1,173,907	6.34	1,062,603	90.52	3,510,500	19.57	25.06
1988	1,258,691	7.22	1,148,799	91.27	3,947,843	12.46	24.18
1989	1,345,722	6.91	1,185,606	88.10	4,671,479	18.33	22.36
1990	1,362,803	1.27	1,095,672	80.40	4,788,873	2.51	22.15
1991	1,556,007	14.18	1,337,371	85.95	4,681,684	−2.24	24.95
1992	1,700,906	9.31	1,474,456	86.69	4,643,380	−0.82	26.81
1993	1,835,348	7.90	1,599,576	87.15	4,693,141	1.07	28.11
1994	1,975,902	7.66	1,722,891	87.20	4,761,475	1.46	29.33
1995	2,134,375	8.02	1,847,743	86.57	4,892,715	2.76	30.37
1996	2,248,872	5.36	1,938,588	86.20	4,942,190	1.01	31.27
1997	2,405,460	6.96	2,021,276	84.03	5,014,580	1.46	32.42
1998	2,525,867	5.01	2,064,675	81.74	5,091,043	1.52	33.16
1999	2,599,702	2.93	2,124,167	81.71	5,108,075	0.33	33.73

Data Sources: *Economic Statistics of Japan* (Honpo Keizai Toukei), Bank of Japan, various issues; *Economic Statistics Annual* (Keizai Toukei Nenpo), Bank of Japan, various issues until 1989; Flow of Funds (Bank of Japan), 1989 to present; *Yusei Gyosei Tokei Nanpo* (Annual Statistics of Ministry of Post and Telecommunications), various issues.

Note: Private-Bank Deposits: up to 1989, Demand Deposits + Time Deposits + CD at All Banks. Private-Bank Deposits: from 1990 to 1999, Demand Deposits + Time Deposits + CD + Nonresident Yen Deposits and Foreign Currency Deposits.

Corporations relied on bank credit rather than on securities to finance operations as part of the main bank or *keiretsu* system in the postwar period or the *zaibatsu* system in the prewar period. Equities were issued primarily to solidify long-term customer relationships between firms and financial institutions, rather than as a method to finance operations. Government debt was marketed through a syndicate system in which groups of financial institutions and securities companies purchased the debt. Prior to liberalization, the syndicate was "captured" in the sense that it was required to purchase debt at above-market prices; however, after liberalization commenced, the syndicate system purchased debt at market prices.

Postal deposits at the end of the nineteenth century represented about 5 percent of total deposits, having declined from a high of around 20 percent at the start of the data (1888) in Figure 2.1. The decline in the market share of postal deposits reflected the return of public confidence in the banking system by the end of the nineteenth century due to serious banking problems in the 1870s. In 1872, Japan adopted the US style of national banking (without a central bank to regulate the overall supply of money). Like the United States, Japan soon found that the lack of a central bank, with private banks allowed to issue the nation's money supply in the form of national bank notes, generated an unstable monetary and financial environment. Once private banks were permitted to issue national bank notes, national bank notes expanded rapidly, the ensuing inflation imposed severe hardship on the economy, and the public lost confidence in the private banks and sought safety in the PSS. In 1882, the Bank of Japan was established as the sole issuer of national bank notes, and it promptly instituted policies to bring inflation under control and limit bank credit; however, it required almost twenty years to retire the previously issued national bank notes.

Postal deposits averaged about 7 percent during the next twenty years, but starting in the 1920s, the percentage of postal deposits steadily increased to a peak of 27 percent in 1946. Banking failures in the late 1920s resulted in a sharp increase in the ratio of postal to total deposits after 1926, but once the banking situation stabilized and government-directed consolidation of the banking system ensued in the early 1930s, the growth of postal deposits stabilized and remained a constant share of total deposits through the end of the war. Bank deposits grew more rapidly than postal deposits in the immediate years after the end of the war, resulting in a sharp decline in the percentage of postal deposits to around 12 percent, which remained at that level during the 1950s. This reflected a return to confidence in private banks and an increase in banking services as Japan recovered from the wartime devastation.

In the 1960s, however, the percentage of postal deposits steadily increased, and by 1985 they reached 31 percent of total deposits. Incentives to hold postal deposits relative to bank deposits were substantial during this period. Banks offered low deposit rates compared to the PSS and in general made no serious effort to attract household deposits by expanding branches, for example. Liberalization had not yet progressed to a stage that provided households with assets other than postal and bank deposits, and postal deposits had important advantages over private-bank deposits because of the *teigaku* deposit, which minimizes interest-rate risk for the deposit holder, compared to private-bank deposits.

The situation changed in the second half of the 1980s, and the growth of postal deposits relative to private-bank deposits declined. Liberalization provided more competition to the PSS by offering increased asset choices to the household sector, and banks became more competitive in attracting household deposits. The Tax Reform Act of 1986 reduced the evasion of income taxes on postal deposits that was widely practiced in the past. In addition, the rapid increase in equity prices attracted nontransaction funds from all depository institutions into the stock market. Since postal deposits were almost entirely time-deposits (nontransaction deposits), the PSS was more likely to lose funds to the stock market than were private banks.

The collapse of asset prices after 1990 reestablished the historical upward trend of the ratio of postal to total deposits. Postal deposits increased as a percentage of total deposits to 34 percent in 1999, the highest percentage achieved over the entire 1888–1999 period.[2] The increase in market share after 1990 can be partly attributed to public concern with growing banking problems. Nonperforming loans and the failure of a number of credit cooperatives and small banks in the first half of the 1990s alarmed the public, and for the first time since the start of reindustrialization in 1950 the public became increasingly concerned about the safety of private-bank deposits. The PSS appeared to many to offer a safer depository for wealth than did bank deposits or other financial assets tied to the money and capital markets. Disintermediation from bank deposits to postal deposits was also encouraged by post-office officials in 1991 and 1992 as they aggressively advertised the relative safety of postal over bank deposits. Postal-deposit growth was further stimulated when the Bank of Japan in July 1991 lowered the discount rate. *Teigaku* deposits, because they pay a fixed interest rate for ten years and can be withdrawn without a penalty after six months, become attractive when the market anticipates a fall in interest rates.

The historical upward trend in postal deposits has also been supported by the PSS's aggressive marketing of payment services (Okina, 2000) in an effort to become a "financial convenience store" like 7-Eleven. In the 1990s, the PSS increasingly collaborated with private financial institutions to establish CD and ATM relationships, debit-card services, Internet banking, and mutual remittance services. The PSS has commenced selling government bonds, travelers checks,

---

[2] As part of the revision of the flow-of-funds accounts, the definition of private banks has been changed to include some previously excluded banks. Hence, the ratio of postal to total deposits is a few percentage points lower than cited in previous publications that use a narrower definition of banks.

and even lottery tickets. Okina (2000) provides a detailed discussion of these new services and their implication for the future development of the PSS.

There are several important implications that can be drawn from Table 2.2 and Figure 2.1. First, the PSS has been a major part of Japanese finance from the first efforts to establish a modern financial system in the second half of the nineteenth century until the beginning of the twenty-first century. Second, the PSS has exhibited an overall upward trend in importance because postal *teigaku* deposits have a significant advantage over private-bank time-deposits, the PSS has had a far more extensive branching system than the private banks, and, until recently, commercial banks have not aggressively channeled services to the household sector. Third, the overall upward trend has been little affected by the official policy of financial liberalization that commenced in the late 1970s, despite obvious contractions between the extensive degree of government financial intermediation implied by the PSS and the FILP and more open and competitive financial structures. Fourth, despite the overall upward trend, fluctuations in the ratio of postal to total deposits have frequently been associated with changes in public confidence in the private-banking system.

The PSS cannot be fully appreciated without considering its role in the FILP or FILP system. In this regard, we need to consider the relationship between the PSS and the FILP, the role of the FILP in the government's annual budget process, and the role of the PSS and FILP in Japan's flow of funds.

2.3. THE PSS AND THE FILP IN THE POSTWAR PERIOD: FLOW-OF-FUNDS PERSPECTIVE

The PSS was an established institution before the FILP program was formulized. The FILP began to evolve in the 1880s in response to banking problems associated with the failure of the national banking system to provide a stable financial and monetary framework to support industrialization. At the time the PSS was established, postal deposits were deposited in private banks with the intent that the government and the private banks would manage the funds. Bank failures and loss of public confidence in the banking system in the 1880s, however, forced the Ministry of Finance to remove postal funds from private banks and thereafter to transfer postal deposits directly to an account at the Ministry of Finance that was managed by the Ministry. The Deposit Bureau of the Ministry of Finance (Trust Fund Bureau in the postwar financial regime) was established in 1885; from that point on, the Ministry of Finance managed postal deposits and other funds deposited in the Deposit Bureau. By 1885, the basic outline of the FILP system was in place; however, it was not until the early 1950s that the system illustrated in Table 1.2 (p. 10) was formalized.

The PSS is the part of Japan's postal system that offers deposit services at every one of the some 24,700 post offices throughout Japan, with over 400 offices in Tokyo alone. The post offices also sell life insurance. The collected funds (postal deposits and insurance premiums) are transferred to the FILP. The FILP combines the funds received with funds from other sources and distributes the funds to government financial institutions, quasi-government corporations, special accounts, local governments, and special firms. Table 1.2 provides a detailed description of the distribution of postal deposits and other funds through the FILP system to FILP-financed entities for amounts outstanding as of 31 March 2000.

Government financial intermediation is not unique to Japan. Every country, whether possessing a rigidly controlled financial system or one subject to significant market forces, incorporates government financial intermediation in some manner to provide subsidized credit to targeted sectors of the economy. In the United States, a variety of government or quasi-government entities, such as the Export–Import Bank, the Federal Farm Credit Bureau, or the Small Business Administration, provide subsidized loans to targeted sectors of the economy. In addition, the US government supports an extensive secondary market system for mortgage loans issued by private financial institutions. Government financial intermediation also exists in more indirect forms; for example, in the United States there is an extensive system of credit unions with tax-free status that gives these institutions a significant comparative advantage in consumer markets compared to private lenders. Although credit unions represent only a small percentage of the total financial assets held by financial institutions, they represent about 11 percent of the total consumer credit outstanding.

Japan is unique, however, in several respects. This point can best be illustrated by comparing government financial intermediation in Japan and in the United States—the financial systems of which represent the two ends of the spectrum of financial regimes ranging from market-directed to state-directed regimes.

First, public financial intermediation in Japan represents a larger part of the flow of funds, compared to the United States; for example, Cargill and Royama (1988) showed that public finance in Japan during the 1975–85 period was significantly larger than in the United States. Second, the sources and uses of funds in the FILP system are separate, which makes it difficult to rationalize the cost of collecting funds with the return on investing funds. The cross-subsidization of normal postal services with deposit-taking understates the cost of postal deposits and hence justifies higher loan subsidies than would be possible if the full cost of collecting funds were transparent. In the United States, government financial intermediation is more transparent because government agencies such as the Ginnie Mae raise funds in the open money and capital market; thus, there is a closer relationship between the cost of funds and the loan subsidization. Third, government financial intermediation in the United States takes a distant second place to market-directed finance. The large role of market-directed finance, especially open money and capital markets, makes it difficult for government financial intermediation to provide large amounts of subsidized credit since the sources of funds for subsidized credit are market sensitive and dependent on open money and capital markets. Open money and capital markets provide less range for nontransparent subsidization of fund collection than is possible with a network of post offices collecting funds. Fourth, the concentration of large amounts of funds at one distribution point—the FILP—provides a rich environment for political influence on how funds are distributed. In this respect, the FILP system as it developed in the postwar period could not likely have been maintained without the PSS to provide low-cost funds. On the other hand, the PSS could have operated in the absence of the FILP as a narrow bank or even a full-service bank with deposit-taking and lending services provided in the same institution. That is, the PSS was a necessary component of the FILP system, since without a large and growing source of postal deposits the FILP system would not likely have existed. It would have been very difficult, in the absence of capital markets and restrictions on capital inflows, for the FILP to fund the type and extent of activities that became commonplace. It is not an accident that the PSS preceded the FILP system.

FILP-financed entities have played a major role in Japanese finance during the postwar period (Ogura and Yoshino, 1988; Yoshino, 1993), especially in the early 1950s as Japan was reindustrializing and rebuilding from the devastation of the war. Of these entities, the government banks have been the most controversial since they are the most dependent on funds provided by the PSS, account for the largest component of funds provided by the FILP system, compete directly with private banks, and are alleged to interfere with monetary policy. Table 2.3 provides a brief description of each of the eight government financial institutions. Previously there were eleven government banks, but as a result of several consolidations in 1999 the number of government banks was reduced to eight as of 2001.

The role of the PSS and the FILP can be quantified by considering five aspects of the flow of funds through the FILP: (1) individual sector assets and liabilities; (2) nonfinancial private corporate-sector sources of funds; (3) trends in industrial dependence on FILP funding; (4) trends in FILP uses of funds; and (5) trends in FILP sources of funds.

2.3.1. *Individual Sector*

Table 2.4 presents the percentage of individual-sector (household) assets[3] allocated to postal deposits and postal life insurance, and individual liabilities owed to banks, private banks, and government banks.

---

[3] The individual sector was previously referred to as the personal sector, which included very small business firms (two or three workers); however, the new individual sector excludes these businesses. Flow-of-funds data since 1997 are thus not completely compatible with previous data. These small businesses are now included in the nonfinancial private corporate sector, previously referred to as the corporate business sector.

Table 2.3. *Eight government financial institutions, 2001*

Government Housing Loan Corporation (1950)
> There was a significant shortage of housing after the Second World War, and demand for housing was further increased as former members of the military services returned to Japan. The private sector constructed 1.6 million houses between 1945 and 1948, while only 40,000 to 50,000 houses were constructed by the public sector. The combined supply of housing was insufficient to satisfy the demand for housing and, in addition, low-income households were largely excluded from obtaining housing funds. The Dodge Plan further reduced the availability of funds to support housing because money supply and bank credit were sharply reduced after 1948. The Government Housing Loan Corporation was established in 1950 to address the shortage.

National Life Finance Corporation (2000)
> A new government bank created by merging the People's Finance Corporation and the Environmental Sanitation Business Finance Corporation.

> *People's Finance Corporation (1949)*
> Private banks at the end of the war continued their focus on lending primarily to large businesses and corporations. Small business firms were unable to raise funds from the market and were forced to resort to unofficial or black markets for needed funds. Small firms found credit even more restricted in 1948 as the Dodge Plan austerity programs were initiated to deal with triple-digit inflation and large government deficits. The lack of credit for small business firms combined with the high inflation rate imposed extreme hardship on small and medium-sized businesses. In an effort to offset the effects on small business firms, the People's Finance Corporation was established in 1949. Despite the name of the corporation, it did not make consumer loans but rather made loans to small business firms. However, in 1978, the People's Finance Corporation initiated education loans to support the parents of high-school and university students.

> *Environmental Sanitation Business Finance Corporation (1967)*
> Sanitation deficiencies were a serious problem for many years after the war in the areas of public baths, laundries, small restaurants, butcher shops, etc. Families and small firms operated these facilities, and their small scale of operation made it difficult to modernize equipment. The Environmental Sanitation Business Finance Corporation was established in 1967 to maintain and improve public sanitation by providing funds to these facilities to upgrade their sanitation equipment.

Japan Finance Corporation for Small Business (1953)
> *Sogo* banks (now referred to as regional banks II) and *shinkin* banks were established in 1951 to assist small businesses because the large private city banks focused primarily on large businesses and corporations. Despite these new institutions, many small business firms had difficulty obtaining credit, especially long-term credit. The Finance Corporation for Small Business was established in 1953 to provide long-term loans to small businesses whose assets were less than 100 million yen or who employed fewer than 300 workers.

Agriculture, Forestry, and Fishery Finance Corporation (1953)
> Immediately following the end of the war, inflation and the subsequent Dodge Plan made it difficult for farmers to obtain private-bank financing. In addition, the land reform

Table 2.3. *(Cont.)*

implemented by the Allied Occupation resulted in a large number of small farms, which further increased agricultural demand for private-bank loans. This corporation was established in 1953 to provide long-term loans to borrowers engaged in farming, forestry, and fishery activities.

Japan Finance Corporation for Municipal Enterprises (1957)
Municipal government had great difficulty raising funds by selling local government bonds because of a general shortage of funds and the lack of developed open money and capital markets. The Corporation was established in 1957 to supply credit to municipal enterprises in order to promote improvements in the water supply, sewage system, hospitals, etc. The Corporation also purchased local government bonds in order to construct local roads, develop land for the promotion of regional industry, etc. The Corporation issued government-guaranteed bonds purchased by regional banks and other institutions, in addition to receiving funds from FILP.

Development Bank of Japan (2000)
A new government bank created by merging the Japan Development Bank and the Hokkaido–Tohoku Development Finance Public Corporation.

Hokkaido–Tohoku Development Finance Public Corporation (1956)
Hokkaido and Tohoku are northern regions of Japan whose development lagged behind other regions in the 1950s. The Corporation was established in 1956 to provide long-term loans to support industrial development in northern Japan and to promote the region.

Japan Development Bank (1951)
The Japan Development Bank was established in 1951 to provide long-term investment funds to industry. The Bank concentrated lending in the electric-power and sea-transport industry, followed by coal mining, iron and steel, fertilizers, and machinery, in that order. In 1988, the Bank started to provide lending for local public infrastructure needs and loans to venture firms judged to be essential for Japan's future.

Okinawa Development Finance Corporation (1972)
Okinawa was under the occupation of the United States until 1972, when it was returned to Japan. The Okinawa Development Finance Corporation was established in 1972 to provide loans to support industry, small business, housing, agriculture and fishery, environmental sanitation, medical sector, etc., in Okinawa.

Japan Bank for International Cooperation (2000)
Formally the Export–Import Bank.

Export–Import Bank (1950)
The Export–Import Bank was established in 1950 to promote exports. The Bank provided long-term funds to finance exports that could not be fully accommodated within the system of preferential treatment being given to short-term export financing by the Bank of Japan. The shipbuilding industry was also supported by loans from the Bank. In 1972, the Bank started to finance projects designed to promote imports and foreign direct investment in Japan in an effort to mitigate increasing international pressure over trade imbalances.

Table 2.4. *Individual postal deposits and postal life insurance as a percentage of assets, and bank loans as a percentage of individual liabilities, 1953–1999*

Fiscal year	Postal deposits	Postal life insurance	Total bank loans	Private-bank loans	Government-bank loans
1953	9.78	4.44	53.06	39.22	13.83
1954	10.80	4.76	52.87	37.70	15.16
1955	10.68	5.14	53.19	37.44	15.76
1956	10.58	5.29	58.35	43.13	15.21
1957	10.26	5.64	56.64	41.89	14.75
1958	9.71	5.78	56.71	42.01	14.70
1959	9.29	5.79	57.67	43.67	14.01
1960	8.60	5.59	59.48	46.47	13.00
1961	8.41	5.56	60.05	47.21	12.84
1962	8.15	5.27	58.51	47.09	11.41
1963	8.29	4.93	56.38	46.96	9.43
1964	8.38	4.26	54.11	45.14	8.97
1965	8.87	4.05	56.63	47.32	9.31
1966	9.24	3.90	58.49	49.27	9.22
1967	9.68	3.69	58.25	49.19	9.05
1968	10.22	3.63	58.77	49.66	9.11
1969	10.65	3.56	58.71	49.86	8.85
1970	11.07	3.57	61.91	52.74	9.18
1971	11.66	3.62	64.49	54.97	9.52
1972	12.02	3.57	70.36	60.82	9.54
1973	12.82	3.72	74.61	64.61	10.01
1974	13.59	3.83	74.16	63.35	10.82
1975	14.38	3.90	72.09	60.67	11.42
1976	15.27	4.04	71.99	60.04	11.94
1977	16.31	4.14	73.86	60.94	12.92
1978	16.99	4.26	74.20	60.76	13.44
1979	17.39	4.40	76.12	61.34	14.79
1980	18.68	4.58	76.46	60.41	16.05
1981	18.74	4.73	76.36	59.57	16.79
1982	18.96	4.88	76.12	58.56	17.56
1983	18.97	5.03	76.63	59.13	17.51
1984	18.97	5.15	76.52	59.20	17.32
1985	19.08	5.29	76.11	58.86	17.25
1986	18.79	5.55	77.60	60.27	17.33
1987	16.01	5.02	80.26	64.17	16.09
1988	15.47	5.10	81.86	66.03	15.83
1989	14.98	5.17	82.62	67.44	15.18
1990	14.28	5.43	82.39	66.89	15.51
1991	15.79	5.87	81.72	65.92	15.80
1992	16.61	6.40	83.13	66.25	16.89
1993	16.97	6.87	84.25	65.60	18.65

Table 2.4. *(Cont.)*

Fiscal year	Postal deposits	Postal life insurance	Total bank loans	Private-bank loans	Government-bank loans
1994	17.66	7.39	83.03	62.81	20.21
1995	18.04	7.14	81.82	62.61	19.22
1996	18.72	8.23	82.25	59.74	22.51
1997	18.68	8.21	80.52	57.98	22.54
1998	19.07	8.43	80.86	57.66	23.20
1999	18.71	8.32	83.37	57.97	25.40

Source: Flow of Funds, Bank of Japan and Ministry of Posts and Telecommunications.

The personal sector in general has increased the percentage of assets allocated to postal deposits and postal life insurance. Postal deposits represented 18.7 percent of personal-sector assets in 1999 (Table 2.4) and 34 percent of total deposits in 1999 (Table 2.2). Assets allocated to postal life insurance increased steadily in the postwar period to represent 8.3 percent of individual assets as of 1999. Postal deposits and life insurance in 1999 represented the largest allocation of individual assets in the postwar period covered by the data in Table 2.4. The percentage of total life insurance accounted for by postal life insurance has steadily increased in the postwar period (Table 2.5), and in the late 1990s postal life insurance represented 30 percent of total life insurance.

Despite the general upward trend in the percentage of assets allocated to postal deposits, there have been two periods when postal deposits became less attractive than other assets. Postal deposits became relatively less important during the late 1950s and the 1960s as banks grew at a very fast rate to accommodate domestic investment spending and as public confidence in the private-banking system was restored. Postal deposits reestablished their upward trend from the late 1960s to the second half of the 1980s. Then postal deposits again declined in importance during the second half of the 1980s as the stock market or "bubble economy" attracted funds to equities and when the exclusion of deposit interest from income taxes up to 3 million yen was eliminated in 1986. At the same time, competition from private banks increased as banks offered expanded products at market rates of interest and increased their branching networks. Postal deposits again reestablished their upward trend after 1990 as the public shifted funds from the stock market and from private banks into postal deposits in response to the collapse of equity prices and the increased awareness of bank failures and problems with nonperforming loans. Expectations of declining interest rates also contributed to the shift of private-bank deposits to the PSS.

The majority of postal deposits held by the personal sector are time-deposits, especially *teigaku* time-deposits (Table 2.2, p. 36). There are two reasons for the relatively small use by the personal sector of demand or ordinary deposits

Table 2.5. *Postal life insurance and private life insurance, 1980–1998*

Fiscal year	Total life insurance	Postal life insurance	Postal life insurance as percentage of total
1980	470,450	114,534	24.4
1981	527,186	133,508	25.3
1982	608,530	154,308	25.4
1983	699,768	178,319	25.5
1984	801,627	203,977	25.5
1985	912,174	231,820	25.4
1986	804,551	239,872	29.8
1987	943,809	290,087	30.7
1988	1,101,850	325,876	29.6
1989	1,291,025	368,471	28.5
1990	1,513,600	415,102	27.4
1991	1,726,042	464,156	26.9
1992	1,905,014	517,835	27.2
1993	2,096,031	578,173	27.6
1994	2,328,005	655,311	28.2
1995	2,587,471	743,450	28.7
1996	2,831,675	842,030	29.7
1997	3,119,091	941,864	30.2
1998	3,296,552	1,007,720	30.6

Source: Ministry of Posts and Telecommunications Annual Statistics;
Bank of Japan, Economic Statistics Annual.

offered by the PSS, despite the fact that postal demand-deposits offer higher interest rates than private-bank demand-deposits. First, postal deposits are not as readily usable a transaction medium as private-bank demand-deposits since post offices cannot offer as many electronic fund-transfer connections as private banks. Any transfer of funds from the PSS to banks is subject to a fee, further discouraging the use of postal demand-deposits as a transaction medium. Okina (2000) however, argues that the past comparative disadvantage of the PSS with regard to transactions services is rapidly being eliminated. Second, the Japanese public utilizes cash for transactions to a large extent, so banks have an advantage over the post office because of their extensive and more available system of CDs. Postal CDs cannot be located outside the post offices, which are closed on Sundays and holidays, thus limiting depositors' access to cash.

On the other hand, the *teigaku* account is superior to any time-deposit offered by private banks. It is a ten-year time-deposit with an option to withdraw the funds after six months. Thus, the deposit-holder has a relatively small level of interest-rate risk. If interest rates increase, the deposit can be withdrawn and redeposited at the higher rate, and if interest rates decline, the deposit is maintained at the rate current when it was established. Private banks have never been officially prevented from offering a *teigaku*-type account, but they have chosen not to because of the considerable interest-rate risk embedded in this type of account. As of 2001, several private banks were offering *teigaku* accounts that compete directly with postal accounts; however, the inherent interest-rate risk of these accounts prevents their use as a major source of funds for private banks.

Table 2.4 also shows personal liabilities to banks, private banks, and government banks. The percentage of liabilities owed to government banks has trended upward over time, especially in the 1990s when the percentage of liabilities owed to private banks declined as a result of the credit crunch. Housing loans provided by the Government Housing Loan Corporation account for most of the increase in the allocation of liabilities to government financial institutions and have been a significant offset to the credit crunch at the private banks, thus further strengthening public support of the FILP system.

2.3.2. *Nonfinancial Private Corporate Sector*

Despite almost two decades of financial liberalization in Japan, reliance on loans from government banks by business has actually increased relative to other sources of funds. Table 2.6 shows that business reliance on government financial institutions declined from 1954 to the early 1970s but then gradually increased over time to 2001. In fact, reliance on government banks in the late 1990s was higher than at any time during the postwar period covered by the data in Table 2.6. The increased reliance on government banks is concentrated primarily in small to medium-sized businesses rather than in the large and more productive corporations in Japan's industrial structure. The reliance on funds from government banks accelerated in the 1990s as private banks greatly restricted credit to increase their capital–asset ratios and reduce their nonperforming loans. Japanese banks are permitted to count 45 percent of capital gains toward tier II capital; although this arrangement appeared to be a major advantage in the late 1980s when equity prices were increasing, it became a constraint on bank lending in the 1990s. As equity prices declined, bank capital also declined. Since banks could not readily raise capital by issuing new equity or subordinate debt, banks restricted the growth of assets to maintain their capital–asset ratios; hence, the credit crunch of the 1990s.

2.3.3. *Trends in Industry–Government-Bank Finance*

Table 2.7 provides information on specific industries in terms of their reliance on private financial institutions, government financial institutions, and bond issues

Table 2.6. *Nonfinancial private corporate bank loans as a percentage of liabilities, 1953–1998*

Fiscal year	Total bank loans	Private-bank loans	Government-bank loans
1953	92.41	82.40	10.01
1954	94.65	83.63	11.02
1955	93.84	82.80	11.04
1956	92.61	82.56	10.05
1957	98.08	87.59	10.49
1958	95.15	85.08	10.07
1959	84.08	75.34	8.74
1960	82.59	74.40	8.18
1961	77.15	69.76	7.39
1962	75.85	68.95	6.90
1963	74.30	67.46	6.83
1964	73.75	66.86	6.89
1965	75.97	68.75	7.22
1966	73.25	66.05	7.20
1967	71.18	64.04	7.13
1968	73.60	66.00	7.59
1969	70.61	63.80	6.81
1970	75.15	68.09	7.06
1971	80.40	73.18	7.22
1972	81.10	74.30	6.80
1973	70.90	64.88	6.01
1974	78.36	71.29	7.06
1975	76.58	69.48	7.10
1976	77.50	70.12	7.38
1977	80.43	72.58	7.85
1978	76.78	68.95	7.83
1979	71.48	63.89	7.59
1980	71.48	63.73	7.75
1981	72.48	64.45	8.03
1982	76.53	68.07	8.46
1983	75.70	67.46	8.24
1984	76.42	68.40	8.02
1985	80.25	72.19	8.05
1986	80.29	72.77	7.52
1987	63.60	55.58	8.01
1988	65.65	57.43	8.22
1989	68.88	60.28	8.59
1990	74.62	65.09	9.53
1991	83.81	72.26	11.55
1992	84.29	71.71	12.58
1993	85.97	72.07	13.91
1994	86.01	71.44	14.56
1995	78.15	64.73	13.42
1996	74.52	61.64	12.88
1997	73.59	60.57	13.01
1998	69.26	56.51	12.74

Source: Flow of Funds, Bank of Japan.

Table 2.7. *Sources of external funds, by industry, 1961–1998*

Industries	Private banks 1961–74	Govt banks	Bonds	Private banks 1975–85	Govt banks	Bonds	Private banks 1986–91	Govt banks	Bonds	Private banks 1992–98	Govt banks	Bonds	Percent change in govt FI from 1986–91 to 1992–98
All industry	80.2	5.4	8.3	79.8	6.0	6.7	76.7	4.8	10.2	73.8	5.2	10.9	9.4
Mining	67.0	20.3	7.0	68.8	16.6	0.3	58.8	20.6	1.2	63.8	18.1	1.8	-12.2
Construction	92.5	1.7	1.9	90.3	3.0	1.7	87.3	2.2	5.8	85.0	2.2	7.1	-1.8
Manufacturing	82.7	4.8	8.1	81.7	5.8	6.6	70.7	5.1	17.0	66.8	6.1	20.1	20.2
Food	86.1	3.5	4.7	82.7	5.3	3.5	71.8	4.6	11.3	72.9	5.7	13.7	21.8
Textiles	85.1	3.3	6.6	83.7	4.7	2.4	81.0	4.5	8.0	75.1	4.9	11.2	10.1
Lumber	—	—	—	85.0	4.7	0.3	83.1	4.4	1.2	81.9	4.8	1.6	10.1
Paper and Pulp	86.7	2.8	6.1	84.7	4.5	4.4	76.2	5.2	11.6	76.0	6.4	11.8	22.6
Chemicals	82.9	3.6	9.0	82.5	4.6	8.1	65.3	4.5	25.0	61.1	5.5	26.5	20.5
Petroleum	—	—	—	83.8	10.5	0.6	71.1	14.4	3.4	72.8	13.3	10.3	-7.5
Ceramics	—	—	—	82.0	6.5	4.9	73.1	6.7	12.1	69.6	6.8	14.2	0.9
Iron and Steel	81.5	3.4	13.2	79.7	6.3	11.2	69.3	5.8	22.6	60.2	6.0	30.7	3.1
Nonferrous metals	81.6	3.5	10.1	82.7	5.5	4.8	68.1	6.6	19.6	60.7	15.1	20.8	128.9
Metal Goods	84.8	5.1	2.5	81.9	6.7	1.3	80.7	7.3	4.9	76.7	8.1	7.2	11.0
General Machinery	83.7	6.2	5.5	80.2	6.8	8.0	71.8	5.4	16.5	69.6	6.6	18.9	22.0
Electrical Machinery	80.7	2.3	14.3	75.7	3.8	14.7	55.8	3.6	31.0	50.5	4.5	34.9	24.4
Transport Machinery	76.3	14.4	7.6	78.1	8.9	9.5	66.7	4.6	24.4	62.8	5.9	29.1	30.1
Precision Machinery	—	—	—	76.2	2.4	11.4	70.2	1.9	22.6	67.0	2.5	22.6	37.3
Wholesale/Retail Trade	90.7	2.9	1.0	88.3	5.2	0.8	82.9	3.8	4.0	79.4	3.5	4.6	-6.4
Transport and Communication	67.2	19.4	8.4	70.8	16.0	7.0	56.3	10.6	26.6	57.4	15.4	20.4	44.4
Land Transport	—	—	—	73.4	16.5	6.2	64.7	12.2	19.0	60.2	16.1	18.7	32.3
Sea Transport	—	—	—	72.0	16.2	4.8	73.1	13.8	4.2	67.1	18.0	5.9	30.3
Electricity Supply	36.0	22.5	40.7	41.4	16.2	42.0	40.0	21.3	38.5	31.2	21.8	46.5	2.4
Services	83.9	3.0	1.0	83.3	2.9	0.5	89.1	1.5	0.9	86.5	1.8	1.5	23.0
Real Estate	—	—	—	75.6	2.5	1.2	84.1	1.3	1.6	79.2	1.7	2.5	26.5

Source: Economic Statistics Monthly (Research and Statistics Department, Bank of Japan): Corporation Statistics Seasonally (Ministry of Finance).

Note: Government bank loans are the sum of loans made by the Japan Development Bank, Export–Import Bank, and Small Business Financial Corporation.

during the postwar period, which is divided into four periods: 1961–74, 1975–85, 1986–91, and 1992–98. The percentage of government bank-loan financing is relatively small for some industries. However, for many industries, government banks provided a significant source of external funds; for example, mining, petroleum, nonferrous metals, transport and communications, and electricity obtained anywhere from 13 to 21 percent of their external funding from government banks during the most recent period (1992–98) presented in Table 2.7.

The allocation of funding across industries reflected two specific objectives of the FILP system: to encourage industries that had the potential to contribute to national development, and to compensate industries adversely impacted by national development. Funding was directed to encourage industries that the government believed would contribute to national development, had the capacity to compete internationally, or were deemed an important foundation for domestic investment and export-oriented growth. In this regard, petroleum, metals, machinery, transportation, communication, and electricity supply depended heavily on government-subsidized bank credit. The FILP system was also used to compensate industries that could not compete and thus contributed to the general objective of mutual support pervasive throughout Japan's economic institutions during much of the postwar period. In this regard, mining, marine transport, and petroleum industries were recipients of subsidized credit.

In terms of dependency on government-bank finance over time, Table 2.7 reinforces the inference from Table 2.6. Industry dependence on government-bank credit increased 9.4 percent from 1986–91 to 1992–98. The increased dependence was widespread. In Table 2.7, there are twenty-five rows of data for industries and subindustry categories, and only four of these rows (mining, construction, petroleum, and wholesale/retail) exhibited a decline in their dependence on government-bank credit over the two most recent periods.

2.3.4. *FILP Uses of Funds*

The FILP reports disbursement of funds across twelve categories ranging from housing to trade/economic cooperation.[4] These separate categories can be grouped into six broad functional categories of FILP lending:

1. Strengthening key industries.
   Industry and technology.
2. Trade/economic cooperation.
   Trade/economic cooperation.

---

[4] The twelve categories are industry and technology; trade/economic cooperation; agriculture, forestry, and fisheries; national land development; regional development; road construction; transportation/communications; small and medium-sized business; housing; living environment; social welfare; and education.

3. Regional Development.
   Agriculture, forestry, and fisheries.
   National land development.
   Regional development.
4. Infrastructure.
   Road construction.
   Transportation/communications.
5. Modernization of low-productivity sectors.
   Small and medium-sized business.
6. Improvement in living standards.
   Housing.
   Living environment.
   Social welfare.
   Education.

Table 2.8 and Figure 2.2 present the percentage distribution of FILP funds for each of the above six broad categories over the period from 1955 to 1999. Strengthening key industries (Category 1) such as electric power, sea transport, mining, and iron and steel was an important focus of FILP funding in the 1950s; however, once the economy achieved a take-off, this allocation absorbed a declining percentage of FILP funds. The same trend is illustrated by the distribution of funds for regional development (Category 3) and infrastructure (Category 4). These were two areas that received significant government

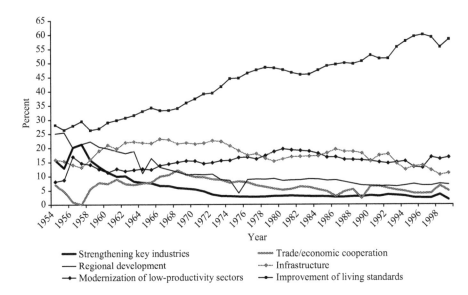

Figure 2.2. *Distribution of FILP lending by function, 1954–1998.*

Table 2.8. *Distribution of FILP funding by function, 1954–1998*

Fiscal year	Strengthening key industries	Trade/ economic cooperation	Regional development	Infra-structure	Modernization of low-productivity sectors	Improvement of living standards
	1	2	3	4	5	6
1954	15.72	6.99	25.10	15.87	8.14	28.18
1955	12.92	4.67	25.50	15.39	8.74	26.42
1956	20.21	0.88	20.04	14.04	16.94	27.90
1957	21.35	0.00	21.38	13.12	14.63	29.52
1958	15.71	5.62	22.29	15.96	14.13	26.29
1959	13.41	7.76	20.41	18.99	12.54	26.89
1960	11.43	7.37	19.79	21.00	11.35	29.07
1961	9.96	8.95	18.88	19.75	12.60	29.85
1962	10.10	7.30	18.09	21.96	11.84	30.70
1963	8.19	6.99	18.84	22.15	12.25	31.58
1964	7.79	7.52	11.04	21.81	12.62	32.99
1965	7.58	7.87	16.34	21.62	12.35	34.24
1966	6.64	9.92	13.21	23.15	13.79	33.28
1967	6.59	10.49	12.36	22.89	14.36	33.32
1968	5.89	12.13	11.55	21.46	14.93	34.04
1969	5.66	10.61	10.55	21.79	15.43	35.95
1970	5.37	9.79	10.68	21.40	15.38	37.38
1971	4.70	9.67	10.56	21.68	14.47	39.10
1972	3.55	8.94	10.76	22.55	14.80	39.40
1973	3.05	8.75	8.78	22.26	15.49	41.67
1974	2.97	7.69	8.54	20.72	15.58	44.49
1975	2.82	8.18	4.02	19.01	16.58	44.68
1976	2.77	7.84	8.83	17.40	16.74	46.42
1977	2.74	6.76	8.99	17.89	16.07	47.55
1978	2.81	6.24	8.94	16.30	17.27	48.44
1979	3.01	5.61	9.17	15.26	18.70	48.24
1980	3.05	5.16	8.46	16.09	19.63	47.62
1981	3.13	5.49	8.65	16.86	19.25	46.61
1982	3.02	6.35	8.73	16.95	19.04	45.91
1983	2.94	6.13	9.07	17.05	18.80	46.01
1984	2.89	5.34	8.99	17.21	18.05	47.52
1985	2.87	4.67	8.53	18.23	16.70	48.99
1986	2.66	2.91	8.67	19.50	16.79	49.47
1987	2.71	4.62	8.05	18.71	15.90	50.00
1988	2.88	5.39	7.44	18.75	15.86	49.69
1989	2.88	2.18	6.83	18.12	15.70	50.66
1990	3.22	6.52	6.69	15.29	15.44	52.83
1991	2.99	6.52	6.53	17.38	14.97	51.61
1992	3.52	5.75	6.63	17.81	14.60	51.69
1993	3.33	5.13	6.45	14.47	14.94	55.68

Table 2.8. *(Cont.)*

Fiscal year	Strengthening key industries	Trade/ economic cooperation	Regional development	Infra- structure	Modernization of low- productivity sectors	Improvement of living standards
	1	2	3	4	5	6
1994	3.06	4.71	6.82	12.37	15.31	57.74
1995	2.49	4.01	7.28	13.53	13.27	59.41
1996	2.42	3.95	6.76	13.84	13.01	60.03
1997	2.42	4.10	6.78	12.17	16.75	59.15
1998	3.60	6.70	7.40	10.50	16.10	55.70
1999	1.80	4.90	7.10	11.10	16.70	58.40

Source: Fiscal and Monetary Statistics Monthly and FILP Report, Ministry of Finance.

funding in the early years of reindustrialization, though infrastructure support has not declined in importance as much has regional development. The distribution of funds for trade/economic development has not exhibited any definite trend over the period covered by the data in Table 2.8 and Figure 2.2. Supporting small business or the modernization of low-productivity sectors (Category 5) has been a continuing goal of the FILP system and, in fact, the allocation of FILP lending to small business has gradually increased over time and has come to represent about 15 percent of the FILP allocation of funds.

The most dramatic trend in the allocation of FILP lending, however, is the allocation of funds to the improvement of living standards (Category 6). As Japan reestablished its industrial power by the 1970s, greater attention was devoted to social programs, to dealing with the adverse effects of economic growth (pollution), and to providing housing to the Japanese people. In the 1990s, the major driving force behind the increased allocation to improvement in standard of living has been housing. Not only has housing become the most important component of FILP funding, but FILP funding for housing has become the most important component of funding for housing from all sources.

Table 2.9 presents more detailed information on the role of government support of the housing sector. Table 2.9 indicates the sources of all housing finance in Japan from 1978 to 1999. Government support of housing has continued to increase over time. In 1977, the percentage of total loans for housing provided by government banks was 23.0 percent, and by 1999 the percentage had increased to 43.2 percent. The Government Housing Loan Corporation provides over 80 percent of government housing loans, and the remaining 20 percent is provided by local governments, the Okinawa Development Corporation, and various government enterprises. At the same time, dependence on the private sector for housing loans has declined from 77.0 percent in 1977 to 56.0 percent in 1999.

Table 2.9. *Distribution of housing loans by government and private institutions, 1977–1999*

Fiscal year	Total government loans	Government banks	Other government loans	Private financial institution loans	Bank loans	Nonbank loans	Ratio of government loans to private loans
1977	23.05	19.47	3.58	76.95	37.54	39.41	0.30
1978	25.15	21.19	3.95	74.85	36.83	38.02	0.34
1979	27.94	23.21	4.73	72.06	34.66	37.40	0.39
1980	30.96	25.14	5.82	69.04	32.66	36.39	0.45
1981	33.44	26.47	6.97	66.56	31.05	35.51	0.50
1982	36.37	28.31	8.06	63.63	28.96	34.67	0.57
1983	38.84	29.81	9.03	61.16	27.18	33.98	0.64
1984	40.83	31.06	9.76	59.17	26.08	33.09	0.69
1985	42.21	31.84	10.36	57.79	25.98	31.82	0.73
1986	42.55	32.11	10.44	57.45	27.10	30.35	0.74
1987	41.86	32.35	9.51	58.14	29.32	28.82	0.72
1988	41.30	32.53	8.77	58.70	35.28	23.42	0.70
1989	39.91	31.83	8.08	60.09	35.69	24.39	0.66
1990	39.78	31.97	7.81	60.22	34.98	25.24	0.66
1991	39.84	31.97	7.87	60.16	34.38	25.78	0.66
1992	41.56	33.36	8.20	58.44	33.27	25.16	0.71
1993	43.73	35.38	8.35	56.27	31.73	24.54	0.78
1994	46.44	38.29	8.15	53.56	30.33	23.23	0.87
1995	47.03	39.27	7.76	52.97	32.81	20.16	0.89
1996	45.87	38.30	7.57	54.13	34.22	19.91	0.85
1997	46.61	39.05	7.56	53.40	35.75	17.65	0.87
1998	45.14	38.07	7.07	54.86	36.88	17.98	0.82
1999	43.21	34.28	8.93	55.69	38.03	17.66	0.78

Source: The Government Housing Loan Corporation Annual: Economic Statistics Annual (Bank of Japan).

About half of private-financial-institution loans are provided by banks (city banks, regional banks level I and II, trust banks, and *shinkin* banks), with the remainder provided by credit cooperatives, labor and agricultural cooperatives, insurance companies, and, until 1995, *jusen* or housing-loan associations.

2.3.5. *FILP Sources of Funds*

Table 2.10 presents information on the sources of funds to the FILP system. Postal deposits have remained a steady source of new funds to the FILP system, ranging from 20 to 30 percent in any given year. There is one notable exception, however. In 1999, the percentage of new funds from postal deposits declined significantly as a large amount of postal *teigaku* deposits began to

Table 2.10. *Sources of FILP funding, 1957–1999*

Year	Special budget	Postal savings	Pensions	Returned funds	Postal insurance	Govt bonds	Total
1957	9.5	25.9	14.5	19.1	19.7	11.4	100
1958	6.5	20.1	13.5	26.3	21.0	12.6	100
1959	6.8	23.7	11.0	21.9	19.5	17.1	100
1960	6.4	24.1	14.7	16.7	19.2	18.9	100
1961	5.8	21.3	17.6	18.3	17.2	19.8	100
1962	5.6	24.1	19.2	15.1	15.7	20.2	100
1963	5.7	24.3	16.6	18.8	13.1	21.5	100
1964	5.7	27.3	17.2	18.2	10.5	21.1	100
1965	2.4	26.1	20.8	19.9	6.2	24.6	100
1966	2.3	28.5	22.3	9.4	8.1	29.4	100
1967	2.7	31.9	22.3	10.0	8.8	24.4	100
1968	2.5	35.4	23.1	9.9	9.5	19.6	100
1969	2.8	37.9	24.5	8.1	10.5	16.2	100
1970	2.7	37.4	27.0	9.1	10.7	13.1	100
1971	1.7	37.7	24.0	13.1	10.1	13.4	100
1972	1.3	43.0	23.4	11.9	10.0	10.4	100
1973	1.1	41.4	21.5	20.0	10.2	5.8	100
1974	0.7	41.4	21.2	22.1	10.4	4.2	100
1975	0.6	44.3	18.7	23.4	8.9	4.1	100
1976	0.6	47.6	19.8	16.0	9.4	6.6	100
1977	0.4	49.8	20.5	12.7	9.4	7.2	100
1978	0.2	51.8	21.3	6.4	10.4	9.8	100
1979	0.2	37.1	14.9	30.5	8.8	8.6	100
1980	0.1	43.5	21.4	20.1	7.7	7.2	100
1981	0.1	32.3	19.3	33.5	8.0	6.8	100
1982	0.1	34.5	17.5	30.6	8.2	9.2	100
1983	0.0	33.4	16.1	29.4	9.4	11.7	100
1984	0.0	28.6	19.1	31.8	9.4	11.1	100
1985	0.1	29.7	18.1	32.5	8.8	10.8	100
1986	0.2	25.5	15.2	38.5	10.5	10.1	100
1987	0.4	24.4	13.3	43.2	11.9	6.8	100
1988	0.3	26.3	7.9	45.5	13.1	7.0	100
1989	0.2	17.2	13.6	48.0	15.9	5.1	100
1990	0.2	12.2	18.0	48.7	16.0	5.0	100
1991	0.1	37.8	15.7	29.8	12.7	3.8	100
1992	0.1	29.1	16.3	38.1	12.5	3.7	100
1993	0.2	23.1	13.4	46.5	12.6	3.6	100
1994	0.2	27.3	13.8	36.7	16.8	5.2	100
1995	0.1	31.0	14.6	32.6	13.7	6.1	100
1996	0.1	22.6	14.4	41.0	16.0	5.9	100
1997	0.1	27.3	13.5	41.9	12.3	5.0	100
1998	0.7	18.6	8.6	57.8	10.3	4.0	100
1999	0.4	9.0	9.9	60.7	14.0	5.9	100

Source: Fiscal and Monetary Statistics Monthly and FILP Report, Ministry of Finance.

mature in early 2000. There was considerable discussion in and outside of Japan about what would happen to the maturing postal deposits (e.g. Alexander, 2000). Returned funds represent payments on past loans made by government financial institutions, which are returned to the Trust Fund Bureau, not to the PSS. In order to compare Table 2.10 with the illustration of the FILP system in Chapter 1 (Table 1.2, p. 10), one needs to keep in mind that the amount of postal deposits in Figure 1.1 represents new deposits and returned funds from previous deposits and loans. Combining new postal savings with returned funds in Table 2.10 provides a measure of the overall importance of the PSS to the FILP similar to that determined in Table 1.2.

2.4. THE FILP SYSTEM AND THE NATIONAL BUDGET

There are two perspectives of the PSS in Japan's economy, depending on whether one focuses on the sources of funds to the PSS or on both the sources and the uses of funds. The PSS can be viewed as an entity that offers deposit services (and life-insurance services) to Japanese households as part of the government's postal-service system. Much of the discussion of the PSS, especially that offered by the Bank of Japan over the years, has focused on postal deposits (e.g. Suzuki, 1987). This perspective, however, is narrow because it ignores what happens to postal deposits once they are received by the government. A more complete perspective is to view the PSS as a major component of the FILP system, which in turn is a component of the national budget-making process. In fact, the FILP is dependent on the PSS, whereas the PSS could stand by itself.

The FILP system is part of the national budget-making process in Japan, but it cannot be regarded merely as a second budget. The general budget is similar in purpose and construction to any government budget in the sense that it records government revenues from taxes, fees, etc., on one side and spending on the other side. The FILP budget is a special feature of Japanese public spending and finance. The FILP budget, although negotiated and determined concurrently with the general budget, is a flow-of-funds budget managed by the Ministry of Finance.

The FILP provides funds to support the special and government-agencies budgets and, to a lesser extent, some of the spending in the general-account budget. The FILP obtains funds from the public in the form of postal deposits, postal life-insurance premiums, contributions to pensions and national welfare, government bond sales, and special accounts. The disbursement of FILP funds is then made to special accounts, government financial institutions, public enterprises or corporations, local governmental entities, and special joint-stock corporations.

The size of the FILP in terms of its sources and uses of funds, the continued and almost uninterrupted growth of postal deposits during the postwar period

(Figure 2.1, p. 34), and the close relationship between the formulation of the general budget and the FILP budget have rationalized the conventional view that the FILP is Japan's "second budget." Although this view is correct in certain respects, referring to the FILP as a "budget" can be misleading because much of the FILP budget involves lending by government financial institutions rather than direct government spending.

A schematic outline of the simultaneous formation of the national budget and the FILP budget is presented in Figure 2.3. The budget-making process commences in August of each year with each ministry and agency drawing up and submitting two budgets to the Ministry of Finance. The first is a general

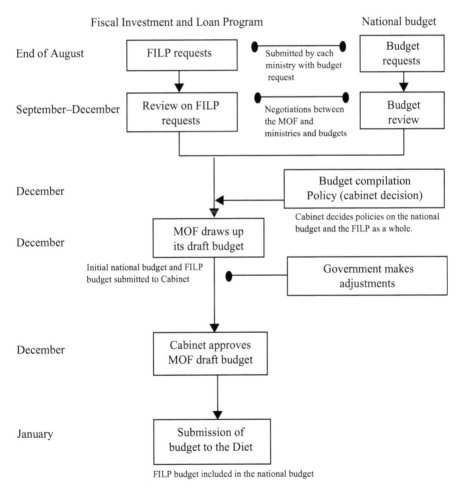

Figure 2.3. *Budget/Fiscal Investment and Loan Program.*
Source: Ministry of Finance (2000, p. 32).

receipts-and-expenditure budget to support the ministry or the agency's annual operations, and the second is a planned allocation of funds to those FILP-financed entities for which the ministry or agency has responsibility. Both requests are developed simultaneously. The general budget is submitted to the Budget Bureau of the Ministry, while the FILP budget is submitted to the Finance Bureau of the Ministry.

An internal review of the two budgets, involving intense negotiations between the Ministry of Finance and the various ministries and agencies, takes place from September through December. The combined budget is then subject to Cabinet approval of the overall general and FILP budget. In December, the Ministry of Finance draws up a draft budget, which is again approved by the Cabinet. The combined budget is then submitted to the Diet in January of the next year. The national and FILP budgets are then negotiated and debated in the budget committees of both the Lower and the Upper House and, once passed by both Houses, become the operating budget for the fiscal year starting on 1 April.

The final result is a set of receipts, spending, and lending plans for each ministry and agency in which their budgets are broken down into the part supported directly by the central and local governments and the part supported by the FILP. The end result is a budget of significant complexity, the outcome of combining a traditional budget with the lending-and-borrowing budget of the FILP. The complexity, either intentional or unintentional, contributes to a nontransparent system of government involvement in the economy.

This process reveals three aspects of the FILP system in Japanese finance. First, the PSS, the FILP, and the government financial institutions are an integral part of government resource-allocation policy; second, the process is complicated and nontransparent; and third, the FILP system is highly politicized by the very nature of the way the FILP budget is determined. Although it may not be correct to refer to the FILP as a second budget because it is more a lending than a spending budget, the integrated nature of the general and FILP budgets provides many opportunities for the FILP budget to respond to political influence. It is well known that Japanese politicians[5] use the budget process to maintain and enhance their political power, so, given the integral role of the FILP system in the budget-making process, a major part of the flow of funds in the Japanese financial system is sensitive to political pressure.

2.5. THE ROLE OF THE PSS AND THE FILP IN THE EVOLUTION OF JAPANESE FINANCE

The previous sections presented a historical perspective of the PSS and FILP system in terms of flow-of-funds statistics and the relationship between the two

---

[5] Cargill *et al.* (1997) provide a summary of the political business-cycle literature in Japan.

institutions and the overall budget-making process. By any reasonable quantitative standard, the influence of the PSS and the FILP is pervasive throughout Japan's economic and financial system. The household sector allocates a significant percentage of assets to the PSS and relies on the FILP system for a significant percentage of housing credit. Small and medium-sized business also relies on the FILP system for credit. Both the household and small and medium-sized business sector have significantly increased their reliance on government intermediation in the 1990s as private banks reduced the rate of growth of assets to increase their capital–asset ratios. In addition to these private-sector beneficiaries of the PSS and FILP, Japan's infrastructure in the broad sense is highly dependent on the two institutions.

The integral role of the PSS and the FILP in the budget-making process adds a political dimension to the PSS and FILP, which, combined with the variety of sectors that benefit from the PSS and FILP, provides these institutions with a significant degree of inertia in the face of financial liberalization.

The previous sections of this chapter focused on the quantitative and political dimensions of the PSS and FILP. The following discussion considers these institutions from a qualitative perspective in terms of how the PSS and FILP system form part of the Japanese financial regime. This is accomplished by reviewing the role of the PSS and FILP in the evolution of Japanese finance starting with the 1868 Meiji Restoration and ending in 2000.

2.5.1. *Prewar Development*

The Meiji Restoration of 1868 represented a political decision within Japan to shift the country from an agricultural and feudal society to an industrial economy to compete and eventually surpass the military and industrial power of the West. Industrialization required a financial infrastructure to institutionalize the saving-and-investment process. The PSS was part of Japan's first efforts to introduce a modern financial infrastructure and was responsible for bringing financial services to both urban and rural areas throughout Japan. It was not regarded as competitive with the national banking system because the latter was concentrated in urban centers and focused on servicing the requirements of the industrial sector. The addition of deposit services to postal facilities was motivated by three considerations—first, many areas outside of the industrial centers of Japan had no banking or financial services; second, commercial banks were designed primarily to serve the interests of business, not households; and third, postal deposits provided the government with a low-cost source of funds to distribute through the Ministry of Finance's Budget Bureau to targeted sectors of the economy. Other functions were added over time; for example, in 1916, the PSS began to offer life insurance.

The financial system evolved slowly until the 1920s and 1930s. Bank failures in the 1920s resulted in efforts of the government to consolidate banks and increase central control over the banking system. War mobilization in the 1930s accelerated the concentration effort and further consolidated banking into a small number of city banks and a larger number of regional banks. The government used the PSS extensively as a funding source for the war effort. The end of the war in 1945 resulted in the complete economic and financial devastation of the economy. The financial system that emerged and reached maturity by the 1950s represented a continuation of prewar trends but was more refined as an instrument of industrial policy.

2.5.2. *Postwar Development Prior to Liberalization*

The beginning of this period was one of economic chaos as Japan shifted to peacetime operation in the face of the almost complete devastation of its industrial capacity. Large government deficits were financed by rapid monetary growth, resulting in inflation rates of 365 percent in 1946, 196 percent in 1947, and 166 percent in 1946. The Dodge Plan implemented in 1949 quickly brought an end to the unstable economic and financial conditions by committing Japan to an austerity program of reduced government spending, lower monetary growth, and fixed exchange rates (360 yen to the dollar). The start of the Korean War in June 1950 allowed Japan to avoid a sharp recession that would have resulted from the Dodge Plan and its restrictive monetary policy.

Postal deposits did not decline after the end of the war as did bank deposits, but they remained flat in 1946. Bank deposits and postal deposits recovered in 1947, and as public confidence returned and wealth started to increase, postal and bank deposits increased. At this point, the PSS entered a period of sustained growth through 1975, and over the entire period increased its share of household wealth relative to banks. The upward trend in market share can be accounted for by six factors.

First, the Ministry of Posts and Telecommunications adjusted deposit rates to changes in rates induced by changes in Bank of Japan policy in such a manner as to provide incentives for households to transfer deposits from banks to the postal system. During periods of easy monetary policy, for example, when deposit rates were reduced, the Ministry of Posts and Telecommunications lagged in adjusting postal rates downward, in order to increase the relative attractiveness of postal deposits.

Second, prior to the Tax Reform Law of 1986 Japan's tax system provided incentives to save by excluding from taxation all interest income of less than 3 million yen. Exclusion from taxation of interest income on small deposits was referred to as the *maruyu* system. Households found it easy to maintain multiple postal deposits so that they could effectively exclude all their interest income from taxation. This flexibility was difficult to achieve in the private banks. Pressure from private banks resulted in some efforts by the Ministry of Finance to reduce the ability to hold multiple accounts, such as the "green card" effort (Feldman, 1986), but by and large, evading taxes through postal savings deposits was a widespread practice and officially tolerated. This advantage was eliminated with the Tax Reform Act of 1986, which extended income taxes to all interest income.

Third, the PSS offered a product mix of deposits that addressed the needs of the household sector far better than those offered by private banks. These included ordinary collection deposits, *teigaku* deposit certificates, time-deposits, housing installment deposits, and education installment deposits. Of these, the *teigaku* time-deposit was the most important source of funds to the PSS and remains the most competitive instrument offered by the PSS. Sakakibara (1991, p. 66) refers to this as the "jewel" of the PSS because of its superiority to any time-deposit issued by private banks.

The *teigaku* time-deposit offers greater liquidity and potential yield than any private time-deposit, especially in periods of fluctuating and uncertain interest rates. The *teigaku* deposit is a ten-year fixed-rate time-deposit that allows funds to be withdrawn after six months with no penalty. The *teigaku* deposit is essentially a long-term deposit with a short-term option to be exercised solely at the discretion of the depositor, and it has been shown to provide the PSS with a significant competitive advantage over bank time-deposits (Kamada, 1993). Table 2.11 illustrates the relative advantage of a *teigaku* deposit compared to a

Table 2.11. *Comparison of the interest rate on a* teigaku *deposit with a ten-year fixed-term bank deposit withdrawn before maturity (contractual rate = 2.45 percent)*

Time period	Effective rate of interest (%)
Bank deposit	
6 months to 1 year	0.1 (equal to ordinary savings account)
In the second year	10 of 2.45 = 0.245
In the third year	20 of 2.45 = 0.49
In the fourth year	30 of 2.45 = 0.74
In the fifth year	40 of 2.45 = 0.98
In the sixth year	50 of 2.45 = 1.2
Teigaku deposit	
6 months to 1 year	0.35
In the second year	0.4
In the third year	0.65
3 years to 10 years	1.2

Source: Chadha, *et al.* (1997, p. 148).

bank time-deposit withdrawn before maturity. Table 2.11 compares a regular ten-year time-deposit offered by a bank with early withdrawal penalties and the *teigaku* deposit, which can be withdrawn after six months with no penalty. The contractual rate on both is 2.45 percent. If the deposit is withdrawn after six months to one year, the private-bank deposit rate is 0.1 percent, whereas the postal deposit rate is 0.35 percent—that is, the effective rate of return on the postal deposit is over three times the effective rate on the private deposit. Although the differential declines with maturity, it remains large. In the third year, the effective rate on the private deposit is 0.49 percent, whereas on the postal deposit the effective rate is 0.65 percent. The *teigaku* deposit's option to withdraw after six months is clearly large.

In addition to the *teigaku* deposit, the PSS provided life insurance, which could not be purchased at private banks. Postal life insurance in 1999 represented about 30 percent of all life insurance in Japan.

Fourth, the PSS was able to service virtually every part of Japan with an extensive system of over 24,500 post offices. This branching network provided the PSS with far more deposit-taking and customer-service offices in Japan than any other financial institution offered. This advantage had the additional benefit of solidifying the political base of the PSS, making it easier to secure and enhance government support. The LDP, which has been a strong supporter of the PSS, aggressively expanded postal offices throughout Japan through a system that allowed private individuals or "special postmasters" to establish post offices.

Table 2.12 reports the number of bank offices and post offices, and the ratio of post offices to bank offices for 1980, 1988, and 1995. In 1980, the PSS had a major advantage over private banks in this regard because the number of bank branches was lower than the number of post offices in every one of Japan's forty-seven prefectures. This advantage has deteriorated in the past decade, however. In 1995, Tokyo, Osaka, and Okinawa had more bank branches operating than post offices, and the number of bank branches increased relative to the number of post offices in every prefecture.

Fifth, the PSS aggressively sought out deposits. PSS officials were paid commissions on their performance in securing deposits. Post offices openly advertised the advantages of postal deposits over bank deposits and adopted a marketing approach to services close to what one would expect from an aggressive private bank.

Sixth, private banks through the early 1970s were focused on servicing the business sector. Although they were critical of the PSS, especially its permitting the blatant use of multiple accounts to allow depositors to avoid income taxes on interest, they were not interested in servicing the household sector. The city banks in particular were continually experiencing excess

Table 2.12. *Bank branches and post offices by prefecture, 1980, 1988, and 1995*

Prefecture	Bank branches 1980	Post offices 1980	Ratio of post offices to bank branches 1980	Bank branches 1988	Post offices 1988	Ratio of post offices to bank branches 1988	Change in ratio from 1980 to 1988	Bank branches 1995	Post offices 1995	Ratio of post offices to bank branches 1995	Change in ratio from 1988 to 1995
Hokkaido	282	1536	5.45	336	1558	4.64	−0.81	533	1548	2.90	−1.73
Aomori	152	341	2.24	195	359	1.84	−0.40	215	363	1.69	−0.15
Iwate	114	406	3.56	145	439	3.03	−0.53	226	446	1.97	−1.05
Miyagi	146	402	2.75	168	434	2.58	−0.17	314	454	1.45	−1.14
Akita	124	393	3.17	158	401	2.54	−0.63	218	400	1.83	−0.70
Yamagata	109	386	3.54	140	397	2.84	−0.71	266	401	1.51	−1.33
Fukushima	112	519	4.63	143	557	3.90	−0.74	298	563	1.89	−2.01
Ibaragi	154	489	3.18	207	509	2.46	−0.72	341	526	1.54	−0.92
Tochigi	107	336	3.14	143	353	2.47	−0.67	242	359	1.48	−0.99
Gunma	120	321	2.68	165	345	2.09	−0.58	229	346	1.51	−0.58
Saitama	323	521	1.61	397	600	1.51	−0.10	524	632	1.21	−0.31
Chiba	303	580	1.91	403	658	1.63	−0.28	564	704	1.25	−0.38
Tokyo	1245	1281	1.03	1594	1360	0.85	−0.18	2032	1490	0.73	−0.12
Kanagawa	413	600	1.45	542	672	1.24	−0.21	679	734	1.08	−0.16
Niigata	203	643	3.17	232	695	3.00	−0.17	368	707	1.92	−1.07
Toyama	118	270	2.29	140	291	2.08	−0.21	209	300	1.44	−0.64
Ishikawa	135	307	2.27	172	340	1.98	−0.30	257	341	1.33	−0.65
Fukui	103	232	2.25	136	249	1.83	−0.42	185	249	1.35	−0.48
Yamanashi	59	251	4.25	77	274	3.56	−0.70	98	273	2.79	−0.77
Nagano	112	665	5.94	145	683	4.71	−1.23	216	679	3.14	−1.57
Gifu	133	418	3.14	190	453	2.38	−0.76	271	453	1.67	−0.71
Shizuoka	286	520	1.82	330	596	1.81	−0.01	444	603	1.36	−0.45
Aichi	339	827	2.44	376	897	2.39	−0.05	726	924	1.27	−1.11
Mie	137	414	3.02	193	457	2.37	−0.65	322	470	1.46	−0.91

Table 2.12. (Cont.)

Prefecture	Bank branches 1980	Post offices 1980	Ratio of post offices to bank branches 1980	Bank branches 1988	Post offices 1988	Ratio of post offices to bank branches 1988	Change in ratio from 1980 to 1988	Bank branches 1995	Post offices 1995	Ratio of post offices to bank branches 1995	Change in ratio from 1988 to 1995
Shiga	90	244	2.71	109	254	2.33	−0.38	190	260	1.37	−0.96
Kyoto	176	442	2.51	207	473	2.29	−0.23	262	482	1.84	−0.45
Osaka	707	978	1.38	797	1074	**1.35**	−0.04	1293	1117	**0.86**	−0.48
Hyogo	267	869	3.25	336	932	2.77	−0.48	598	957	1.60	−1.17
Nara	108	302	2.80	126	316	2.51	−0.29	181	323	1.78	−0.72
Wakayama	76	310	4.08	87	318	3.66	−0.42	169	314	1.86	−1.80
Tottori	93	234	2.52	105	244	2.32	−0.19	133	246	1.85	−0.47
Shimane	70	355	5.07	80	379	4.74	−0.33	113	379	3.35	−1.38
Okayama	127	493	3.88	155	530	3.42	−0.46	254	534	2.10	−1.32
Hiroshima	190	635	3.34	232	686	2.96	−0.39	433	706	1.63	−1.33
Yamaguchi	132	387	2.93	150	411	2.74	−0.19	224	419	1.87	−0.87
Tokushima	100	231	2.31	115	240	2.09	−0.22	185	241	1.30	−0.78
Kagawa	113	198	1.75	137	220	1.61	−0.15	210	222	1.06	−0.55
Ehime	125	367	2.94	149	396	2.66	−0.28	257	400	1.56	−1.10
Kochi	66	310	4.70	82	329	4.01	−0.68	164	331	2.02	−1.99
Fukuoka	283	721	2.55	473	769	1.63	−0.92	747	792	1.06	−0.57
Saga	74	195	2.64	99	202	2.04	−0.59	154	205	1.33	−0.71
Nagasaki	144	429	2.98	218	443	2.03	−0.95	317	450	1.42	−0.61
Kumamoto	99	534	5.39	126	560	4.44	−0.95	235	570	2.43	−2.02
Oita	104	384	3.69	132	405	3.07	−0.62	195	408	2.09	−0.98
Miyazaki	87	287	3.30	124	307	2.48	−0.82	176	311	1.77	−0.71
Kagoshima	104	685	6.59	136	718	5.28	−1.31	212	717	3.38	−1.90
Okinawa	124	134	1.08	152	166	**1.09**	0.01	205	186	**0.91**	−0.18

Source: Annual Economic Statistics of Japan, Bank of Japan and Minryoku, *Asahi-Shinbun* News Paper Company.

demand for credit from the corporate sector. Regional banks in contrast were not subject to the same pressure for loans but could easily channel excess funds to the interbank market. Banks frequently criticized the relative growth of the PSS but never made it a major issue. During that time, banks were operating under conditions of excess demand for loans, had easy access to funds at the Bank of Japan discount window, and believed they needed to offer few loans or other financial services to the household sector (Cargill, 1986; Suzuki, 1980). Corporate demand for funds was intense, and corporations had no alternatives in the form of domestic money and capital markets or external markets. Consequently, banks had a secured demand for funds and a secured deposit base from the business sector, since corporations were required to maintain large compensating balances and businesses were prohibited from holding postal deposits. Thus, the relative growth of the PSS during the 1946–75 period was as much the outcome of actions implemented by the PSS as of inaction on the part of the private banks to pursue the household sector with any degree of aggressiveness.

These six factors account for the relative growth of the PSS during the postwar period up to 1975. It might also be argued that the government deposit guarantee of postal deposits also accounted for the upward trend in the share of postal deposits, because Japan lacked a deposit-insurance system until 1971. Prior to the establishment of the Deposit Insurance Corporation in 1971, financial supervision and regulation operated with an explicit policy of no failures of financial institutions or markets. Even after 1971, deposit insurance was not regarded as an important component of the government deposit-guarantee system in Japan. Thus, with the exception of the late 1940s, the household sector perceived no difference in the degree of government deposit guarantees between the PSS and private financial institutions.

The perception that all deposits were subject to a government guarantee was reinforced by the economic and financial performance of the Japanese economy during the 1950s and 1960s. Japan's real GDP grew at annual rates of 10 percent, thus characterizing this period as the High-Growth Period in postwar Japan. Rapid growth was accompanied by mild "growth recessions" and moderate inflation (at least through the late 1960s). There were no publicly announced failures of private depositories, and the government's bailout of Yamaichi Securities Company in 1965 illustrated the willingness of the regulatory authorities to support a policy of no failures of financial institutions and markets.

The prewar development of the FILP paralleled the growth of the PSS, since the PSS was a major funding source for the FILP. The expansion of the FILP system would not have been as significant if the PSS had not expanded to the degree that it did throughout the postwar period. The growth of FILP funding was designed to benefit other groups than those targeted by the PSS. First, FILP funding was an important part of rebuilding Japan's infrastructure after the complete devastation of the war. Second, FILP funding supported sectors excluded from obtaining credit through the banking system, either because of their size (small and medium-sized businesses), because they lacked a *keiretsu* relationship, or because of their location (rural as opposed to urban). Third, FILP funding supported residential housing, which was essentially ignored by the banking system and thus was part of the *quid pro quo* between the government and the public to provide benefits (housing, high rates of economic growth, high rates of real wage growth, etc.) in exchange for limited and low-yielding financial assets. Fourth, FILP funding to low-productive sectors of the economy was part of the overall system of mutual support and limited bankruptcy. Fifth, the FILP played an important role in absorbing government debt. Figure 2.4 presents the amount of FILP funds allocated to purchase government bonds; thus, the FILP became part of the syndicate of banks and securities companies that subscribed to government debt.

Not only did the Japanese economy achieve significant economic growth after the Second World War and by the 1960s had completely recovered from the effects of the war, but the Japanese financial regime reached full maturity during this period. The characteristics of this regime defined a financial system fundamentally and functionally different from Western financial systems. Even Western financial systems that had a meaningful amount of government regulation and

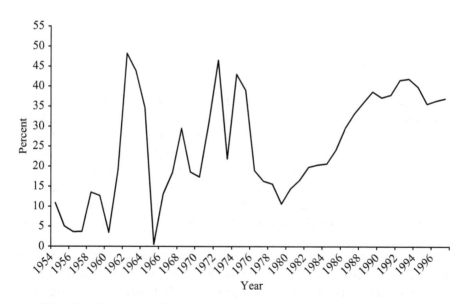

Figure 2.4. *Percentage of outstanding government bonds held by FILP, 1954–1997.*

control, such as the US system, differed significantly from the Japanese financial regime. The essential elements of the Japanese regime became a model for other Asian economies wishing to duplicate Japan's impressive growth record.

2.5.3. *The Preliberalization Financial Regime*

The following elements define the core features of the Japanese financial regime—or "old" financial regime—that reached maturity in the 1950s and 1960s. Many of the elements are not unique to Japan but rather represent a collection of government financial policies designed to achieve stable and sustained economic growth in the context of minimizing risk and bankruptcy (Cargill, 1999).

1. The financial system is viewed as an instrument of industrial policy.
2. The financial system is designed to transfer the majority of funds from surplus units to deficit units through intermediation markets, primarily banking channels.
3. The financial system is designed to encourage household saving but at the same time to limit household access to the financial system for consumer and mortgage credit.
4. Highly leveraged nonfinancial businesses dominated by large business groups are the primary recipients of bank finance. These business groups were called *zaibatsu* before the war and *keiretsu* after the war. Smaller business firms obtain credit from small private banks and government banks.
5. Foreign financial institutions are prohibited or restricted to limited participation in the financial system, and external debt is avoided.
6. Government credit-allocation policies, including extensive interest-rate controls to maintain a low cost of capital, play a major role in allocating funds through intermediation markets and mirror the government micromanagement of the real sector.
7. Financial regulation and supervision are designed with opaqueness and nontransparency in mind, in order to provide an environment more conducive for political favors and concessions to be struck between politicians, government bureaucrats, and the business sector.
8. The Bank of Japan lacks independence and serves as an agent of the government via the Ministry of Finance, in order to ensure a steady flow of credit to the business sector and to provide funds to support weak financial institutions.
9. A system of pervasive deposit guarantees is maintained through regulation, "convoy" approaches to dealing with troubled institutions or markets, and the discount window of the Bank of Japan. These policies are designed to ensure a policy of "no failures of financial institutions or markets" that is supported by opaque financial regulation, supervision, and central bank policy.

10. Reliance on long-term multi-dimensional relationships between banks, individual borrowers, and business groups to assess and monitor risk—the "customer relationships" that play a relatively small role in Western financial systems. In many cases, these relationships are viewed as more important than the basic economic considerations of the lender–borrower relationship.

The financial system is thus an instrument of industrial policy maintained and protected by mutual support, restraints on competition, and insularity. This regime was designed to achieve a specific set of objectives: to support reindustrialization, support domestic investment and export-led economic growth, encourage high household savings rates, ensure international isolation, and ensure that household savings were directed to the business sector rather than used to support consumer or housing expenditures.

These objectives were achieved by a rigidly regulated and administratively controlled financial system in which market forces played a small role in the flow of funds. In fact, as of 1975, Japan had the most rigidly regulated and internationally isolated financial system among the industrial countries.

Households were largely excluded from the financial system as demanders of funds; however, every effort was made to ensure high household savings that would in turn be available to the business sector. In this regard, the PSS played two important roles. First, the extensive system of post offices throughout Japan brought deposit services to virtually every segment of the population. The large banks were concentrated in the major industrial centers of the country and had little incentive to establish branching networks outside of these industrial areas away from their borrowing customers; more important, the Ministry of Finance through the early 1970s limited branching by large banks to restrict competition with regional banks. Second, the fact that the PSS did not make loans and the reliance of households on postal deposits reinforced the view that the household sector was a supplier, not a demander, of funds from the financial system.

Funds deposited in the PSS were transferred to the government to support government enterprises, such as agencies responsible for transportation and roads, to government banks, and to the special budget. The government banks served several purposes. First, government banks provided subsidized loans to encourage investment. Second, government bank loans were used to placate sectors of the economy excluded from the financial system, such as households demanding mortgage loans or small businesses demanding development loans. Third, government bank loans had a "leading indicator" or "cowbell" effect, in that they indicated which industries the private banks could safely support. Fourth, government enterprises and government banks supported activities, such as the construction of infrastructure, but because of their externalities could not easily be financed by private banks. Fourth, the FILP system assisted the government's efforts to market debt after general deficit-financing bonds were authorized in 1965. Figure 2.4 illustrates the amount of outstanding government bonds held by the FILP over the 1954–98 period and illustrates the importance of FILP purchases of government bonds in the government's debt program.

This financial regime served Japan well in the postwar period.[6] By any reasonable standard, economic growth after 1950 was impressive for the next two decades (Table 1.1, p. 3). In fact, this period is referred to as the High-Growth Period because of sustained real GDP growth averaging 10 percent per annum, interrupted by only mild "growth recessions" and accompanied by moderate inflation. Financial stability was also impressive. There were no officially declared failures of banks, and the government showed in its 1965 bailout of Yamaichi Securities Company that it would use whatever policy was required to maintain a policy of no failures of financial institutions or markets.

2.5.4. *The Start of Financial Liberalization*

Japan's impressive growth was interrupted in the early 1970s by a short but turbulent period in economic performance. Policy errors on the part of the Bank of Japan, resulting from political interference with monetary policy and an attempt to limit yen appreciation, generated high rates of inflation. As monetary policy sought to bring inflation under control in 1973, oil-price shocks and the previous 1971 "Nixon shocks" adversely impacted Japan. A system of price controls on oil, oil-related products, and certain consumer goods, such as toilet paper, also contributed to instability by further limiting supply. By 1975, however, the macroeconomic situation was under control. The Bank of Japan had adopted price stability as a policy objective, had achieved a degree of political independence from the Ministry of Finance and the government in order to pursue price stability, and was freed operationally to pursue price stability by termination of the fixed exchange-rate system. The return to stability marked the end of the High-Growth Period. The Japanese economy's natural growth-path shifted downward from the 10 percent annual rate to a 3–6 percent annual growth rate (Table 1.1, p. 3).

The return to macroeconomic stability was not the only financial event occurring in the early 1970s. In the 1970s, a new set of economic, political, and technological forces emerged that rendered the old financial regime increasingly incompatible with its environment. The conditions upon which the old

---

[6] Lee (1992) argues that the Japanese and Asian financial structures based on the core principles outlined above are superior to more market-oriented systems used in Western economies under the specific circumstances experienced by Asian economies.

regime relied could not be maintained. Japan was not unique in this regard—virtually every financial system in the industrial world prior to the 1970s was regulated and administratively controlled to some extent. These financial systems increasingly conflicted with the new environment, and deregulation or financial liberalization became a worldwide phenomenon by the 1980s.

2.5.5. *Increasing Conflict with the New Financial Environment and the PSS and FILP*

In 1975, Japan possessed one of the most rigidly regulated and administratively controlled financial systems in the world. However, a variety of internal and external forces initiated a process of financial liberalization. The catalyst for liberalization internally came from a fundamental shift in the flow of funds after 1975, which generated a consensus to liberalize financial markets. Prior to 1975, central government deficits were small, the household surplus was large, and the corporate-sector deficit was large. The financial system was designed to transfer the large surplus of the household sector to the corporate sector. After 1975, the natural growth-path of the Japanese economy shifted downward in response to high energy prices and the completion of the reindustrialization process that was driven by domestic investment. As a result, the corporate-sector deficit declined, while at the same time the government sector became a large deficit sector as tax revenues declined and fiscal policy was used to offset the adverse effects of the oil-price shocks.

The shift in the flow-of-funds pattern brought pressure on the rigidly regulated financial system and generated sufficient political incentive to move toward more open and competitive markets. The Ministry of Finance needed the assistance of the banks and securities companies to market the increasing amount of debt needed to finance the deficits. The banks viewed liberalized markets as means to reestablish market share lost when corporate demand for funds declined in response to lower investment spending. Securities companies viewed liberalized markets as means to expand their business. Corporations viewed liberalized markets as means to enhance profits by managing liquidity freed up by the reduced dependence on bank credit and the need to maintain compensating bank balances. Thus, the shift in the flow of funds established a *quid pro quo* between the Ministry of Finance, which set and administered the regulatory parameters of the financial system, and the various participants in the financial system.

There were important external pressures that also provided incentives to liberalize financial structures. These included advances in computer and telecommunications technologies that made it easier for innovation to circumvent regulations, the shift from a managed to a floating exchange-rate system

after 1973, and pressure from the United States to liberalize and international-
ize domestic markets as a policy to reduce trade imbalances.

As an outcome of internal and external forces, Japan embarked on a gradual
liberalization process after 1975. The liberalization efforts eventually eliminated the majority of interest-rate controls, permitted enhanced competition
between different segments of the financial system, established domestic
money and bond markets, and greatly reduced restrictions on the inflow and
outflow of capital. Although these were nontrivial structural changes, the
Japanese financial system remained wedded to many elements of the old
regime. In fact, in terms of the financial supervision and regulation framework,
there was little change in either attitude or policy. This would become apparent
in the 1990s.

The liberalization process during the 1975–85 period also took place in an
environment of impressive macroeconomic stability. Inflation had been brought
under control by 1975, real GDP growth was stabilized in the 3–6 percent range,
and growth recessions were few and minor. Most significant, Japan was able to
absorb the oil-price shocks of 1979–80 without the inflation–disinflation process
that characterized the responses of all but a few of the other industrialized
economies. By 1985, Japan emerged as the second largest economy and the
largest creditor nation in the world, and the publication of books claiming that
Japan would soon dominate the world economy and financial system grew
faster than Japan's GDP. In hindsight, much of the macroeconomic stability
could be attributed to Bank of Japan policy, which after 1975 focused on price
stability. In addition, the Bank of Japan achieved a degree of operational and
political independence that contrasted sharply with its legal foundation, which
dictated that the Bank of Japan be an agent of the Ministry of Finance (Cargill
et al., 1997).

In this new environment of greater competition and openness in the financial
system and a more flexible monetary policy, the PSS and FILP came under
increasing criticism from private banks, the Bank of Japan, and a few academics. Private banks lost market share after 1975 as a result of reduced corporate
demand for investment funding in an environment of slower economic growth
and, as a result, bank deposits grew more slowly than they had in the past, while
at the same time postal deposits increased their market share. Corporations no
longer needed to maintain large compensating balances to solidify a customer
relationship; in fact, by the end of the 1970s, banks had lost the ability to
impose the previously high compensating balances on their corporate customers. Banks argued that the PSS had an unfair regulatory advantage that was
no longer compatible with an open and competitive financial system. The PSS
was able to cross-subsidize its deposit-taking activities with the nondeposit-
taking functions associated with postal obligations; the PSS could offer life

insurance, whereas private banks were not permitted to do so; the PSS was not required to pay for deposit insurance, hold reserves against deposits, maintain a capital requirement, or pay income taxes, and it had an extensive government-subsidized branching network as part of its postal responsibilities; and the PSS offered the popular *teigaku* deposit that paid an effective interest rate higher than any bank deposit because of its option feature. These advantages made it difficult for banks to compete for deposits at the very time that banks were being required to be more competitive. Banks argued, for example, that although there was no serious regulatory reason why they could not offer a *teigaku* deposit, they could never offer the same interest rates as those offered by the PSS since they lacked any of the subsidies provided to the PSS.

Private banks raised issues about FILP lending to support housing and the business sector. As banks lost market share to reduced corporate demand, they increasingly turned to housing and small-business lending as a way to mitigate the lost market share. In fact, banks played a significant role in the growth of *jusen* mortgage lending in the 1980s as a means to mitigate lost loan demand from the corporate sector.[7]

The PSS also came under criticism from the Bank of Japan during the 1975–85 period. The Bank of Japan found itself in heated discussion with both the Ministry of Posts and Telecommunications, responsible for regulating the PSS, and the Ministry of Finance, which formulated and administered the majority of financial regulation in Japan (Suzuki, 1987, p. 150). The Bank of Japan argued that the PSS interfered with monetary policy by timing its interest-rate changes when monetary policy changed as a ploy to attract depositors. For example, in response to the lower interest rates induced by Bank of Japan policy, the Ministry of Posts and Telecommunications lagged its downward interest-rate adjustment, thereby inducing disintermediation from private banks and complicating the task of controlling the money supply. The Bank of Japan, as a strong advocate of financial liberalization, argued that the very existence of the PSS, given its regulated advantages, made it more difficult to liberalize the private-banking system. The Ministry of Finance and the Bank of Japan also conflicted over the PSS. The Ministry of Finance, on the one hand, indicated support for liberalization, but on the other hand—and more impor-tant—it was unwilling to seriously modify the PSS because the PSS was a major source of government funding. The Bank of Japan view, like that of private bankers, found little support.

Aside from issues of competition and interference with monetary policy, pri-vate banks and the Bank of Japan criticized the PSS and the FILP as inconsistent

---

[7] Cargill *et al.* (1997) provide a detailed discussion of the *jusen* industry and the role of private banks in establishing the housing-loan companies.

with the goals of financial liberalization. In this regard, some academics expressed their opposition to the high degree of government financial intermediation based on the PSS and the FILP.

The criticism, however, paled in comparison to the support that the PSS and the FILP received from the public, business, regulatory authorities, and politicians. The economic and political property rights established by government intermediation were pervasive throughout Japan, so without any obvious difficulties with either the PSS or the FILP, there was little enthusiasm to reform these institutions.

2.5.6. *Asset Inflation, Postal Deposits, and the Bubble Economy*

The macroeconomic performance during the 1975–85 period covered up fundamental weaknesses in the economy, especially in the financial system. Japan's financial liberalization during the 1975–85 period proceeded at a slow, steady pace with few disruptions to the real or financial sectors, especially when compared to the United States. What started as a smooth transition changed dramatically in the second half of the 1980s, however, with the sharp run-up in asset prices and booming economic and monetary growth characterizing the "bubble economy." This set the stage for the economic and financial distress of the 1990s.

The percentage of postal to total deposits declined in the second half of the 1980s for three reasons. First, the Tax Reform Act of 1986 ended the *maruyu* system in which interest income up to 3 million yen was exempt from income taxes. The PSS had benefited from lax enforcement of the 3-million-yen limit because there was no effective limit on the number of accounts that an individual could open at the post offices at that time. Although postal officials were nominally required to ensure that the limit was enforced, widespread violation of the law was permitted because it gave postal deposits a significant advantage over bank deposits. Banks were under tighter regulations to enforce the limit. The tax-exempt interest income of 3 million yen was replaced with a uniform tax of 20 percent on all interest income for individuals 65 years or younger.

Second, the liberalization of interest rates and an increased number of deposit products offered by banks, such as large CDs and money-market certificates, brought greater competition to the PSS for household deposits.

Third, the decline in bank market share as a result of reduced corporate demand for credit provided incentives for banks to pursue the household market for loan and deposit services. As banks became more willing to offer consumer and mortgage-loan services, they were better able to compete with the PSS, since the latter could offer only deposit services. Banks, for example, expanded their branching networks to attract deposits (Table 2.12). Although the number of post offices in 1995 exceeded the number of bank offices every-where, with the exception of Tokyo, Osaka, and Okinawa, the relative advantage declined from 1988 to 1995 in every other prefecture.

2.5.7. *Financial Distress and Disintermediation from Bank to Postal Deposits in the 1990s*

The economic and financial crisis following the collapse of equity and land prices in 1990 and 1991 raised new concerns about the PSS. The share of postal deposits sharply increased after 1990 (Figure 2.1, p. 35) as the public lost confidence in the banking system and began to doubt the ability of the government to maintain a policy of no failures of financial institutions or markets. For the first time in postwar Japan, the government officially closed eleven small credit cooperatives over the 1991–95 period. In addition, the shift from private-bank to postal deposits resulted from the public's expectation that interest rates would decline along with the slowdown in economic activity. In fact, there was concern in 2000 and 2001 that the PSS might experience an outflow of funds as the ten-year deposits came to maturity. This did not occur, however, and most of the funds remained with the PSS despite extremely low interest rates, suggesting that in the public's view postal deposits represented the most secure financial asset.

The disintermediation of funds, often with the encouragement of post-office officials, threatened the stability of banks and complicated efforts to deal with the nonperforming loan problem. The presence of the PSS essentially established a bimodal system of deposit guarantees that further interfered with efforts to deal with the financial distress and complicated the liberalization process. At one end of the spectrum, the large city and regional banks were viewed as "too big to fail," and at the other end, the PSS enjoyed a government guarantee. In between were a large number of small banks and other depository institutions whose deposit-guarantee status was uncertain, given that for all practical purposes the two deposit-insurance corporations operated by the government were insolvent by the end of 1994. Although no depositor lost funds when some small institutions were closed in the first half of the 1990s, the failures, combined with the problems experienced by the Deposit Insurance Corporation, raised concern in the minds of the public about the safety of bank deposits.

Four official actions were taken to stem the disintermediation of funds from bank to postal deposits and to restore public confidence in bank deposits. First, in 1993 the Ministry of Posts and Telecommunications instructed individual post offices to cease using the problems of the banking system as a market instrument to attract deposits. Second, in 1994 the Ministry of Finance and the

Ministry of Posts and Telecommunications reached an agreement that the PSS would set deposit rates "close to" private-bank deposit rates. Third, in 1995 the Deposit Insurance Corporation was reorganized, expanded, provided with new authority to deal with troubled institutions, and recapitalized. Fourth, the Ministry of Finance in 1995 announced a complete deposit guarantee for the entire private-banking system, scheduled to be removed on 1 April 2001. The deposit guarantee, however, was extended in late 1999 to 1 April 2002.

The series of steps taken by the government after 1990 is discussed in detail in Cargill *et al.* (1997, 2000). In most instances, the government actions were inadequate and failed to resolve the growing financial distress. A major part of the problem was the unwillingness of the government to depart from the old financial regime, especially to depart from the past policies of nontransparency, forgiveness, and forbearance in dealing with troubled institutions. In addition, policymakers believed that the asset deflation would be short and that recovery would improve bank balance sheets. Economic stagnation intensified the financial distress, since it was more difficult to eliminate nonperforming loans in the absence of economic growth. By late 1997, financial distress came close to financial panic in the face of the failures of the Hokkaido Takushoku Bank and the Yamaichi Securities Company. This was the first instance of the failure of large financial institutions in Japan. In the first part of the 1990s, only small credit cooperatives and banks failed, and regulatory authorities argued that the financial distress was largely confined to small and poorly managed institutions. At the same time, the economy declined in the fourth quarter of 1997, followed by a decline in real GDP for all of 1998 (Table 1.1, p. 3), when the economy began to exhibit negative real GDP growth quarter after quarter.

Aside from official actions to stem the disintermediation of bank deposits to postal deposits mentioned above, no specific action was taken with respect to the PSS. In fact, the PSS contributed to the government's policy of forgiveness and forbearance. Postal life-insurance funds were used on several occasions to support prices on the Tokyo Stock Market, and on numerous occasions members of the LDP called on the PSS to use its liquidity to provide aggressive support for equity and land prices in general. The existence of the large holdings of liquidity by the PSS thus may have had the effect of reducing pressure to adopt needed but painful resolution policies because it provided a psychological fall-back position.

The intensification of financial problems in late 1997 and 1998, however, resulted in a change in attitude and the emergence of a "new" financial supervision and regulation framework that departed from the old financial regime. Most significant from the perspective of this study is that, for the first time, serious reform effort was directed toward the PSS and FILP system and a "new" PSS and FILP system was established to commence on 1 April 2001.

2.5.8. *Demographic Changes and the Need to Increase the Rate of Return on Savings*

The financial distress of the 1990s revealed fundamental problems with the PSS. Although the expansion of FILP lending in the late 1990s offset some of the adverse effects of the private-bank credit crunch, the continued expansion of FILP lending will have adverse long-term effects on the Japanese economy. Declining population and the aging of population in the absence of significant advances in productivity will lower the standard of living over the coming decades. In this context, the benefits of the FILP system, in terms of offsetting the credit crunch, compensating less-productive sectors, or maintaining political power, must be balanced against the long-term cost of lost opportunities to enhance productivity. Independent of the need to liberalize and modernize the financial system, the rapidly changing demographic environment in Japan places a premium on reforming the FILP system to provide institutions that will allocate savings to high-return investments.

2.5.9. *Increasing Role of the PSS in the Payments System*

Okina (2000) provides detailed documentation of the new services offered by the PSS designed to make it Japan's "financial convenience store" for households. This is especially apparent in providing payment services not only with private financial institutions but with nonfinancial business firms such as NTT Data and All Nippon Airways. These developments suggest that the PSS intends to become a major part of Japan's payments system and is increasingly shifting emphasis from providing store-of-wealth financial assets to providing transaction assets. Aggressive actions in this direction provide another factor accounting for the continued growth of the PSS in the 1990s and, at the same time, highlight the small window of opportunity to reform the PSS. As the PSS becomes more integrated into the payments system, the task of reforming and eventually privatizing it will become more difficult.

2.6. CONCLUDING COMMENT

The PSS and the FILP have been major components of Japanese finance from the beginning of industrialization in the second half of the nineteenth century until the present, and they formed an important part of an overall financial infrastructure that reached maturity in the early years of the postwar period. The Japanese economy achieved impressive economic and financial success under this system. As a result, key elements of the Japanese financial infrastructure served as a model for other Asian economies wishing to duplicate Japan's economic record.

The PSS and the FILP represented an attitude that government allocation of real and financial resources was a necessary part of economic development, and although these two institutions were subject to some criticism, they were a widely supported part of Japanese finance. Even after Japan adopted an official policy of financial liberalization, the PSS and the FILP continued to increase their roles. Postal deposits increased their market share, and the private sector became more dependent on loans from government financial institutions. In the 1980s and especially in the 1990s, the PSS and the FILP came under more criticism, though they continued to receive widespread support. However, by the end of the 1990s, the PSS and the FILP were increasingly viewed as inconsistent with the type of modern financial system envisaged by the Big Bang proposal of November 1996 and as unresponsive to the critical need of the Japanese economy to raise the rate of return on investment to offset the anticipated decline and aging of the population.

3

Flow-of-Funds Model of the Postal Savings System and Fiscal Investment and Loan Program

3.1. INTRODUCTION

The previous chapter reviewed the role of the PSS and the FILP in Japan's financial system from several perspectives. First, in quantitative terms, the PSS and FILP are large and pervasive institutions, and few aspects of Japan's economy are immune to their influence. Second, despite an official policy of financial liberalization since 1976, the PSS and the FILP have increased their role in the economy. Third, the PSS and the FILP represent an integral part of a policy to institutionalize the savings and investment process and they thus contributed to the regime's focus on directing credit to specific sectors of the economy, maintaining segmented financial markets, limiting household access to the financial system as a source of funds (borrowing), stimulating household saving, providing credit to small and medium-sized businesses, compensating unproductive sectors, and supporting infrastructure spending. Fourth, the PSS and especially the FILP system are an integral part of the budget-making process and hence are sensitive to political influence.

Many policymakers and observers argue that irrespective of whatever reforms are required in the future, the PSS and FILP made significant and positive contributions to Japan's economic performance. Japan's growth record from the second half of the nineteenth century to the late 1980s, excepting wartime and a few other periods, is clearly consistent with this view. Even advocates of reform acknowledge that the PSS brought financial services to many parts of rural Japan and, as the FILP system evolved in the postwar period, worthwhile projects were funded that would not likely have found funding in the absence of government financial institutions to support them. In particular, the FILP played an important role in reestablishing Japan's infrastructure after the almost complete devastation of the war and contributed to the improved living conditions of the population through regional development and housing. However, others argue that although the PSS may have stimulated saving by extending deposit services throughout Japan and that government banks provided funding for projects that otherwise might not have been funded, these positive effects were offset by unproductive and low-yielding investment spending because of the lack of a framework to evaluate projects in terms of costs and benefits and/or because FILP decisions were overly sensitive to political influence.

Thus, although one can generally point to positive aspects of either the PSS or the FILP, the real issue is whether the combined effect of the PSS and the FILP was positive, zero, or negative and, even if one can isolate a positive combined effect, whether the combined positive effect has diminished over time. The question can be addressed from a theoretical and empirical perspective. This chapter presents a formal model of the PSS and the FILP, and the following chapter reviews the empirical evidence.

The formal or theoretical framework provides a schematic outline of how the PSS and the FILP function and the specific channels through which they influence the financial system and economy. Irrespective of whether the combined effect is positive, negative, or zero, the formalization of the PSS and the FILP is a worthwhile objective since it provides a clear view of how government intermediation influences the flow of funds. More important, however, the formal model will identify the channels through which the PSS and the FILP influence the economy and provides a framework to isolate those cases where a clear positive impact of the PSS and the FILP can be identified.

Irrespective of the outcome of the debate over the past role of the PSS and FILP, there is a general consensus that the PSS and FILP are candidates for reform if Japan is to evolve to the type of financial structure outlined by the Big Bang announcement of November 1996 and meet the needs of a rapidly changing economic and demographic environment. The June 1998 legislation and subsequent administrative decisions initiated a process that may result in fundamental change. It is also possible to be pessimistic about the ultimate outcome of the reforms.

Financial liberalization started in Japan during the late 1970s and, despite over two decades of reform efforts, the PSS and the FILP by 2000 had assumed their largest and most important role in the Japanese financial system compared to any previous time in their history. Postal deposits now represent a larger percentage of total deposits (bank and postal deposits combined) than at any time covered by the data in Chapter 2; the individual sector (previously the personal sector) has increased its dependence on government bank finance; small and medium-sized businesses have increased their dependence on government bank finance; and the FILP budget continues an upward trend as a percentage of GNP. The PSS complicated the deposit-guarantee system in the 1990s as concern was raised over the ability of the government to manage the financial distress. Once the Deposit Insurance Corporation becomes the primary safety net when the complete deposit guarantee is removed after 31 March 2002, the PSS has the potential to destabilize the system should public confidence in the banking system and/or the Deposit Insurance Corporation wane. The projected decline in population and other demographic factors place importance on ensuring that savings are allocated to high-yielding projects, and there are questions as to whether the extensive system of government financial intermediation, despite the impending reforms, can accomplish this task.

Reform of the PSS and the FILP over the coming years is uncertain, judged by Japan's less-than-enthusiastic willingness to depart from the old regime in the past. Reform could result in a major redesign of the FILP system accompanied by ultimate privatization of the PSS, or the widespread support of the PSS and FILP could mute the reforms so that in essence little change occurs.

The next chapter reviews empirical evidence on the various roles played by the PSS and the FILP in postwar Japan. However, before presenting the empirical evidence, the present chapter presents a simple flow-of-funds model of the PSS and the FILP, focusing on government banks. The model captures the institutional structure as it existed throughout postwar Japan until 1 April 2001. The model is then extended to incorporate the institutional changes that became effective on 1 April 2001.

3.2. FLOW-OF-FUNDS MODEL

A flow-of-funds model incorporating the PSS and the government banks will highlight important relationships between private and public finance in Japan. The flow-of-funds model is based on a model framework originally developed by Yoshino (1987), although it is extended in several significant ways.

First, the model is bifurcated into a pre- and post-1994 version to incorporate the 1994 agreement between the Ministry of Finance and the Ministry of Posts and Telecommunications over the setting of postal-deposit rates. Second, the loan market is extended to allow for the fact that government-bank loans do not always compete with private-bank loans; that is, government banks make loans that would not be made by private banks either because of externality considerations or because of considerations such as political influence. Third, the model incorporates the role of branches (convenience factor) in the demand for government and private-bank deposits based on the importance of this factor in accounting for the high percentage of household deposits held in the PSS. Fourth, the post-1994 version of the model is developed both for the prevailing institutional conditions up to 1 April 2001, when legislation and administrative decisions initiated in 1998 became effective. The model is then modified to incorporate the reforms and, as a result, it will focus on the essential difference between the "old" and the "new" PSS and FILP.

3.3. SECTORS AND RELATIONSHIPS: THE "OLD" PSS AND FILP

The model is based on a three-sector decomposition of the financial system: (1) the combined Bank of Japan (BOJ), FILP, and government sector; (2) the private-banking sector; and (3) the nonbank or private sector consisting of the nonfinancial business and the individual sector. The model and comparative static results are bifurcated by two periods: pre- and post-1994. In the pre-1994 period, the rate on government deposits is different from the rate on private-bank deposits, whereas in the post-1994 period, the two rates are assumed equal. The Ministry of Posts and Telecommunications, prior to 1994, set the government deposit rate independently of the private-bank deposit rate.

After 1994, the Ministry of Posts and Telecommunications agreed to set the rate "close to" the private-bank deposit rate and would accept whatever deposit level the public was willing to hold at that rate.[1] This did not, however, eliminate the advantage that the PSS enjoyed relative to private banks. The PSS continued to operate an extensive branching network, and the *teigaku* deposit remained a desirable deposit. The importance of the branching network is demonstrated in empirical estimates of the demand function for postal savings reported in the next chapter. The PSS has also continued to offer the *teigaku* deposit, which provided significant insurance against declines in the interest rate. As of early 2001, about twenty private banks were issuing *teigaku* deposits, though these deposits were not aggressively advertised, and private banks in general were unwilling to allow these deposits to become a meaningful source of funds, given their inherent interest-rate risk.

The variable definitions are presented in Table 3.1. The functional relationships are summarized in Tables 3.2 and 3.3. Table 3.4 presents the flow-of-funds matrix for the complete model. In Table 3.4, columns 2–4 are sector columns, column 5 is the interest-rate column, and column 6 is the market equilibrium for each asset listed in rows 1 through 9.

In row 1 of Table 3.4, high-powered money supplied by the government is equal to the demand for high-powered money by private banks to meet reserve requirements and the demand for high-powered money by the private sector for use as currency:

$$H^{G} = kD^{B}(\cdot) + H^{N}(\cdot) \tag{3.1}$$

The symbol $(\cdot)$ indicates that the demand for high-powered money by the private sector is a function of other variables.

---

[1] See Chapter 1, fn 8.

Table 3.1. *Variable definitions*

The "Old" Model

Sectors

G	Government sector, including Bank of Japan
N	Non-bank or private sector
B	Private bank sector

Variables

H^G	High powered money supplied by the government (Bank of Japan)
H^N	High powered money held by the nonbank or private sector
BJL	Bank of Japan loans
D^B	Private bank deposits
D^G	Government bank deposits (deposits in PSS)
L^G	FILP loans, where $L^G = L_1^G + L_2^G$
L_1^G	Government loans to the backward sector that do not compete with private bank loans
L_2^G	Government loans to borrowers that also have the ability to obtain loans from private banks

L^B, l^B Supply of bank loans:

L^B	Supply of loans in market where both government and private banks supply loans
l^B	Supply of loans in market where only private banks supply loans. Government bank loans supplied to a fixed "backward" sector not dependent on private bank financing

L^N, l^N Demand for bank loans:

L^N	Demand for loans in market where private sector demands both government and private banks loans
l^N	Demand for loans in market where private banks sector demands only private-bank loans. "Backward" private sector depends on government bank supplied loans

k	Private bank reserve requirement ratio
B^G	Government bonds
B^B	Government bonds held by private banks
B^N	Government bonds held by non-bank or private sector
W^N	Non-bank or private sector wealth
DEB	Accumulated government debt
r_L, r_1	Loan rate for loan market with both government and private bank loans and loan rate for loan market only with private bank loans, respectively
r_B	Government bond rate
r_{DG}	Government bank deposit rate or PSS deposit rate
r_{DB}	Private bank deposit rate
r_G	Government bank loan rate
n^G	Number of government bank branches (number of post offices)
n^B	Number of private bank branches

Additions to the "New" Model

Additional sectors

$FILP$	New FILP in which government banks issue bonds or participate in Ministry of Finance issued bonds, referred to as FILP bonds
PSS	New PSS which purchases government bonds and FILP bonds

Additional variables

B^{FILP}	Bonds issued by government banks or FILP earmarked bonds issued by Ministry of Finance
B^{PSS}	Bonds purchased by the PSS

Table 3.2. *The "old" model relationships*

(1) $H^G = kD^B(r_L, r_1, r_{DG}, r_{DB}, r_B) + H^N(r_L, r_1, r_{DG}, r_{DB}, r_B, W^N, n^G, n^B)$

(2) $BJL = BJL^*$

(3) $L_2^G + L^B(r_L, r_1, r_{DG}, r_{DB}, r_B, k) = L^N(r_L, r_B, y)$

(4) $l^B(r_L, r_1, r_{DG}, r_{DB}, r_B, k) = l^N(r_1, r_B, y)$

(5) $D^G = D^G(r_{DG}, r_{DB}, r_B, y, n^G, W^N)$

(6) $D^B = D^B(r_{DG}, r_{DB}, r_B, y, n^B, k, W^N)$

(7) $B^G + B^B(\cdot) = B^N(\cdot)$

(8) $\Delta DEB = \Delta W \text{ or } (G - T) = (I - S)$

Balance sheet identities

(9) $L^G + BJL + DEB = H^G + D^G + B^G$

(10) $kD^B + L^B + l^B + B^B = D^B + BJL$

(11) $W^N + H^N + D^G + D^B + B^N - L^N - l^N$

Table 3.3. *Relationship between assets, interest rates, net wealth, and government loans in the "old" model*

	r_L	r_1	r_B	W^N	r_{DG}	r_{DB}	L^G	n^G	n^B
H^N	−	−	−	+	−	−	0	0,−	0,−
L^B	+	−	−	0	−	+	+,0	0	+
L^B	−	+	−	0	−	+	−,0	0	+
L^N	−	0(+)	+	+	0	0	0	0	0
L^N	0(+)	−	+	+	0	0	0	0	0
D^G	−	−	−	+	+	−	0	+	−
D^B	−	−	−	+	−	+	0	−	+
B^B	−	−	+	0	−	+	−,0	0	0
B^N	−	−	+	+	−	−	0	0,−	0,−

Table 3.4. *Flow-of-funds matrix for the "old" model*

	1	2 Government and central bank G	3 Private banks B	4 Private sector N	5	6
1	*HPM*	$-H^G$	$+kD^B$	$+H^N$		$H^G = kD^B + H^N$
2	BOJ loans, BJL	$+BJL^*$	$-BJL$			$BJL = BJL^*$
3	Loan mkt 1	$+L_1^G$		$-L_1^G$	r_G	$L_1^G = L_1^{G*}$
4	Loan mkt 2	$+L_2^G$	$+L^B$	$-L^N$	r_L	$L_2^G + L^B = L^N$
5	Loan mkt 3		$+l^B$	$-l^N$	r_1	$L^B = l^N$
6	Private bank deposits, D^B		$-D^B$	$+D^B$	r_{DB}	$D^B = D^B$
7	Govt bank deposits, D^G	$-D^G$		$+D^G$	r_{DG}	$D^G = D^G$
8	Bond market, B	$-B^G$	$+B^B$	$+B^N$	r_B	$B^G = B^B + B^N$
9	Net wealth	$-DEB$		$+W^N$		$W^N = DEB$
10	Sector balance	$L_1^G + L_2^G + BJL + DEB = H^G + D^G + B^G$	$kD^B + L^B + l^B + B^B = D^B + BJL$	$W^N = H^N + D^G + D^B + B^N - L^N - l^N$		

Bank of Japan loans are assumed fixed in row 2:

$$BJL = BJL^*$$ (3.2)

The loan market is divided into three separate markets. The first loan market represents loans made by government banks to a "backward" sector, L_1^G. The backward sector does not compete with loans made by private banks, and the term *backward* is used to signify that the sector is removed from the private-bank loan market. As a result, the backward sector can be either productive or unproductive. In the case of a productive backward sector, externalities in which social marginal benefits exceed private marginal costs limit the ability of this sector to borrow from private banks. In contrast, the unproductive backward sector is precluded from private-bank borrowing because of its low rate of return on investment. Row 3 of Table 3.4 specifies this loan market:

$$L_1^G = L_1^{G*}$$ (3.3)

The amount of loans provided to the backward sector is fixed and administratively determined.

The second loan market represents loans made by government banks to sectors such as housing or business that compete directly with loans made by private banks, L_2^G. Loans made by private banks in this market are designed as L^B. Row 4 of Table 3.4 specifies the second loan market consisting of both government and private-bank loans:

$$L_2^G + L^B(\cdot) = L^N(\cdot)$$ (3.4)

where

$$L^G = L_1^G + L_2^G$$ (3.5)

The rate on government loans, r_G, is administratively determined and set lower than the private-bank rate, r_L. The private-bank loan interest rate in the second loan market, r_L, is determined when the supply of loans is equal to the demand for loans, according to expression (3.4) and row 4 of Table 3.4.

The third loan market represents loans made by private banks that do not compete with loans made by government banks, l^B, and is indicated by row 5 of Table 3.4. Row 5 illustrates the part of the loan market in which only private banks supply loans to the private sector. Borrowers in this market do not have a choice between borrowing from the government or private banks but must rely exclusively on private-bank credit for their needs.

The supply and demand for loans in the third loan market consists of private-bank loans and private-sector demand for loans, respectively:

$$l^B(\cdot) = l^N(\cdot)$$ (3.6)

The private-bank deposit market (row 6) equilibrium rate, r_{DB}, is determined by:

$$D^B(\cdot) = D^B(\cdot) \tag{3.7}$$

In row 7, the government deposit rate, r_{DG}, on postal deposits is determined exogenously until 1994 or set equal to the private-bank deposit rate after 1994.

$$D^G = D^G(\cdot) \tag{3.8}$$

The government bond market (row 8) equilibrium rate, r_B, is determined by:

$$B^G = B^B(\cdot) + B^N(\ ) \tag{3.9}$$

where B^G represents the net issue of government bonds, excluding bonds held by the FILP; B^B represents bonds held by private banks; and B^N represents bonds held by private nonbank sectors.

Net wealth (row 9) in terms of stocks is defined as:

$$W = DEB \tag{3.10}$$

where DEB represents the net debt of the government sector. In terms of flows, the change in wealth represents saving less investment, and the change in net debt represents the difference between taxes and government expenditures.

$$\Delta W = \Delta DEB \tag{3.11}$$

or

$$(I - S) = (T - G) \tag{3.12}$$

Row 10 indicates the balance sheet constraints for each of the three sectors. Functional forms are presented in Tables 3.2 and 3.3. The relationship between the three sectors in terms of the variable definitions is illustrated in Figure 3.1. Figure 3.1 incorporates some additional detail; for example, the FILP receives not only postal deposits but also pension premiums and part of the postal life-insurance premium. The combined funds are transferred to government banks (and nonbank government entities), which in turn make loans to the private sector. The essential flow, however, is from the private sector to the government banks through the FILP. Part of the government-bank loans compete directly with private-bank loans.

The model describes in a formal manner the interrelationships between the PSS, FILP, and government banks and private banks as they existed in the postwar period through 31 March 2001. The model is bifurcated into a pre- and a post-1994 period to reflect the 1994 reform that changed the relationship between government-bank deposit rates (postal deposits) and private-bank deposit rates. The model is solved for the pre-1994 period by setting the government deposit

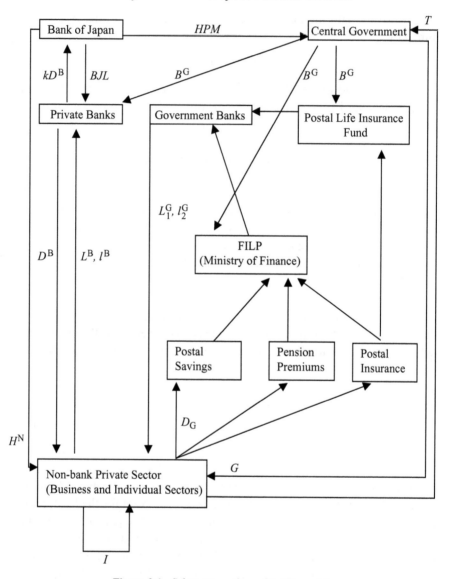

Figure 3.1. *Schematic outline of "old" model.*

rate independently of the private deposit rate and solved for the post-1994 period by setting the two rates equal to each other. The solved model provides comparative static results to determine how the presence of the PSS and the FILP influence financial variables in general and provides a framework to evaluate issues raised about the effect of the PSS and the FILP on economic activity and monetary policy. The comparative static results, however, are relatively insensitive to whether the model is considered from a pre- or a post-1994 perspective. To simplify matters, the following discussion of the model is based on the post-1994 reform that establishes equality between the government-bank and private-bank deposit rates.

3.4. COMPARATIVE STATIC RESULTS OF THE "OLD" MODEL

The model can be used to provide insight into two issues frequently raised about the PSS and the FILP. First, the model can be used to illustrate the effect on the economy of a change in government-bank loans and deposits. The PSS and the FILP have been alleged to have had positive effects on Japan's growth in the past by providing loans to sectors that contributed positively to Japan's economic growth. Under what conditions does the model support the conventional wisdom about the contribution of government financial intermediation to Japan's postwar growth record?

Second, the model can be used to illustrate how changes in government-bank loans and deposits influence the impact of monetary policy. The Bank of Japan has argued for many years that the PSS interferes with monetary policy by complicating the channels of monetary policy and/or by providing incentives for deposits to disintermediate from private to postal deposits. The end result is that monetary policy has a less-predictable effect on income and imposes a disproportionate impact on the banking system. Does the model support claims made by the Bank of Japan?

3.4.1. *Changes in Government Bank Loans*

There are three cases to consider, depending on which type of government-bank loans are issued. In all three cases, increases in government-bank loans are associated with a shift in deposits from private to government banks.

1. Increase in government-bank loans to unproductive backward sectors; that is, loans to small, inefficient business firms or loans to support bridge and road systems with low rates of utilization.
2. Increase in government-bank loans to productive backward sectors, such as infrastructure, with high rates of return from society's perspective but which, because of externalities, are excluded from obtaining private-bank loans.
3. Increase in government-bank loans to sectors that already have access to private-bank loans; that is, government banks and private banks compete directly in the loan market.

The impact on the economy resulting from changes in government-bank loans is measured by the associated aggregate demand and, where applicable, by the aggregate supply effects.

In the first case, the increase in loans to the unproductive backward sector reduces private-bank loans to sectors that have a choice between government and private banks and to sectors that rely only on private banks. This is because deposits are shifted from private banks to government banks to support increased government-bank lending to the unproductive backward sector. As a result, the supply of bank loans decreases, causing lending rates r_L and r_1 to increase. Higher private-bank loan interest rates lower private investment and hence reduce total income generating a negative demand effect. Since the loans are made to an unproductive backward sector, the increase in government-bank loans has a negative aggregate supply effect. The negative aggregate demand effect is thus reinforced.

In the second case, the increase in government-bank loans is made to a productive backward sector. In this case, there is still a negative aggregate demand for the same reasons as in the first case. However, there is now a positive aggregate supply effect, because loans to the productive sector increase the overall productivity of the economy. The net result is dependent on the relative magnitudes of the aggregate demand and aggregate supply effects.

In the third case, government-bank loans are made to sectors that have a choice between borrowing from either government or private banks. Housing loans or loans to small businesses would fall into this category. In this case, the shift from private-bank lending to government-bank lending lowers the bank loan rate, r_L, thus increasing investment spending. At the same time, the reduced availability of funding for loans made to those sectors that do not have a choice between government and private-bank lending results in a higher bank loan rate, r_1, and thus reduces investment spending. The opposite movements in the two private bank rates can be explained more fully by considering that the private bank faces two markets, each with a supply and demand function. In the first market, where loans do not compete with government banks, the supply function shifts to the left as deposits are transferred from private to government banks; hence, with an unchanged demand function and a reduced supply, r_1 increases. In the second market, demand is sensitive to government bank loans because borrowers have a choice to borrow from either private or government banks, the demand function shifts to the left as a result of increased lending by the government banks. Other things held constant, the loan rate, r_L, will decline. In addition, the increased lending by the government banks indicate to private banks that these types of borrowers are worthy ("cow bell" effect) and hence, banks shift funds from the first to the second market; thereby lowering the loan rate r_L, more and increasing the loan rate r_1 higher. The net effect will determine whether the increase in government-bank loans increases or reduces total income. There is no aggregate supply effect.

Thus, the comparative static results suggest that there is no unambiguous case in which increased government-bank lending increases income. In some cases, such as loans to backward but unproductive sectors, the effect is negative. In the other cases, the effect depends on the combination of several factors that may render the net effect either positive or negative.

3.4.2. *Changes in Government Bank Loans and Monetary Policy*

Monetary policy is measured by changes in high-powered money and the M2 money supply (Currency + Private Bank Deposits) resulting from changes in either Bank of Japan loans (BJL) and/or changes in the Bank of Japan discount rate. Monetary policy designed either to stimulate or to slow down the economy will be influenced by the existence of government-bank deposits and loans. The effect, however, will depend on the type of government loans being made. Consider an expansionary monetary policy.

The direct effects of Bank of Japan policy are reflected by decreases in both r_L and r_1 by private banks. Lower bank rates for both types of loans will increase investment spending and hence increase aggregate demand. The extent to which this policy is reinforced or offset depends on the nature of government-bank lending.

To the extent that deposits are shifted from private banks to government banks to support loans to the unproductive backward sector, the direct stimulative effects of Bank of Japan policy will be offset by higher private-bank loan rates. The net effect will depend on the combined aggregate demand effects of Bank of Japan policy (positive) and the disintermediation effect (negative).

To the extent that deposits are shifted from private banks to government banks to support loans to the productive backward sector, however, the direct effect of monetary policy is reinforced. Both effects will increase income.

To the extent that deposits are shifted from private banks to government banks to support loans to the competitive sector, the net effect depends on the combined influences of three effects. The three effects are the direct effect of Bank of Japan policy, the effect of higher r_1 on investment, and the effect of lower r_L on investment.

In the case of loans to the productive backward sector, the presence of government banks will reinforce an easy monetary policy since government-bank lending increases private-bank lending, which in turn reduces the interest rate and increases investment spending. In the other two cases, the presence of government banks provides some degree of offset to easy monetary policy.

These results are the same for restrictive monetary policy—that is, only in the case of loans to the productive backward sector will restrictive monetary policy be reinforced. All other types of loans will offset restrictive monetary policy.

3.5. THE "NEW" PSS AND FILP

Legislation in 1998 and administrative decisions in 2000 set into motion a reform process that commenced on 1 April 2001. It will take several years for the reforms to fully evolve and before further reforms are possible. The 1998 legislation called for a separation of the PSS from the FILP and will require government banks to finance future lending through the sale of bonds. These bonds can be issued with or without government guarantee. Government banks can also obtain funds from bonds issued by the Ministry of Finance. The PSS plans to allocate 80 percent of its funds to the purchase of government bonds and other safe assets.

The simple model can be modified to shed light on how the "new" PSS and FILP differ from the old structures. The model needs to be modified because postal deposits will now be used to purchase government bonds, FILP bonds, or FILP agency bonds. The funds raised by selling the FILP bonds hereafter (defined to include FILP agency bonds) will then be used to support the three sectors used in the model:

$$\text{PSS} > \begin{cases} \text{Goverment Bonds} \\ \\ \text{FILP Bonds} \end{cases} > \begin{cases} \text{Unproductive Backward Sector} \\ \\ \text{Productive Backward Sector} \\ \\ \text{Competing Sector} \end{cases}$$

The most important change is to expression (3.9). The government-bond market rate is now determined by:

$$B^G + B^{FILP} = B^B(\cdot) + B^N(\cdot) + D^G(\cdot) \tag{3.13}$$

The government-bond market now consists of normal government bonds and FILP bonds, which will be issued by individual government banks or by the Ministry of Finance, with funds earmarked for government banks. The bonds will be purchased by private banks, private nonbank sectors, and the PSS, and FILP bonds will be indistinguishable from general government bonds. This leads to the assumption that the PSS allocates all funds to the purchase of government bonds when in fact only 80 percent will be so allocated. The Ministry then lends to the three sectors in the same manner that the government banks lent to the three sectors under the old FILP system. The inherent logic of the reform is that, in a formal sense, little has changed.

Table 3.5. *The "new" model relationships*

(1) $H^G = kD^B(r_L, r_l, r_{DG}, r_{DB}, r_B) + H^N(r_L, r_l, r_{DG}, r_{DB}, r_B, W^N, n^G, n^B)$
(2) $BJL = BJL^*$
(3) $L_2^G + L^B(r_L, r_l, r_{DG}, r_{DB}, r_B, k) = L^N(r_L, r_B, y)$
(4) $l^B(r_L, r_l, r_{DG}, r_{DB}, r_B, k) = l^N(r_l, r_B, y)$
(5) $D^G = D^G(r_{DG}, r_{DB}, r_B, y, n^G, W^N)$
(6) $D^B = D^B(r_{DG}, r_{DB}, r_B, y, n^B, k, W^N)$
(7) $B^G + B^{FILP} = B^B(\cdot) + B^N(\cdot) + D^G(\cdot)$
(8) $\Delta DEB = \Delta W$ or $(G-T) = (I-S)$

Balance sheet identities
(9) $BJL + DEB = H^G + B^G$
(10) $kD^B + L^B + l^B + B^B = D^B + BJL$
(11) $W^N + H^N + D^G + D^B + B^N - L^N - l^N$
(12) $L_1^G + L_2^G = B^{FILP}$

Table 3.6. *Flow-of-funds matrix for the "new" model*

1	2 Government and central bank G	3 New FILP	4 New PSS	5 Private banks B	6 Private sector N	5	6
1 *HPM*	$-H^G$			$+kD^B$	$+H^N$		$H^G = kD^B + H^N$
2 BOJ loans, BJL	$+BJL^*$			$-BJL$			$BJL = BJL^*$
3 Loan mkt 1		$+L_1^G$			$-L_1^G$	r_G	$L_1^G = L_1^{G^*}$
4 Loan mkt 2		$+L_2^G$		$+L^B$	$-L^N$	r_L	$L_2^G + L^B = L^N$
5 Loan mkt 3				$+l^B$	$-l^N$	r_l	$L^B = l^N$
6 Private bank Deposits, D^B				$-D^B$	$+D^B$	r_{DB}	$D^B = D^B$
7 Govt bank deposits, D^G			$-D^G$		$+D^G$	r_{DG}	$D^G = D^G$
8 Bond market, B	$-B^G$	$-B^{FILP}$	$+B^{PSS}$	$+B^B$	$+B^N$	r_B	$B^G = B^B + B^N$
9 Net Wealth	$-DEB$				$+W^N$		$W^N = DEB$
10 Sector balance	$BJL + DEB = H^G + B^G$	$L_1^G + L_2^G = B^{FILP}$		$kD^B + L^B + l^B + B^B = D^B + BJL$	$W^N = H^N + D^G + D^B + B^N - L^N - l^N$		

Table 3.5 presents the new model relationships with the new bond-market equation (expression (7)) and a new constraint that requires government-bank lending to equal FILP bonds (expression (12)), and the list of variables is extended in Table 3.1. The new flow-of-funds matrix for the expanded model is presented in Table 3.6, and a new flow-of-funds diagram is presented in Figure 3.2. In Figure 3.2, the FILP is removed. Funds provided by the private sector in the form of postal deposits, postal insurance premiums, and pension

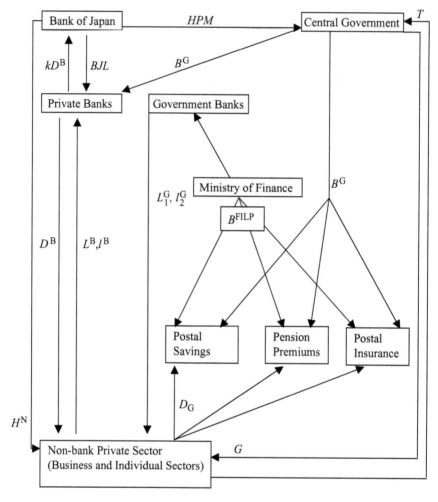

Figure 3.2. *Schematic outline of "new" model.*

premiums are now used by the PSS (and insurance and pension funds) to purchase FILP bonds as well as general government bonds. The funds raised by selling FILP bonds are transferred to the government banks through the Ministry of Finance. The government banks then make loans to the private sector, some of which compete directly with loans to the private sector from the private banks.

The logic of the reforms and how they are incorporated into the model essentially means that the comparative static results of the previous model remain unchanged. In the previous model, government banks collected deposits and made loans, while in the new model, government banks (or the Ministry of Finance) sell bonds to the PSS, which collects the deposits. Hence, the only change is that we now separate the PSS from the FILP, but the PSS remains the funding agent for the government banks. Although the formal model is unaffected by this institutional change, the reform is not necessarily trivial, as we discuss in Chapter 5.

3.6. SUMMARY OF THE MODEL

The only positive case for the PSS and FILP system that emerges from the simple flow-of-funds model is when the government banks lend to the backward, but productive, sector of the economy. Even this case requires the positive-supply effect to be greater than any possible negative-demand effect. In any other loan situation, the PSS and FILP are likely to have an adverse impact on the economy either in terms of lower economic growth or more difficult monetary policy. The question of which case is the more likely thus depends on the type of loans that have been supported by postal deposits in the postwar period.

The model also indicates that the reform process initiated in 1998 will not fundamentally change the conclusions. This is because the PSS remains the funding source of the government banks, but instead of transferring deposits to the government banks as if they represented one institution, the government banks will now sell bonds to the PSS. The real issue is not how the government banks obtain their funding but how they allocate their assets to the three sectors identified in the model. In this regard, the reforms have the greatest potential for changing the FILP system because the method of finance may become more transparent and market sensitive. The more market sensitive and transparent, the more likely it is that the government banks will reduce loans to the unproductive backward sector, but they will continue to compete with private banks in some loan markets.

The flow-of-funds model on which these implications is dependent is, of course, very simple. The model is static, the behavioral assumptions are simple, the model assumes a closed economy, and the model assumes segmented loan markets. Nonetheless, the model sheds light on an important component of Japanese finance. First, it formalizes the interaction of the PSS and the FILP with the rest of the economy; second, it compares and contrasts the old and new PSS and FILP; and third, it shows that, at best, the case for a positive contribution of the PSS and FILP to economic development is ambiguous.

3.7. CONCLUDING COMMENT

The comparative static results of the model suggest that whether the PSS and the FILP have had a positive effect on economic growth depends on the type of loans made by government banks. Government banks contribute positively to economic growth only when government-bank loans finance projects that are productive from society's view but would not otherwise be completed because of externalities or because of lack of access to the private-loan market. That is, the positive argument relies on some degree of market failure. However, this effect needs to be offset with the negative-demand effect of reduced lending by private banks. Loans for any other purposes within the parameters of the model either lower income or have an ambiguous effect on income. Thus, the view that the PSS and the FILP have positively contributed to Japan's economic growth may be exaggerated, at least within the framework of this model.

Monetary policy may be reinforced by the existence of government banks in the case where government-bank loans finance spending by the productive backward sector. This outcome, however, depends on the underlying parameters in the model. Otherwise, the existence of government-bank deposits and loans offsets monetary policy to some degree. The comparative static results support arguments by the Bank of Japan that the PSS and the government financial institutions that it supports are more likely to interfere with monetary policy than to reinforce monetary policy.

The model further suggests that the reforms introduced on 1 April 2001, might not significantly change the situation, since the only analytical difference is that instead of the government bank lending (postal) deposits to the three sectors, postal deposits are used to purchase FILP bonds, which in turn provide funds for the government bank to lend to the three sectors as before. In point of fact, however, there are significant differences that will be discussed in the concluding chapter.

4

Empirical Issues and Results

4.1. INTRODUCTION

During the period from 1950 to 1975, when the Japanese financial regime reached maturity, the PSS and the FILP played important roles in transferring funds from surplus to deficit units, judged by their importance in Japan's flow of funds and the various roles assigned to the PSS and the FILP in the financial system and economy. Comparative static results derived from a flow-of-funds model, however, suggest that whether the PSS and the FILP system contributed positively to economic growth is not clear, and only in those cases where some degree of market failure existed can a case be made that the PSS and the FILP raised productivity and economic growth. The model is static, however, and any potential contribution to Japanese economic growth in the postwar period is likely to be time-variant. Judged by Japan's economic performance through the early 1970s, it would be hard to argue that the PSS or the FILP adversely affected economic growth. In addition, it is likely that the PSS and FILP made positive contributions to Japan's economic development in the early 1950s, given the need to rebuild the infrastructure after the Second World War, provided a take-off platform for various industries, and provided services to raise the standard of living. The question, then, is whether the PSS and FILP made an identifiable positive contribution over the postwar period considered as a whole and, more important, whether we can identify those subperiods for which the PSS and FILP made a positive contribution and those for which a positive contribution cannot be identified.

After 1975, Japan's financial regime began a transition in response to new economic, technological, and political forces that conflicted with institutions embedded in the old regime, which had been designed to limit competition, limit risk, and limit bankruptcy through a system of mutual support. During the next fifteen years, the role of the PSS and the FILP credit-allocation program continued to expand despite the official policy of financial liberalization. Measured by household response, political influence, and the relative increase of postal to total deposits in the household flow of funds, the PSS and FILP became even more important than in the first part of the postwar period. Despite the success of the PSS and the FILP, however, concern was expressed in some quarters about the compatibility of the PSS and FILP with more open and competitive financial institutions and markets, and about the ability of the Bank of Japan to conduct monetary policy effectively. In the wake of the collapse of asset prices in 1990 and 1991, new concerns were raised about the PSS. The PSS complicated Japan's extensive system of deposit guarantees and at various times in the first half of the 1990s induced disintermediation of deposits from private banks to post offices.

The rapidly changing demographic features of Japan in the 1990s also raised concern about the large amounts of funds transferred through the PSS and the FILP. Projections of declining population, especially working-age population, place a premium on high-rate-of-return investment in order to raise labor productivity. The PSS and FILP, in the view of many observers, constrain the rate of return on investment because large amounts of the funding are allocated to low-productivity sectors either to compensate losers (mutual support) or to maintain and enhance the political power of bureaucrats and politicians with little regard to rate-of-return considerations.

The PSS and the FILP for all practical purposes were ignored in the government's response to the financial distress in the first half of the 1990s, in the 1996 Big Bang proposal, and in the subsequent legislation passed in 1997 that initiated significant change in Japan's monetary and financial policy institutions. The PSS and FILP system, however, could not be ignored for long. The June 1998 legislation set the stage for reform by ending the link between the PSS and the government banks (and other government entities) dependent on postal deposits. The subsequent administrative decisions regarding portfolio strategy essentially established a narrow-bank framework for the PSS, but even a government narrow bank retains the ability of the government to channel funds much as they were channeled under the previous system.

It is not clear at this point how far reform of the PSS and FILP will proceed. Before discussing the June 1998 legislation and subsequent administrative decisions, as well as the various reform scenarios, there are a number of empirical issues that need to be addressed regarding the role of the PSS and FILP in postwar finance. Information on several relevant empirical questions will provide important background information on how to proceed with further PSS and FILP reform. Combined with the quantitative overview and the theoretical model presented in Chapters 2 and 3, respectively, the empirical information presented in this chapter will complete the overview of the role of government finance in Japan's postwar financial infrastructure. We will then be in a position to evaluate the reform process initiated in 1998.

4.2. EMPIRICAL ISSUES

4.2.1. *What is the Magnitude of the Subsidy of the FILP System to Japanese Industry?*

The PSS and FILP system has been frequently rationalized on the basis of some degree of market failure in the private-banking sector. Government banks provide loans to productive industries that for a variety of reasons would have been unable, or would have found it difficult, to obtain credit from private banks. These loans correspond to the backward-but-productive-sector loans in the formal model developed in Chapter 3—that is, there is a certain degree of market failure that justifies government provision and subsidization of loans to targeted sectors of the economy. The cost of borrowing from government banks is subsidized by setting a lower effective loan rate than that offered by private banks. The lower effective loan rate can be achieved either by setting a lower nominal rate than offered at private banks or even by setting a rate equal to the private-bank rate since private banks imposed a compensating deposit-balance requirement as part of the loan. Compensating balance requirements, however, declined in importance after 1980, and by the late 1990s they became extinct for all practical purposes. Takeda (1985) provides statistics on the importance of compensating balances prior to the start of liberalization and the degree to which they declined in importance through the early 1980s.

Two empirical issues are important with regard to the subsidy to industry: the magnitude of the differential between the effective loan rates on government and private banks in the postwar period and the relative magnitude of the interest-rate subsidy to Japanese industry. Industry and bank balance-sheet information can be utilized to estimate the interest-rate spread and the importance of the interest-rate subsidy over time to provide evidence on these two issues.

4.2.2. *Has Credit Allocation at Subsidized Interest Rates Had an Identifiable Impact on Industry Investment Spending?*

Clearly, subsidized credit directed to a specific sector will increase investment spending in that sector. The more appropriate issue, however, is whether credit-allocation policies have positively and significantly increased the overall level of industry investment. There are three channels through which FILP credit-allocation policies may have had an overall positive effect on investment spending and hence economic growth.

First, government-bank loans increase the supply of credit. This is referred to as the quantitative effect of the FILP system. Second, the interest-rate subsidy increases expected profit, and higher expected profits generate higher rates of investment spending. This is referred to as the low-interest-rate effect of the FILP system. Third, the FILP system serves as an indicator and, like the bell on the cow, signals private banks to advance loans to a specific borrower and/or a specific industry. This is referred to as the "cowbell" effect of the FILP system.

Figure 4.1 illustrates these three effects. The line D_1 represents the demand for funds to support investment spending as a function of the private-bank loan rate in the absence of government-bank loans. The line S_1 represents the supply of loans to finance investment in the absence of government-bank loans. In the absence of government-bank credit, the equilibrium rate of investment spending is I_1.

The quantitative effect is represented by a rightward shift in the supply function to S_2 and a higher level of investment spending at I_2. The cowbell effect is represented by a further rightward shift in the supply function from S_2 to S_3 and a further increase in investment spending to I_3. The low-interest-rate effect is represented by a rightward shift in the demand for funds from D_1 to D_2 and a further increase in the level of investment spending from I_3 to I_4. The demand function shifts to the right because of the subsidy provided by the government banks at any given private-bank loan rate.

There are three empirical issues to be considered. First, can these effects be identified; second, if identifiable, what are their magnitudes and third, have their significance and magnitude changed over time? These empirical issues can be investigated by estimating the coefficients of industry investment, which in turn can be used to simulate the effects of government-bank loans into the three effects.

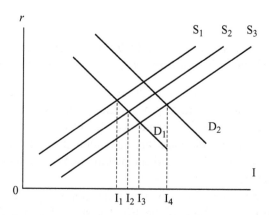

Figure 4.1. *Three effects of FILP lending on investment spending.*

4.2.3. *Has the PSS Interfered With and Complicated Bank of Japan Monetary Policy?*

The Bank of Japan, as an early advocate of financial liberalization, has been critical of the PSS and FILP since the early 1980s. The Bank of Japan at various times has raised three issues about the role of the PSS in the financial system, although its main focus has been on the influence of postal deposits in the transmission of monetary policy.

The first argument focuses on the incompatibility of the PSS with a policy of financial liberalization. The size of the PSS and the large role of government banks in allocating subsidized credit to favored sectors renders the PSS and FILP system inconsistent with the goal of financial liberalization. A financial institution insulated from market forces that plays such a large role in the flow of funds cannot coexist with a policy of liberalization. The second argument is a more specific version of the first and stresses the lack of a level playing field in the competition for household deposits. The Bank of Japan, as an advocate of liberalization, has argued that the presence of the PSS creates an uneven playing field in the competition for household deposits. The third and probably the most important criticism from the Bank of Japan's perspective is the argument that the PSS complicates monetary policy. The PSS encouraged disintermediation of funds from private banks to post offices in the past by delaying changes in deposit rates and because of the superiority of the *teigaku* deposit during periods of declining interest rates. During periods of increasing interest rates, the *teigaku* deposit becomes less attractive and funds are transferred to the banking system, thus again interfering with monetary policy. In many respects, it was pressure from the Bank of Japan that led to the 1994 agreement between the Ministry of Finance and the Ministry of Posts and Telecommunications to set postal-deposit rates "close to" those set for private-bank deposits.

This issue can be addressed from two perspectives. First, a qualitative review of past monetary policy, especially policy errors, can suggest whether past policy mistakes can be reasonably attributed to the presence of the PSS. Second, models of the money-supply process can indicate whether the money-supply process is significantly influenced by the presence of postal deposits.

The Bank of Japan has emphasized the role of postal deposits in complicating the transmission of monetary policy; however, one could argue that FILP lending is at least equally responsible for interfering with monetary policy. To the extent that postal deposits provide the major part of FILP funding, there is little distinction between focusing on postal deposits and on FILP lending. Unfortunately, this line of inquiry would be difficult to pursue, since only annual data on FILP lending are generally available. In addition, FILP lending needs to be considered from the perspective of the loan market. Since we are focused here on the money supply, which is a key variable in Bank of Japan policy (Cargill *et al.*, 1997), focusing on postal deposits seems appropriate.

4.2.4. *What Influences the Relative Demand for Postal Deposits Compared to Private-Bank Deposits and Does the PSS Have an Advantage in Competing with Private Banks?*

Postal deposits represented 34 percent of household deposits in 1999. The share of postal deposits as a percentage of household assets has exhibited an upward trend in the postwar period, especially after 1975. These trends are interpreted differently, depending on one's view of the PSS. Supporters of the PSS and the PSS itself argue that postal deposits provide features that private banks are able but unwilling to offer. Critics of the PSS argue that the government-provided advantages of postal deposits create an uneven playing field between the PSS and the banks. It is not an issue of whether private banks are willing to provide these services, but rather that private banks are unable to provide the same services as the PSS. Banks are required to satisfy reserve requirements, are required to be members of the Deposit Insurance Corporation and hence pay deposit insurance premiums, are subject to regulatory oversight, are required to pay taxes, and must meet minimum capital requirements. None of these constraints are relevant to the post office. In addition, the post office is able to cross-subsidize deposit services by locating them in post office facilities, an arrangement that accounting systems have difficulty unraveling along functional lines. The Ministry of Posts and Telecommunications does make an effort to decompose costs into three categories: postal deposits, postal life insurance, and mail services, based on the number of staff assigned to each, but nonetheless there remain opportunities for cross-subsidization.

These advantages manifest themselves in three forms. First, the advantages provide the PSS with the ability to adjust interest rates in such a manner as to encourage disintermediation from private banks. Second, the advantages make it possible for the PSS to raise the majority of deposits by issuing *teigaku* deposits that have embedded in them significant interest-rate risk. Third, the ability to utilize the extensive post-office facilities spread throughout Japan, especially in areas unable to support full banking services, provides a significant convenience advantage to the PSS.

These and other issues relating to the market share of postal deposits to total deposits can be quantified by estimating postal deposit-demand functions over time and across Japan's forty-seven prefectures.

4.2.5. *What Role Does the PSS Play in Japan's Deposit-Guarantee System in General, and Does the PSS Have the Potential to Generate Financial Instability?*

The financial liberalization process has not progressed smoothly in a variety of countries. Banking problems in one form or another were a prominent feature of the international financial landscape in the late 1980s and 1990s, suggesting to some observers that the banking problems were the outcome of liberalization. The correlation between banking problems and financial liberalization has led some observers to suggest that financial liberalization is the primary cause of these financial crises.[1] In the context of financial problems in Asia, Russia, and Latin America in 1998 following the Asian financial crisis of 1997, some observers have argued either for a slower liberalization process or for a return to government-managed financial systems.

These arguments are at best misleading since they fail to distinguish between the process of liberalization and liberalization per se. Liberalization itself is not the problem; rather, the problem is embedded in the political economy of liberalization. Three particular manifestations can be identified.

First, the system of mutual support between financial institutions, finance ministries, and politicians in the majority of developing economies allows them to resist the exposure of their protected and nontransparent financial structures to the rigors of market forces. Market methodology (which places emphasis on transparency, limited government-directed credit allocation, direct money and capital markets, financial disclosure, and the willingness to accept business failures as a normal part of the market process) clashes with the Asian financial regime. As a result, liberalization progressed slowly in countries such as Japan and South Korea—and then only after considerable political and economic pressure was brought to bear on the regulatory authorities.

Second, even economies that possess a more general acceptance of market forces have an incentive to pursue unbalanced liberalization, especially with regard to government deposit guarantees. The self-interest of the regulatory authorities and politicians provides incentives to pursue liberalization policies that increase portfolio diversification powers without significantly modifying the risk incentives embedded in, and the administration of, government deposit guarantees. An unbalanced liberalization process can also be created by attempts to maintain certain sectors of the financial system—for example, the mortgage or consumer-finance sectors in the US economy—in a relatively privileged position.

---

[1] Borio, Kennedy, and Prowse (1994), for example, argue that liberalization and financial disruptions are causally related. Nakajima and Taguchi (1995) suggest that deregulation in Japan encouraged banks to adopt risky loan and investment strategies.

Third, the old financial regime, with its emphasis on nontransparency and its belief that government can manage market forces, biases any regulatory response to a shock toward delay, forgiveness, and forbearance. The first reaction in this regime is to deny the problem and, once denial is no longer credible, to adopt accounting gimmicks clouded in nontransparency in order to understate the problem and give troubled institutions time to "work their way out of the problem."

The problems that have been encountered during the past decade largely revolve around the government's administration of the deposit-guarantee system. The PSS in Japan is particularly important in this regard. Postal deposits are guaranteed (postal deposits are limited to 10 million yen), and although bank deposits are insured up to the same limit by the Deposit Insurance Corporation, postal deposits have complicated the guarantee system. First, public confidence in the Deposit Insurance Corporation was weakened in late 1994 when for all practical purposes the Deposit Insurance Corporation became insolvent, in the sense that it lacked sufficient reserves to bail out any more failed institutions (Cargill *et al.*, 1996, 1997, 2000). The second and much smaller insurance agency that insures deposits of small cooperative institutions was also insolvent. Deposit insurance reform started in 1995 when the decision was made to adopt a US-style deposit-insurance system as the safety net for the financial system. To provide a transition and to restore confidence in Japan's banking system, the Ministry of Finance in late 1995 announced a complete deposit guarantee on all private bank deposits scheduled to be removed 1 April 2001. The economy and financial system did not improve and in fact, deteriorated significantly in the last part of the 1990s. In December 1999, the government extended the removal of the complete deposit guarantee one year and instead of imposing the limit on all deposits of 10 million yen at one time, the government decided to phase-in the new limits over a two-year period. On 1 April 2002, the complete guarantee was replaced by a 10 million yen deposit-insurance limit on time deposits. Transaction and other deposits remained subject to the complete guarantee scheduled to be replaced 1 April 2003, with a 10 million yen deposit-insurance limit.

Thus, given the lack of experience with a meaningful deposit-insurance system, the failure of deposit-insurance in the early 1990s, and the troubled phase-in of the new deposit-insurance system, it is unlikely the public views a 10 million yen postal deposit in the same light as a 10 million yen private bank deposit insured by the Deposit Insurance Corporation.

Examination of flow-of-funds patterns between post offices and private banks by prefecture may reveal the degree to which funds were disintermediated from private banks to the PSS. Even in the absence of clear evidence of disintermediation, the existence of a large PSS complicates the deposit-insurance system planned for Japan's future financial system as the primary safety net for deposits.

4.2.6. *In the Context of Nonperforming Loans in the 1990s, Do Government Banks Have a Nonperforming Loan Problem?*

Financial distress in the 1990s has been exacerbated by the lack of transparency regarding nonperforming loans. In the early 1990s, the Ministry of Finance reported nonperforming loans only for the twenty-one largest banks combined, and the nonperforming-loan definitions significantly understated the magnitude of the problem because the definitions were narrow and relied on bank reporting. Even when the Ministry of Finance released nonperforming-loan statistics by bank, the estimates were generally regarded as understatements. There was even less information provided about nonperforming loans at credit cooperatives and other nonbank financial institutions. Many private estimates of nonperforming loans before 1998, for example, were often twice the size of those reported by the Ministry of Finance. In early 1998, the Ministry of Finance, the Bank of Japan, and the newly operational Financial Supervisory Agency adopted more transparent and realistic measures of nonperforming loans. Although still subject to question, the nonperforming-loan estimates provided by government agencies and private banks at the end of the 1990s were generally regarded with somewhat more credibility than in the early 1990s.

There is little meaningful information, however, about nonperforming loans held by government banks, which until recently were not required to disclose nonperforming loans. Credit risk may be a problem, especially in light of increased lending by these institutions to housing and, to a lesser extent, to small and medium-sized business. Regulatory authorities minimize the problem of nonperforming loans at government banks because they argue that loans are collateralized, government- bank loans have first claim on assets, and FILP lending agencies closely evaluate and monitor credit risk. These, however, are the same arguments that were used to argue that private banks did not need to be concerned with nonperforming loans in the early 1990s. Government banks have begun to release information on nonperforming loans on the same basis as private banks. In addition to possible nonperforming loans held by the government banks, there may be a problem with many of the assets held by the other FILP entities, especially local government debt, or with the ability to generate sufficient revenue to cover expenditures (Doi and Hoshi, 2002).

One indirect indication of the potential problem can be obtained by examining the balance sheets of the government banks for information about bad loan reserves in the light of general economic conditions in the 1990s. Low levels of loss reserves in the context of the negative economic growth experienced in 1998 and 1999 suggest that there may be a serious problem that has yet to be revealed. The complexity of the FILP system makes it easy to shift the results of bad loan decisions on the part of the FILP to various special accounts and off-budget areas; for example, the Japan National Railroad, once a heavy borrower from the FILP, continues to operate with a large deficit carried by the government, with no evidence that the deficits will be paid off in the near future.

4.3. FILP SUBSIDIES BY INDUSTRY AND OVER TIME

FILP lending to industry is approximated by combining the "Strengthening of Key Industries," "Modernization of Low-Productivity Sections," and the "Trade and Economic Cooperation" categories discussed in Chapter 2 with respect to Figure 2.2 (p. 55). In the early 1950s, the "Trade and Economic Cooperation" category should be included in loans to industry; however, over time, this lending function has focused increasingly on activities outside of Japan. In any event, "Trade and Economic Cooperation" are considered industry loans. Using this standard, FILP funding to industry has represented about 20–30 percent of the FILP lending budget during the postwar period. Most of this funding was provided by the Japan Development Bank, the Export–Import Bank of Japan, and the Small Business Finance Corporation. Table 2.3 (p. 46) provides some historical information on these three banks and indicates institutional changes in the first two banks.

Table 2.7 (p. 53) provides insight into the relationship between industries and government banks in postwar Japan. First, all industries combined reduced their reliance on private-bank credit as a source of external funding. In the period 1961–74, all industries obtained 80.2 percent of their external funds from private financial institutions, primarily banks. This clearly reflects the dominance of the bank-finance model in Japan. However, by the 1986–91 period the share of private-bank credit declined to 76.7 percent, and by the 1992–98 period the share declined to 73.8 percent. Reliance on capital markets increased over the period, as would be expected from the development of open money and capital markets in Japan. Reliance on government financial institutions, however, has not changed significantly over the entire period covered by Table 2.7. Prior to the start of financial liberalization, all industry obtained 5.4 percent of its external funding from government banks, but after 1974 all industry obtained on average 5.3 percent of its external funding from government banks. This is not a dramatic decline, and between the 1986–91 and 1992–96 periods the dependency on government banks increased to 9.4 percent. The reduced reliance on private-bank credit and increased reliance on bond markets are relatively more significant, however.

There are substantial changes in the allocation of government-bank credit to various industries. Construction and manufacturing increased their reliance on government banks for external funding, whereas mining, transport and communications, services, and real estate reduced their reliance.

The statistics suggest that Japanese industries continue to rely on government-bank credit, although not to the extent that they rely on private-bank credit. No one industrial sector obtained more than 21.8 percent of its external funding (electricity supply) from government banks in the most recent period. However, the fact that every industrial category listed in Table 2.7 obtained anywhere from 1.7 to 21.8 percent of its external funding from government banks in the 1992–1998 period suggests that FILP funding remains a nontrivial source of funding for Japanese industry on a broad scale, especially in light of the increased reliance on government-bank credit in the past two decades.

FILP funds provide two advantages: favored access to credit, and loan rates lower than those in the private market. It is difficult to quantify the magnitude of the first element since it depends on the political power of a specific industry and on the overall industrial policy of Japan. It is, however, possible to approximate the interest rate on government-bank loans relative to the interest rate on private-bank loans and thus measure the interest-rate differential. The differential can then be used to measure the importance of the interest-rate subsidy to the specific industry. The interest-rate differential and the size of the subsidy by industry can then be reviewed over the postwar period to access trends in the subsidy.

The interest rate paid by a given industry for private and government-bank loans in a given year can be derived in the following steps. First, balance-sheet and income statements for each industry provide outstanding amounts of bank loans (private-bank and government-bank loans combined), bank deposits (businesses are normally not permitted to hold postal deposits), and bank interest expenses (private-bank and government-bank loan interest combined). Second, combined with information obtained from private banks on their outstanding loans and interest receipts from each industry, each industry's loan and interest expense is decomposed into private-bank loan and interest expense, and government-bank loan and interest expense.

An estimate of the effective loan rate charged by private banks to any industry is defined by:

$$er = \frac{((r^{L}*LB) - (r^{d}*DB))}{(LB-DB)} \tag{4.1}$$

where

er = the effective private-bank loan rate
r^{L} = the posted private-bank loan rate
LB = amount of private-bank loans
r^{d} = interest rate on one-year time-deposits
DB = amount of one-year time-deposits held as a compensating balance.

Expression (4.1) incorporates a feature of the Japanese financial system that required firms to hold compensating balances at the bank in order to establish and maintain a customer relationship. As a result, the posted loan rate under-states the cost of borrowing from private banks. Compensating-balance requirements became less restrictive and more flexible as financial liberaliza-tion increased the sources of funds available for business firms and as business firms reduced demand for credit when the economy shifted to a lower natural-growth path after 1975. Compensating-balance requirements continually declined in importance after 1980, and by the 1990s they became nonexistent for all practical purposes. The opportunity cost of the compensating balance is approximated by the one-year bank time-deposit rate applied to the level of time deposits held by the industry. In the absence of any reasonable basis to decompose deposits into compensating and voluntary, the assumption that all of the deposits held by a firm are compensating will bias the effective loan rate upward and overstate the size of the subsidy provided by government banks.

The interest rate charged by government banks, in contrast, is the effective interest rate, since government banks did not impose a compensating-balance requirement because they obtained their funds directly from the FILP.

The difference between the effective private-bank loan rate (expression (4.1)) and the government-bank rate is calculated on a quarterly basis from 1960:1 to 1995:4 and is presented in Figures 4.2–4.9 for all industries combined and for mining, manufacturing, wholesale, transport and commu-nications, electricity, services, and real estate individually. Interest rates charged by private banks exceeded government-bank interest rates until the mid-1980s; however, the gap narrowed as liberalization increased competition

Figure 4.2. *Private bank−government bank interest rate (all industries), 1961 : 1–1995 : 4.*

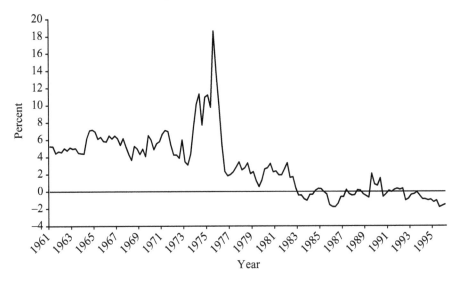

Figure 4.3. *Private bank−government bank interest rate (mining), 1961 : 1–1995 : 4.*

Figure 4.4. *Private bank−government bank interest rate (manufacturing), 1961 : 1–1995 : 4.*

in the banking industry, increased businesses' access to nonbank forms of domestic and external credit, and effectively abolished compensating-balance requirements.

By the second half of the 1980s, there was essentially no difference between private-bank and government-bank interest rates, and after 1993 government

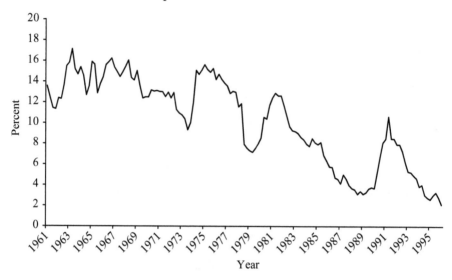

Figure 4.5. *Private bank−government bank interest rate (wholesale), 1961 : 1−1995 : 4.*

Figure 4.6. *Private bank−government bank interest rate (transport and communications),*
1961 : 1−1995 : 4.

loan rates actually exceeded private-bank loan rates. This reflects the credit-crunch conditions of Japanese banking in the wake of the collapse of asset prices. Firms have increasingly resorted to government financial institutions to offset the decline in the availability of private-bank credit.

The interest-rate gap for each industry can also be used to quantify the magnitude of the subsidy to that industry. The interest-rate gap times the amount of

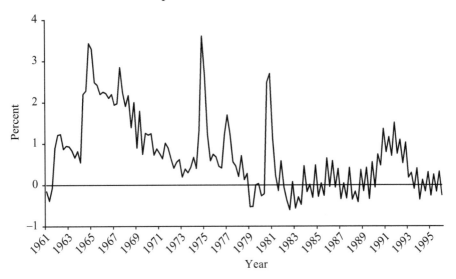

Figure 4.7. *Private bank−government bank interest rate (electricity), 1961 : 1–1995 : 4.*

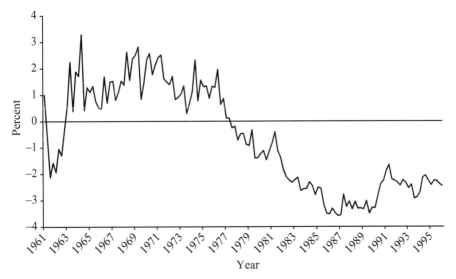

Figure 4.8. *Private bank−government bank interest rate (services), 1961 : 1–1995 : 4.*

government loans held by each industry quantifies the interest-rate subsidy provided by the FILP system:

$$s = (er - gr) * LG \qquad (4.2)$$

where

s = interest-rate subsidy
er = effective private-bank loan rate
gr = government-bank loan rate

Empirical Issues and Results

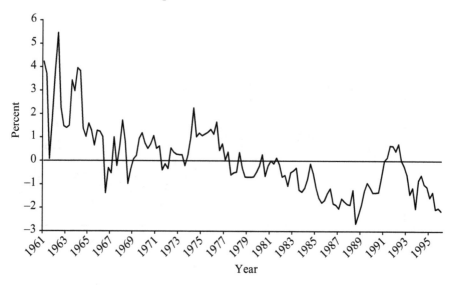

Figure 4.9. *Private bank−government bank interest rate (real estate), 1961 : 1–1995 : 4.*

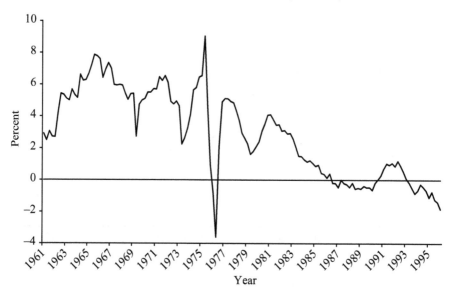

Figure 4.10. *Subsidy as percent of after-tax profits less dividends for all industries,*
1961 : 1–1995 : 4.

LG = government loans held by each industry.

The interest-rate subsidy for each industry can be normalized by expressing the amount of the subsidy as a percentage of each industry's after-tax retained earnings. This provides an estimate of the relative importance of the interest-rate subsidy to that industry. Unfortunately, the statistics on after-tax retained earnings (after-tax income less dividends) fluctuate and are influenced by the oil-price shocks of the early 1970s and the economic and financial distress of the 1990s. Thus, the interest-rate subsidy as a percentage of after-tax retained earnings fluctuates and exhibits sharp changes over time.

Figure 4.10 presents the normalized interest-rate subsidy for all industries[2] using after-tax income as the normalization variable. Despite some sharp fluctuations over time, the interest-rate subsidy was fairly large before 1975. The subsidy ranged from 3–5 percent of after-tax retained earnings for manufacturing, to 15–30 percent of after-tax retained earnings for transport and communications and for electricity. In the past two decades, however, the subsidy has become less important. The all-industry subsidy was also expressed as a percentage of before-tax income less dividends and generated a pattern virtually identical to Figure 4.10.

This result is consistent with the view that the financial system was used as an instrument of industrial policy and that FILP funding provided meaningful subsidies to favored sectors and to firms within the favored sectors. Estimates of the interest-rate subsidy decline significantly after 1975. This declining trend is the outcome of relatively higher government loan rates, increased competition in providing private-bank loans, and the reduced compensating-balance requirements imposed by private banks since 1975.

FILP funding has been distributed across a broad spectrum of Japanese industry in the postwar period. The dependence on government-bank loans by industry has not changed dramatically over the past several decades, although the interest-rate subsidy embedded in FILP funding has declined significantly as private banks have been forced to offer more competitive loan rates and dispense with compensating balance requirements. The elimination of the subsidy in the context of increasing business reliance on government-bank loans suggests that government banks may have lowered their credit standards in order to invest the considerable sums collected through the PSS, and it may further suggest increased credit risk. In the past when the loan subsidy was positive, a quality borrower would select a government bank over a private bank because of the price difference; however, without a significant price advantage, the quality borrower is more likely to select a private bank to satisfy its borrowing needs.

4.4. IMPACT OF THE SUBSIDY ON INDUSTRIAL INVESTMENT SPENDING

A simultaneous model of industrial investment in Japan is estimated to quantify the effect of government-bank loans on investment spending in manufacturing

---

[2] The normalized subsidy for mining, manufacturing, wholesale trade, transport and communications, electricity, services, and real estate also exhibited a similar pattern as would be expected from the behavior of the interest-rate spread illustrated in Figures 4.3–4.9.

and nonmanufacturing industries. The model is estimated over the period from 1965 to 1998. The results presented in this study are based on results presented in Yoshino and Nakata (1997), Nakata (2001), and Yoshino *et al.* (2001).

The model consists of four equations: corporate demand for funds, corporate supply of funds, private-bank-loan supply of funds, and corporate bond supply. Variable definitions are presented in Table 4.1.

Corporate investment or demand for funds is specified by the following equation:

$$\frac{I_t}{K_{t-1}} = a_1 + a_1 \rho_t^e + a_2 r_t + a_4 \left[\frac{p_t^I}{(1-\tau)p_t} \right] + a_5 \left[\Delta \left(\frac{p_t^L}{(1-\tau)p_t} \right) \right] \quad (4.3)$$

where $r_t = b r_t^B + (1-b) r_t^L$

The demand for funds or investment is measured by the ratio of investment spending at time t to the capital stock at time $t-1$, I_t/K_{t-1}. Investment spending

Table 4.1. *Variable definitions*

I_t/K_{t-1}	Gross investment rate
I_t	Gross investment (including land)
K_t	Capital stock (including land)
ρ_t^e	Expected profit rate
r_t	Interest rate on external funds, excluding government-bank loans
r_t^B	Corporate-bond interest rate
r_t^L	Private-bank effective loan rate
p_t^I	Price of investment goods
p_t	GDP deflator
p_t^L	Land price
τ	Effective tax rate
r_t^c	Call rate (collateralized overnight)
r_t^{d1}	Time-deposit rate (regulated)
r_t^{d2}	Time-deposit rate (unregulated)
D_t	Deposits at all banks
LB_t	Loans and discounts at all banks
$D1$	Dummy variable for 65Q3–85Q3
$D2$	Dummy variable for 85Q4–98Q1
$Land_t$	Market value of land owned by firms
$Risk_t$	Default risk ratio
CF_t	Internal funds
LB_t	Private-bank loans for equipment
B_t	Corporate-bond issues
LG_t	Government-bank loans for equipment
$Time$	Time trend
$RCAP_t$	Share of large firms to total capital
ROP_t	Share of large firms to total (ordinary) profit
GOP_t^j	Growth rate of the jth industry profit
GOP_t	Growth rate of all industry profit

depends on the following: (1) the expected rate of return on investment measured by the industry profit rate, ρ_t^e; (2) the real rate of interest measured as a weighted average of the rate on corporate bonds and the private bank loan rate, r_t; (3) the ratio of the price of investment goods to the after-tax output price, $p_t^I/(1 - \tau)p_t$; and (4) the change in the ratio of the price of land to the after-tax output price, $\Delta(p_t^L/(1 - \tau)p_t)$. The rate of investment spending is negatively related to the interest rate and positively related to the other three variables.

The corporate supply of funds is a definitional equation that identifies four sources of funds to support investment spending: (1) internal funds; (2) private bank loans; (3) government bank loans and; (4) funds raised by issuing corporate bonds.

$$p_t^I I_t = CF_t + \Delta LB_t + \Delta LG_t + \Delta B_t \tag{4.4}$$

The total supply of funds to be invested is measured by the price of investment goods and the amount of real investment at time t, $p_t^I I_t$. By definition, the supply of funds to support investment equals the sum of internal corporate funds, CF_t, change in private bank loans, ΔLB_t, change in government bank loans, ΔLG_t, and corporate bond issues, ΔB_t. Corporate internal funds and government bank loans are considered exogenous in the estimation procedure.

The supply of private bank loans is:

$$r_t^L = c_0 + c_1 r_t^c + c_2 \left[(r_t^c - r_t^d) \frac{D_t}{LB_{t,}} \right] D1 + c_3 \left[(r_t^c - r_t^d) \frac{D_t}{LB_{t,}} \right] D2 \\ + c_4 \Delta LB_t + c_5 \Delta LG_t + c_6 Land_{t,} + c_7 Risk_t \tag{4.5}$$

The private-bank loan supply function expresses the private-bank loan interest rate, r_t^L, as a function of the following variables: (1) the call or interbank interest rate, r_t^c; (2) the difference between the call rate and the deposit rate times the deposit loan ratio, $(r_t^c - r_t^d)D_t/LB_t$ adjusted for a dummy to account for the conversion of *sogo* banks into regional banks II in 1985 : 4 (*D1* and *D2*); (3) change in private bank loans, ΔLB_t; (4) the change in government bank loans, ΔLG_t; (5) the market value of land, $Land_t$; and (6), the default loan loss ratio to total loans for private banks, $Risk_t$.

Corporate bonds are issued according to:

$$\frac{\Delta B_t}{(\Delta B_t + \Delta LB_t)} = d_1 Time + d_2 RCAP_t + d_3(GOP_t^j - GOP_{t,}) \\ + d_4 ROP_t + d_5 \left[\frac{\Delta B_{t-1}}{(\Delta B_{t-1} + \Delta LB_{t-1})} \right] \tag{4.6}$$

Corporate bond issues, ΔB_t as a percentage of total funds raised, is a function of the following variables: (1) time trend, *Time*; (2) the ratio of capital of large firms to capital for all firms, $RCAP_t$; (3) rate of growth of profit of the jth industry minus the growth rate of industry ordinary profit, $GOP^j_t - GOP_t$; (4) the ratio of profits of large firms to total profits, ROP_t; and (5) lagged bond issues, $\Delta B_{t-1}/(\Delta B_{t-1} + \Delta LB_{t-1})$.

The three equations are estimated via instrumental variables for manufacturing and nonmanufacturing industries over the period from 1965:3 to 1998:1. The coefficient estimates for the investment function are presented in Tables 4.2 and 4.3 for manufacturing and nonmanufacturing, respectively. The coefficient estimates for the private-bank supply function using the bank rate as the left-hand side variable are presented in Tables 4.4 and 4.5 for manufacturing and nonmanufacturing, respectively. The coefficient estimates for the corporate-bond issue equation are presented in Tables 4.6 and 4.7 for manufacturing and nonmanufacturing, respectively. In the majority of cases, the variable coefficient estimates generate the anticipated sign and were generally significant at the 5-percent level of confidence.[3]

The three estimated equations are substituted into the corporate-supply-of-funds equation to obtain a reduced-form equation for corporate investment. In addition to the three influences discussed above (quantitative effect, low-interest- rate effect, and cowbell effect), the model also provides information on the influence of land values and risk:

1. *Quantitative Effect of Government-Bank Loans.* The addition of government-bank loans increases investment spending by increasing the overall supply of funds to the corporate sector.
2. *Low-Interest-Rate Effect of Government-Bank Loans.* The interest-rate subsidy is reflected as an increase in expected profits, which in turn increases investment spending in the corporate sector.
3. *Cowbell Effect of Government-Bank Loans.* Government-bank loans provide information to the private banks and thereby reduce risk of private-bank

---

[3] The regression results reported in Tables 4.2–4.7 incorporate constant and coefficient dummy variables. They are included to incorporate a variety of events that likely generated a shift in the relationship between the dependent variable and the repressors. The dummy variable for a given event covers different time periods in each equation based on statistical significance and expected coefficient sign; that is, once a dummy variable was included for a given event, the exact time period for the variable was empirically determined. The following events for each table are listed in order of the constant and coefficient dummy variables presented in each table. Table 4.2: first oil-price shock, recession, recession, high-growth period, recession, high-growth period, second oil-price shock, interest-rate liberalization period, and high-growth period. Table 4.3: second oil-price shock, post-liberalization up to start of asset inflation, Plaza Accord, high-growth period, recession, high-growth period, recession, and recession. Table 4.4: recession, recession, asset-inflation period, decline in call rate, easy monetary policy, high-growth period, post-first oil-price shock, FILP loans used as counter-cyclical policy, and financial distress. Table 4.5: first oil-price shock, recession, recession, asset-inflation period, decline in call rate, easy monetary policy, post-first oil-price shock recession, financial distress, asset-inflation period, and financial distress. Table 4.6: post-Plaza Accord, recession, pre-liberalization, post-liberalization, and pre-liberalization. Table 4.7: high-growth period, Plaza Accord, pre-liberalization, Plaza Accord, post-liberalization, and pre-liberalization.

Table 4.2. *Investment function for manufacturing, expression 4.3,*
1965 : 3–1998 : 1 (R²(Adjusted) = 0.97; DW = 1.80)

Parameter	Period	Estimate	t-value
Constant term		5.132	18.5**
Const. D1	73Q2–73Q4	−1.007	−8.72**
Const. D2	84Q4–85Q3	−0.421	−4.48**
Const. D3	92Q1–98Q1	−0.772	−11.9**
Expected profit ratio		0.356	14.4**
Coef. D	65Q3–73Q4	0.802	18.2**
Coef. D	90Q2–98Q1	−0.171	−6.06**
Interest rate		0.055	8.89**
Coef. D	65Q3–75Q2	−0.068	−7.49**
Coef. D	78Q1–80Q3	−0.127	−8.77**
Coef. D	87Q1–98Q1	−0.068	−8.21**
Relative price of inv. goods		−1.034	−10.1**
Relative price of land		−5.135	−11.5**
Coef. D	67Q1–70Q1	28.47	4.28**

Note: Period: 1965Q3–1998Q1; * and ** indicate statistically significant at
10- and 5-percent level, respectively. Const. D = Constant Dummy Variable.
Coef. D = Coefficient Dummy Variable.

Table 4.3. *Investment function for nonmanufacturing, expression*
4.3, 1965 : 3–1998 : 1 (R²(Adjusted) = 0.86; DW = 1.60)

Parameter	Period	Estimate	t-value
Constant term		4.395	19.2**
Const. D1	79Q1–79Q4	0.262	3.41**
Const. D2	81Q3–88Q3	0.233	5.44**
Const. D3	85Q3–86Q2	0.223	2.99**
Expected profit ratio		0.572	9.85**
Coef. D	65Q3–73Q2	0.836	12.5**
Coef. D	95Q4–98Q1	0.417	7.99**
Interest rate		0.006	2.06**
Coef. D	65Q3–73Q4	0.037	4.40**
Coef. D	92Q2–98Q1	0.064	5.86**
Relative price of inv. goods		0.784	8.98**
Relative price of land		1.484	2.38**
Coef. D	90Q4–98Q1	4.896	5.32**

Note: See Table 4.2.

lending to certain industries. That is, the private-bank loan-supply function
includes government-bank loans as a positive influence.

4. *Land-Value Effect.* Increases in the value of land increase private-bank
   lending as a result of increased collateral.

Table 4.4. *New loans for equipment funds from private banks—manufacturing industry, expression 4.5, 1965 : 3–1998 : 1 (R^2(Adjusted) = 0.95; DW = 1.55)*

Parameter	Period	Estimate	*t*-value
Const. D1	84Q4–86Q1	−1.519	−6.42**
Const. D2	93Q2–98Q1	2.246	8.05**
Call rate		1.322	7.65**
Coef. D	85Q4–91Q2	−0.343	−10.4**
Coef. D	Call Rate Down	−0.217	−8.62**
Deposit ~	85Q3	−1.609	−19.1**
Deposit	85Q3 ~	−0.765	−7.47**
Private banks' loan		4.95E-06	9.27**
Coef. D	65Q3–66Q4	6.67E-06	5.29**
Coef. D	76Q1–78Q3	−1.32E-06	−6.16**
Government banks' loan		−4.36E-06	−2.52**
Coef. D	97Q2–98Q1	−9.84E-06	−2.95**
Market value of land		−7.94E-08	−11.1**
Default loan loss ratio		3.508	7.06**
Coef. D	95Q4–98Q1	−1.552	−2.21**

Note: See Table 4.2.

Table 4.5. *New loans for equipment funds from private banks— nonmanufacturing industry, expression 4.5, 1965 : 3–1998 : 1 (R^2(Adjusted) = 0.95; DW = 1.53)*

Parameter	Period	Estimate	*t*-value
Const. D1	73Q1–73Q3	−2.317	−3.43**
Const. D2	84Q4–86Q1	−1.370	−6.25**
Const. D3	93Q2–98Q1	1.697	5.58**
Call rate		1.298	6.28**
Coef. D	85Q4–91Q3	−0.282	−7.26**
Coef. D	Call Rate Down	−0.099	−5.88**
Deposit ~	85Q3	−1.454	−16.1**
Deposit	85Q3 ~	−0.692	−7.61**
Private banks' loan		0.43E-06	4.91**
Coef. D	70Q3–74Q1	1.12E-06	7.54**
Coef. D	76Q1–78Q3	−0.51E-06	−4.98**
Government banks' loan		−2.13E-06	−2.89**
Coef. D	97Q2–98Q1	−1.91E-06	−2.20**
Market value of land		−2.22E-08	−5.84**
Coef. D	89Q4–91Q2	−0.61E-08	−3.79**
Default loan loss ratio		4.236	8.63**
Coef. D	96Q1–98Q1	−1.315	−2.03**

Note: See Table 4.2.

Table 4.6. *Access to bond market for manufacturing industry, expression 4.6, 1965 : 3–1998 : 1 (R^2(Adjusted) = 0.89; DW = 1.89; Durbin h = 1.03)*

Parameter	Period	Estimate	t-value
Constant term		0.040	2.16**
Const. D1	85Q4–87Q1	0.421	4.62**
Const. D2	92Q2–95Q4	−0.126	−2.80**
Share of large firms capital		0.928	7.62**
Coef. D	65Q3–83Q4	−0.692	−3.58**
Growth rate of profit: difference from all industry		−0.002	−0.66
Coef. D	86Q4–98Q1	0.033	2.26**
Share of large firms: ordinary profit		−0.011	−2.07**
Lagged dependent variable		0.489	8.12**
Coef. D	65Q3–83Q4	0.485	3.21**

Note: See Table 4.2.

Table 4.7. *Access to bond market for nonmanufacturing industry, expression 4.6, 1965 : 3–1998 : 1 (R^2(Adjusted) = 0.59; DW = 2.07)*

Parameter	Period	Estimate	t-value
Constant term		0.005	−0.45
Const. D1	65Q3–72Q1	0.080	−2.76**
Const. D2	85Q2–86Q2	0.245	3.25**
Share of large firms: capital		0.016	−0.50
Coef. D	65Q3–84Q4	0.070	−1.08
Coef. D	85Q2–86Q2	0.616	5.16**
Growth rate of profit: difference from all industry		0.004	1.85*
Coef. D	85Q1–98Q1	0.006	−1.12
Share of large firms: ordinary profit		−0.002	−0.35
Lagged dependent variable		0.225	1.80*
Coef. D	65Q3–84Q4	0.279	1.79*

Note: See Table 4.2. Durbin's *h* statistic could not be calculated; thus, an alternative method introduced in Durbin and Watson (1971) was employed. First-order serial correlation was rejected.

5. *Default-Loan-Risk Effect.* Increases in default risk reduce private-bank lending.

The quantitative effect is measured by using the actual changes in government-bank loans to determine the effect on investment spending. The interest-rate effect is measured by using the actual interest-rate subsidy to change expected

Table 4.8. *The impact of FILP loans on manufacturing investment evaluated at the equilibrium, 1965 : 3–1998 : 1, (Unit: Real/Million Yen. In ( ), the share to the gross investment is shown (Unit: %))*

	Government banks' new loans for equipment funds			Market value of land owned by firms	Default risk ratio
	Cowbell effect	Quantitative effect	Low interest rate effect		
65Q3–69Q4	1,185	1,828	88,101	11,035	−9,326
	(0.05)	(0.09)	(4.16)	(0.53)	(−0.46)
70Q1–74Q4	3,619	4,320	105,485	27,308	−8,478
	(0.11)	(0.13)	(3.49)	(0.85)	(−0.26)
75Q1–80Q4	8,132	9,404	56,520	42,102	−20,805
	(0.32)	(0.36)	(1.44)	(1.60)	(−0.81)
81Q1–85Q3	—	—	—	—	—
	(—)	(—)	(—)	(—)	(—)
85Q4–86Q4	—	—	—	—	—
	(—)	(—)	(—)	(—)	(—)
87Q1–91Q4	12,478	14,894	1,078	102,487	−10,309
	(0.26)	(0.32)	(0.11)	(2.07)	(−0.22)
92Q1–95Q4	16,092	19,207	−3,980	112,585	−28,915
	(0.36)	(0.43)	(−0.13)	(2.51)	(−0.63)
96Q1–98Q1	15,333	8,538	−15,037	86,748	−19,904
	(0.36)	(0.21)	(−0.39)	(2.11)	(−0.48)
89Q1–91Q2	15,047	17,961	5,809	127,069	−7,714
	(0.28)	(0.34)	(0.18)	(2.37)	(−0.14)
97Q2–98Q1	25,980	9,044	−14,311	84,230	−24,061
	(0.59)	(0.20)	(−0.35)	(1.92)	(−0.54)

Note: During 1981Q1–1986Q4, the estimated parameter of the interest rate in the investment function did not satisfy the negative sign condition. The effects thus cannot be evaluated at the equilibrium. The same situation occurred for 1975Q1–1980Q4.

profits and hence investment spending. The cowbell effect is measured by determining the effect of government-bank loans on the supply of private-bank loans, which in turn influence investment spending.

Tables 4.8 and 4.9 provide relative measures of each of these effects on corporate investment according to selected subperiods over the 1965 : 3–1998 : 1 period. The results support several observations. First, the land-value effect and the default effect appear to be important in the more recent periods. Both effects before 1990 are small and account for a relatively small impact on corporate investment spending. Second, the cowbell effect is seldom important. It accounts for less than 1 percent of investment spending in the manufacturing sector for each of the subperiods and, except for the 1990s, has no meaningful

Table 4.9. *The impact of FILP loans on nonmanufacturing investment evaluated at the equilibrium, 1965 : 3–1998 : 1, (Unit: Real/Million Yen. In ( ), the share to the gross investment is shown (Unit: %))*

	Government banks' new loans for equipment funds			Market value of land owned by firms	Default risk ratio
	Cowbell effect	Quantitative effect	Low interest rate effect		
65Q3–69Q4	3,257	657	130,774	17,670	−44,398
	(0.17)	(0.03)	(6.94)	(0.93)	(−2.38)
70Q1–74Q4	6,621	4,443	151,916	31,724	−30,498
	(0.20)	(0.13)	(4.73)	(0.95)	(−0.96)
75Q1–80Q4	2,483	543	59,209	6,055	−9,127
	(0.08)	(0.01)	(1.96)	(0.19)	(−0.32)
81Q1–85Q3	4,464	901	6,372	9,546	−10,581
	(0.10)	(0.02)	(0.22)	(0.21)	(−0.23)
85Q4–86Q4	5,068	1,023	−57,243	13,226	−16,035
	(0.09)	(0.02)	(−0.98)	(0.23)	(−0.28)
87Q1–91Q4	9,934	2,005	−37,624	54,421	−12,302
	(0.11)	(0.48)	(−0.53)	(0.54)	(−0.13)
92Q1–95Q4	248,188	50,103	−74,344	666,885	−407,681
	(2.39)	(0.41)	(−0.77)	(6.33)	(−3.82)
96Q1–98Q1	283,617	40,586	−51,541	633,663	−385,596
	(2.84)	(0.41)	(−0.52)	(6.46)	(−3.88)
89Q1–91Q2	10,999	2,220	−20,207	73,665	−9,634
	(0.11)	(0.02)	(−0.25)	(0.71)	(−0.09)
97Q2–98Q1	392,972	41,826	−53,259	27,870	−471,793
	(3.78)	(0.40)	(−0.51)	(6.04)	(−4.52)

effect on nonmanufacturing investment. The relative importance of the cowbell effect in the 1990s for nonmanufacturing is probably being picked up by increased lending to small businesses. Third, the quantitative effect is never more than one-half of 1 percent of investment for either the manufacturing or nonmanufacturing sectors. Fourth, the low-interest-rate effect has the highest positive effect on corporate investment, but only in the period prior to 1975. The low-interest-rate effect is small after 1975.

The results suggest that the three effects of the FILP system on investment spending are small, even before 1975. Although the low-interest-rate effect was at its largest before 1975, it still accounts for less than 7 percent of investment spending. All three effects, with the exception of the cowbell effect in the 1990s, are small after 1975. Thus, although the FILP system appears to have had a small but positive impact on corporate investment prior to 1975, the effects have subsequently become very small for all practical purposes.

4.5. POSTAL SAVINGS AND BANK OF JAPAN POLICY

The influence of the PSS (and FILP) on monetary policy is a complex issue for at least three reasons. First, Bank of Japan policy throughout much of the postwar period has been successful, given the operating environment at any particular time. Thus, for long periods in postwar Japan, it would be difficult to argue that the PSS seriously interfered with monetary policy. In fact, the 1975–85 period is regarded as the high point of Bank of Japan policy (Cargill *et al.*, 1997) in terms of macroeconomic policy outcomes, but it was during this same period that the PSS grew rapidly relative to private banks and that the PSS attracted increasing criticism. Second, the Bank of Japan made several policy errors in the postwar period. Easy monetary policy contributed to the "wild inflation" of the early 1970s, easy monetary policy in the second half of the 1980s fueled the bubble economy, tight monetary policy in the early 1990s contributed to recession, and the less-than-aggressive easy monetary policy in the late 1990s permitted a gradual decline in the price level. These policy errors had adverse effects on the economy, but none can even remotely be traced to the existence of the PSS or the FILP. That is, the presence of the PSS and the FILP and their upward-growth trend cannot be held responsible for Bank of Japan policy failures. Third, modeling monetary policy to incorporate the presence of the postal savings system presents a number of difficult issues, given the changes in operating environment for monetary policy resulting from external factors, structural changes brought about by financial liberalization, and financial distress.

The first two points suggest that whereas there may be some theoretical justification for the claim that the PSS adversely influences the conduct of monetary policy, the practical relevance of the issue is not large. A simple VAR and structural model of Bank of Japan policy can shed some additional light on the issue.

Several VAR models of the money-supply process were estimated using M2+CDs as the money-supply measure. M2+CDs excludes postal deposits. It seems reasonable to argue that if the existence of postal deposits interferes with monetary control, VAR equations for the money-supply process should be statistically sensitive to the presence of postal deposits. That is, postal deposits in one form or another would significantly influence the money-supply process. The VAR equations are estimated using quarterly data over the period from 1978:3 to 1985:1 and from 1985:2 to 1997:4. Variables are measured as growth rates, with the exception of the call-rate of interest.

Table 4.10 presents estimates for several variations of the VAR equation. Only one equation estimate indicates a significant postal-deposit effect at one of the two lags. All other estimated equations indicate that the growth rate of postal deposits contributes no explanatory influence to the money-supply process in Japan.

Table 4.10. *VAR model of money-supply process with influence of postal deposits 1978 : 3–1997 : 4 (Money Supply = M2 + CDs)*

Variable	Estimated coefficient	Standard error	*t*-statistic
1978 : 3–1985 : 1			
M2CD(−1)	0.441983	0.265316	1.66587
M2CD(−2)	0.208097	0.206721	1.00665
POST(−1)	−0.27097	0.253957	−1.0670
POST(−2)	0.459571	0.283491	1.62111
1985 : 2–1997 : 4			
M2CD(−1)	0.962048	0.146699	6.55796**
M2CD(−2)	−0.02970	0.142593	−0.20830
POST(−1)	−0.11774	0.136220	−0.86434
POST(−2)	0.163705	0.138509	1.18190
1978 : 3–1985 : 1			
C	4.88023	1.52457	3.20105**
CALL(−1)	−0.36099	0.184375	−1.9579
CALL(−2)	0.023799	0.224139	0.106178
M2CD(−1)	0.035545	0.235119	0.151177
M2CD(−2)	0.296130	0.170122	1.74069
POST(−1)	−0.356392	0.228163	−1.5620
POST(−2)	0.574390	0.237402	2.41949*
1985 : 2–1997 : 4			
C	−1.42152	0.784352	−1.8123
CALL(−1)	0.063573	0.289923	0.219276
CALL(−2)	−0.304443	0.288200	−1.0563
M2CD(−1)	0.810487	0.144070	5.62567**
M2CD(−2)	0.263166	0.161860	1.62589
POST(−1)	0.112948	0.149023	0.757920
POST(−2)	0.128776	0.138602	0.929106

Note: All variables with the exception of the call rate, CALL, are annualized quarterly growth rates.

There are well-known problems with VAR-model estimation. In order to determine the robustness of the VAR results, we expand a structural money-demand–money-supply model originally developed by Rhodes and Yoshino (1999) to include postal deposits. The model consists of a money-supply function (4.13) based on definitions and relationships (4.7) through (4.12).

The money-supply function is determined by the following:

$$MS = CUR + DEP \tag{4.7}$$

$$CUR = cDEP \tag{4.8}$$

$$HPM = RES + DEP \tag{4.9}$$

$$k = RES/DEP \tag{4.10}$$

$$\frac{MS}{HPM} = \frac{(c(r)) + 1)}{(k + c(r))} \tag{4.11}$$

$$MS = \left\{ \frac{(C(r) + 1)}{(k + c(r))} \right\} HPM \tag{4.12}$$

$$MS = f(1/r, 1/k, HPM) \tag{4.13}$$

where

MS = Currency (C) + Deposits Except Postal Deposits (DEP)
c = Currency deposit ratio
HPM = High-Powered Money defined as Deposits (DEP) + Reserves (RES)
k = reserve requirement
r = short-term interest rate.

The money demand is determined by the following:

$$MD = f(r, Y, Land) \tag{4.14}$$

where

Land   = Value of land as a measure of wealth
DEP   = $aLOAN + bFILP + DEP0$
LOAN = Loans made by private banks
FILP   = FILP loans
DEP0 = Core deposits at private banks.

The view that the PSS interferes with monetary policy can be illustrated by considering the case of an easy policy. Let's assume that an easy monetary policy induces the disintermediation of private-bank deposits to postal savings, and thereby induces a decline in core private-bank deposits, *DEP0*. This would occur as expected interest-rate declines induce a shift from private-bank to PSS *teigaku* deposits. However, the increase in FILP lending supported by the disintermediation will likely end up increasing private-bank deposits by the coefficient *b*. FILP lending is used for infrastructure and other types of spending and thus, a major portion of the received funds (the *b* fraction—i.e. *bFILP*) is eventually deposited into private-bank deposits. This will be combined with core deposits already in the private banks and deposits created through the bank-lending process, *aLOAN*. Therefore, it is unlikely that an increase in postal savings will decrease money supply. Likewise, in the case of tight monetary policy, it is unlikely that a reduction in postal savings will increase the money supply, though the model does allow for some offset to monetary policy.

2SLS and 3SLS estimates of the structural model are obtained for the period from 1972:2 to 1999:3, using high-powered money and the call rate as the policy instrument. The estimates support the hypothesis that postal deposits do

Table 4.11. *2SLS estimates of money supply-and-demand model, 1972 : 2–1999 : 3*

Variable	Coefficient	Standard Error	*t*-statistic	*P*-value
Money Supply Equation; Adjusted $R^2 = 0.98$				
Constant	1.04245	0.667830	1.56096	[0.119]
LHPM(−1)	1.14888	0.165413	6.94553	[0.000] log(HPM) (+)
RCALL(−1)	−0.026756	0.652640E-02	−4.09965	[0.000] $1/r$ (−)
RRES	0.123462E-04	0.386778E-05	3.19205	[0.001] $1/k$ (+)
LPOST(−1)	−0.039820	0.105387	−0.377845	[0.706] log(Postal savings)
Money Demand Equation; Adjusted $R^2 = 0.99$				
Constant	1.57270	0.505604	3.11054	[0.002]
RCALL	0.020526	0.331718E-02	6.18785	[0.000] $1/r$ (+)
LGDP	1.02038	0.045206	22.5720	[0.000] log(Y) (+)
LAND	0.549766E-02	0.928249E-03	5.92261	[0.000] Asset Price (+)

Note: All variables are quarterly levels expressed as natural logs with the exception of the call rate and reserve requirements.

not significantly influence the response of the income to changes in monetary policy. The *t*-values on the postal-savings coefficient are insignificant at conventional levels in all estimates of the model. Table 4.11 reports the 2SLS estimates using high-powered money as the Bank of Japan instrument.

These results, though based on simple models of monetary policy, combined with the theoretical results in Chapter 3 and a qualitative review of the success and failure of monetary policy in the postwar period, suggest that the PSS and FILP have not been a practical constraint on Bank of Japan policy. There are reasonable arguments that can be made to support reform of the PSS and the FILP, but interference with monetary policy is not one of those arguments. The problems experienced by monetary policy in the past cannot be attributed to either the PSS or the FILP, and at the same time, the Bank of Japan has been able to pursue successful policy in the past despite the presence of the PSS and FILP.

4.6. DEMAND FOR POSTAL DEPOSITS RELATIVE TO BANK DEPOSITS

The relative growth of the PSS has led many to argue that this growth has been at the expense of the private banks. Among the many advantages that the PSS enjoys over private banks, two are of special importance.

First, *teigaku* deposits until recently were issued only by the PSS. These deposits minimize interest-rate risk for the depositor to a greater extent than any deposit offered by private banks. During periods when interest rates are expected to decline, *teigaku* deposits are attractive because they lock in the interest rate. During periods when interest rates are expected to increase, depositors prefer to hold funds in short-term bank deposits. In addition, abstracting from interest-rate expectations, the *teigaku* deposit provides a higher ex-post return than a standard ten-year time-deposit because it allows the depositor to withdraw funds after six months without penalty (Table 2.11, p. 65).

Second, the PSS offers more convenience in the form of branches than do private banks. Table 2.12 (p. 67) presented the ratio of private-bank branches to post offices for each of Japan's forty-seven prefectures in 1980, 1988, and 1995. In 1980, post offices outnumbered bank branches in all forty-seven prefectures (ratio greater than 1.0 in Table 2.12 for all prefectures). In 1995, the situation began to change as banks more aggressively sought out deposits by expanding branches. In all prefectures, the ratio of post offices to bank offices declined, and in Osaka and Tokyo, the number of bank offices exceeded the number of post offices. The greater convenience offered by the PSS also suggests that even during periods when interest rates are expected to increase the PSS is not as disadvantaged as might be expected. The lower-convenience factor of private banks to post offices throughout most of Japan suggests that at any interest rate, there is resistance to shift from *teigaku* deposits to short-term bank deposits.

Yoshino has published several studies estimating the relative demand for postal deposits to bank deposits (e.g. 1996). The most recent and complete set of demand functions is provided in Yoshino and Sano (1997) and Wada (2000). The following time-series – cross-section model is estimated:

$$\left(\frac{PD}{BD}\right)_{tj} = a_0 + a_1\left(\frac{NPO}{NBB}\right)_{tj} + a_2 I_{tj} + a_3(\Delta BTD - \Delta PS)_t,$$
$$+ a_4 IRate_t + a_5 Large_t + a_6 RBII_t \qquad (4.14)$$

The ratio of postal to bank deposits at time t for prefecture j, $(PD/BD)_{tj}$, depends on the following factors: (1) the relative convenience of post offices to banks measured by the ratio of the number of post offices to the number of bank branches, $(NPO/NBB)_{tj}$; (2) household income, I_{tj}; (3) the difference between the change in the interest rate on bank time deposits and the interest rate on postal savings, $(\Delta BTD - \Delta PS)_t$; (4) a dummy variable to represent periods of increasing interest rates, $IRate_t$; (5) a dummy variable to represent large cities, $Large_t$, used to adjust the interest rate spread variable; and (6) and a dummy variable equal to one after 1985Q3 to represent the reclassification of *sogo* banks into regional banks II, $RBII_t$.

The model is estimated using annual data over the period from 1980 to 1995 for the forty-seven prefectures in Japan. The coefficients are estimated by a fixed-effects model, and the results are presented in Table 4.12.

The results reveal several significant implications about those factors that influence the choice between postal and bank deposits. First, the ratio of the number of post offices to the number of bank branches, as a measure of convenience,

Table 4.12. *Demand for postal deposits relative to private-bank deposits,*
1980–1995 (47 prefectures)

Dependent variable	Postal savings/private-bank deposits	
Independent Variable	Estimated Coefficient (*t*-value)	
Ratio of post offices to private banks	0.124	(11.1)
Household income	−0.021	(−1.7)
Spread between private-bank time-deposit and postal savings rate changes	−0.005	(−0.2)
Spread between private-bank time-deposit and postal savings rate changes adjusted for large-city dummy variable	−0.062	(2.0)
Dummy variable for periods of increasing interest rates	−0.124	(−15.2)
Dummy variable for regional bank reorganization	−0.087	(−5.3)
R^2 (adjusted)	0.92	

is significant. Measured by the beta coefficient, the ratio of post offices to bank branches is the most important determinate of the choice between postal and bank deposits. The convenience variable is significant in every specification estimated.

Second, the income variable is negative but insignificant at the 5-percent level when the dependent variable is measured as the ratio of postal to bank deposits. However, when the dependent variable is measured as the ratio of all bank deposits to postal deposits (not presented), household income has a significant and positive effect on the ratio of bank to postal deposits; that is, the higher the level of household income, the higher the ratio of bank to postal deposits. To the extent that one regards the income variable as significant, the results suggest that the 10-million-yen limit on postal deposits per individual and the effectiveness of enforcement policy on the part of the PSS may be a binding constraint for some individuals. It may also suggest that higher-income individuals require services more available at private banks than at the post office, as well as reflect the greater proportion of higher-income households in Tokyo and Osaka, where banks now offer more branching convenience than the post office does.

Third, the interest-rate-spread coefficient is negative but insignificant, suggesting that the PSS has not timed interest-rate changes to induce disintermediation; however, the variable is negative and significant when adjusted for a large-city dummy. Expression (4.14) was estimated without the large-city dummy variable adjustment of the interest-rate-spread variable (not presented). In this case, the interest-rate-spread variable was negative and significant at the 5-percent level of confidence. If the spread variable is positive, this means that the change in bank-deposit rates minus the change in postal-deposit rates increases the relative attractiveness of bank deposits, thereby shifting deposits from the PSS to private banks. Finding a negative and significant spread under some conditions is consistent with the claim that the PSS has timed interest-rate changes to induce disintermediation. At the same time, this practice essentially ceased after the 1994 agreement between the Ministry of Posts and Telecommunications and the Ministry of Finance to set postal-deposit rates "close to" private-bank deposit rates.

Fourth, the dummy variable to indicate periods of increasing interest rates is significant and has the anticipated negative sign. Periods of increasing interest rates, to the extent that they imply expectations of higher interest rates in the future, will provide incentives to shift from long-term *teigaku* deposits to short-term bank deposits.

Fifth, the dummy variable for the reclassification of *sogo* banks into regional banks—Rank II is significant and has the anticipated negative sign. *Sogo* deposits were not included in the definition of all bank deposits; however, once these institutions were reclassified as banks, their deposits then became part of all bank deposits.

The results suggest that branching has been an important advantage offered by the PSS relative to private banks, while at the same time bank deposits are positively correlated with household income. Until the early 1970s, the Ministry of Finance restricted branching to protect small banks and credit cooperatives and as a result, the PSS benefited. In the 1970s, the Ministry of Finance adopted a more flexible approach and began to permit increased branching. In fact, the establishment of the Deposit Insurance Corporation in 1971 was a response to concerns from smaller depository institutions that increased branching would be harmful to banks and reduce public confidence. The Ministry of Finance increasingly relaxed restrictions on branching and in 1990, the law restricting branching was repealed. Thus, the private banks did have some constraints on competing with the PSS, but these constraints became less important over time. As a result, complaints from private banks about the unfair advantage enjoyed by the PSS may reflect an unwillingness on the part of private banks to offer more convenience in the form of branching rather than inherent advantages of the PSS.

4.7. PSS AND PRIVATE BANKS: DEPOSIT FLIGHT

The influence of the PSS on the financial system changed significantly after 1990. The collapse of asset prices, subsequent recession, market insolvency of the two deposit-insurance agencies by 1994, and the problem of banks and other financial institutions with nonperforming loans heightened the public's awareness of government deposit guarantees. Although the Ministry of Finance in 1995 guaranteed all deposits in private institutions through 31 March 2001, and in late 1999 extended the guarantee to 31 March 2002, there have been several instances of shifts of funds from private banks to the PSS, especially in response to publicized failures of larger banks, insurance companies, and securities companies.

Figure 4.11 indicates the number of official failures of depository institutions by prefecture from 1992 to 2002. Depository institutions include ordinary banks, *shinkin* banks, and credit cooperatives. In some instances the failed institution was closed, but in most other cases, they were merged with another institution. The official date of the closure or announcement of a closure lags the point in time the public became aware the institution was in trouble. Thus, the public would commence shifting deposits away from an institution before the official announcement the institution was to be closed.

The PSS has denied that its actions have had an adverse effect on the banking system; however, the destabilizing effect of postal deposits during times of financial distress has a well-known precedent. In Japan's history, for example, movements in postal deposits relative to total deposits can be partly accounted for by problems in the private-banking system, such as in the 1880s and the 1920s. The economic history of the United States also supports the view that

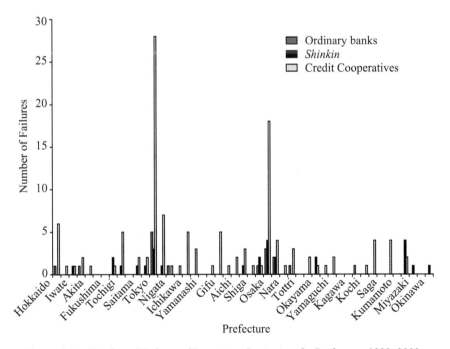

Figure 4.11. *Number of Failures of Depository Institutions by Prefecture, 1992–2002.*

postal deposits can be a destabilizing element in the financial system in times of financial distress. The US postal-deposit system was established in 1910, but it was never as extensive nor did it offer as many services as the PSS in Japan. The US system did not gain widespread public support and was ended in 1966; however, it did play an important and destabilizing role during the Great Depression (Kuwayama, 2000; O'Hara and Easley, 1979).

There are several problems in determining whether the PSS contributed to the financial distress of the 1990s. First, the demand-for-postal-savings model discussed above is based on annual data, and interest-rate variables are constant across prefectures. This makes it difficult to use the model to isolate the impact of specific bank failures in specific parts of the country. Second, the date used to indicate a bank failure is difficult to establish, especially when regulatory authorities engage in nontransparent policies designed to protect weak institutions. The official failure date is clearly inappropriate because the market will surely have become aware of the impending official recognition of the insolvency well before the official date. But what date prior to the official date would one employ? Third, even if reasonable bank-failure dates could be established, one would need to correlate these with disaggregated prefecture data. This data is difficult to compile and is not publicly available.

Notwithstanding these problems, we make an effort to determine the extent of deposit flight from private banks to the PSS during the 1990s. This is done in two steps. First, we examine aggregate growth-rate data on private and postal deposits to determine whether deposit growth is consistent with the hypothesis that the PSS induced disintermediation during some part of the 1990s. Second, we obtained a detailed set of annual data on private-bank and postal deposits by prefecture over the period from 1981 to 1998. Focusing on those prefectures that experienced bank failures both small and large, we can review the flow of funds into and out of private banks and the PSS.

These two empirical approaches are clearly simple and fail to account for other possible variables that might have influenced the shift in funds from private banks to the PSS. At the same time, evidence consistent with the deposit-flight hypothesis suggests that policymakers need to consider the potential for instability that a postal-savings system may bring to the financial system.

Figures 4.12–4.16 present quarterly growth rates (annualized) for all bank deposits, *shinkin* bank deposits, credit cooperative (*shinkumi*) deposits, agricultural credit cooperative deposits, and postal deposits over the period from 1990:1 to 1997:12. In general, there is a negative association between postal-deposit growth and private- bank-deposit growth. The measured correlation coefficient between postal deposits and each of the four private deposits is -0.65, -0.45, -0.44, and -0.10, respectively. The fact that the deposit changes at private banks include both individual and business deposit changes makes it difficult to isolate the flow of individual deposits from private banks

Figure 4.12. *All bank deposits, 1990 : 1–1997 : 12.*

Figure 4.13. Shinkin *deposits, 1990 : 1–1997 :12.*

to the PSS. At the same time, the relative rates of growth among the institutions illustrated in Figures 4.12–4.16 are suggestive.

The second approach is to compare all-bank total-deposit flows, individual bank-deposit flows, and postal-savings flows in each year from fiscal years 1991 to 1998 in those prefectures that experienced bank failures in the 1990s.

Figure 4.14. *Credit cooperation* (shinyokumi) *deposits, 1990 : 1–1997 : 12.*

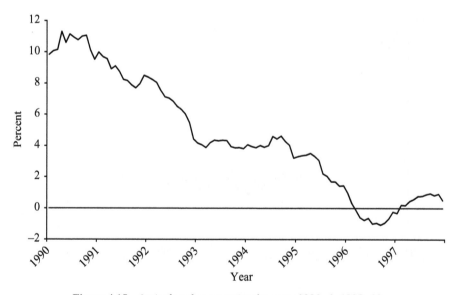

Figure 4.15. *Agricultural cooperative deposits, 1990 : 1–1997 : 12.*

All-bank total-deposit flows and postal-savings flows were also obtained for the period from 1981 to 1989; however, individual-deposit flows for all banks were unavailable prior to 1990. The selected prefectures are Fukui, Fukuoka, Gifu, Hokkaido, Hyogo (capital city is Kobe), Iwate, Kanagawa, Miyagi, Osaka, Shizuoka, Tokyo, and Wakayama. Table 4.13 presents the ratio of postal-savings

Figure 4.16. *Postal deposits, 1990 : 1–1997 : 12.*

Table 4.13. *Ratio of postal-savings flows to individual bank-deposit flows by selected prefecture, 1980–1981 to 1988–1989, and 1990–1991 to 1997–1998*

Prefecture	1980–81 to 1988–89	1990–91 to 1997–98
Fukui	0.88	2.05
Fukuoka	0.57	1.66
Gifu	0.86	1.81
Hokkaido	1.00	2.34
Hyogo	0.82	2.55
Iwate	1.21	0.82
Kanagawa	0.51	1.10
Miyagi	0.66	1.18
Osaka	0.26	Negative movement
Shizuoka	0.72	1.30
Tokyo	0.10	Negative movement
Wakayama	1.14	3.90

flows to all-bank deposit flows for each of the selected prefecture for two periods: 1980–81 to 1988–89 and 1990–91 to 1997–98. In Osaka and Tokyo—the two largest cities in Japan with the most bank failures—during the 1990s, the flow of funds into the PSS was positive and the flow of all-bank deposits was negative. In the other prefectures, the flows into the PSS increased relative to the flows into the banks in the 1990s. These results reinforce the results obtained for aggregate deposits illustrated in Figures 4.12 and 4.16, but in addition, they suggest that the most dramatic shift of funds occurred in Osaka and Tokyo.

The most revealing flows, however, are reflected by the flows of individual bank deposits and the postal-savings flows. The problem with total bank deposits is that they include both individual and business deposits, and businesses are normally prohibited from holding postal deposits. In general, the two flows are positively related; however, there are several notable exceptions supporting the view that the PSS may have been viewed as a safe haven by individuals.

Figures 4.17 through 4.21 present the three sets of deposit flows for the 1990s in Hokkaido, Tokyo, Osaka, Hyogo, and Wakayama. In the case of Hokkaido (Figure 4.17), postal-deposit flows were about four times the size of individual bank-deposit flows; however, in 1997–98 (from 31 March 1998 to 31 March 1999), postal inflows exceeded individual bank inflows by a factor of seventeen. This shift in the pattern of flows probably reflects concern over the failure of Hokkaido Takushoku Bank, the nineteenth largest bank in Japan and the largest bank ever to fail in Japan since the start of reindustrialization in 1950 up to that point.

In Tokyo (Figure 4.18), individual bank-deposit flows were negative in 1991–92, whereas postal-deposit flows were positive. The Ministry of Finance in the early 1990s took the unprecedented action of declaring several small credit cooperatives insolvent and thus raised concern among depositors about the safety of the banking system overall. The fact that the Ministry of Posts and

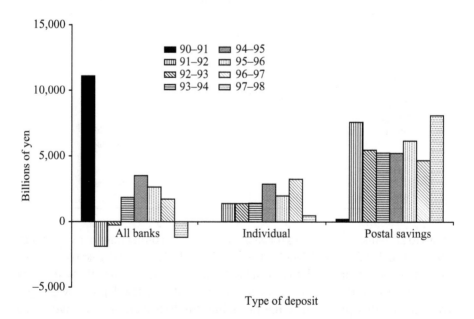

Figure 4.17. *Deposit flows: Hokkaido, 1990–1998.*

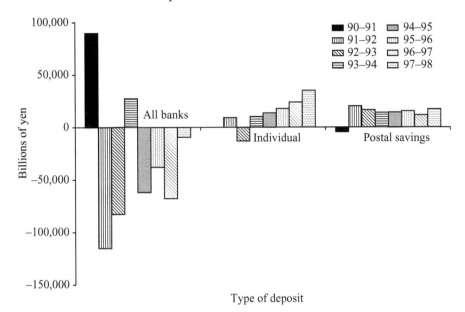

Figure 4.18. *Deposit flows: Tokyo, 1990–1998.*

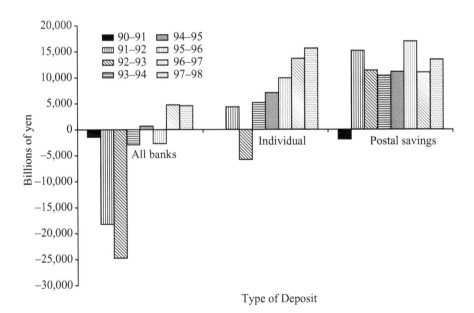

Figure 4.19. *Deposit flows: Osaka, 1990–1998.*

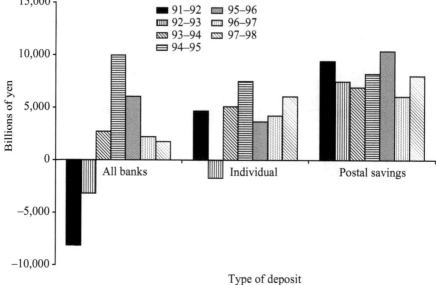

Figure 4.20. *Deposit flows: Hyogo, 1990–1998.*

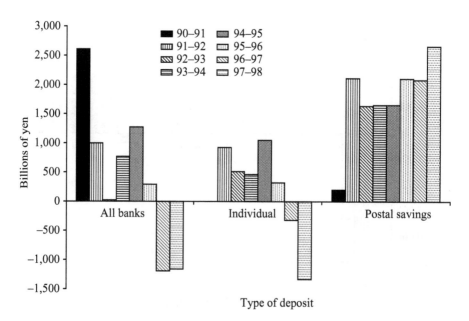

Figure 4.21. *Deposit flows: Wakayama, 1990–1998.*

Telecommunications was also emphasizing the safety of postal deposits rela-tive to private-bank deposits also played a role in the shift of deposits. On the other hand, postal deposits in 1990–91 showed a small decline while individ-ual bank deposits increased. The same pattern of flows occurred in Osaka (Figure 4.19). Hyogo (Figure 4.20) indicates an increase in postal deposits while individual bank deposits declined in 1992–93. Wakayama (Figure 4.21) indicates the same pattern, but for the two most recent years illustrated.

Okina (2000) also found evidence of disintermediation for the failure of Hokkaido Takushoku Bank (Hokkaido) and the Hanwa Bank (Wakayama). Outstanding postal balances increased above the national average in both Hokkaido and Wakayama during times of financial distress; in Hokkaido, indi-vidual deposit balances at private institutions increased significantly less than the national average, and in Wakayama, individual deposit balances at private institutions declined.

The fact that we, along with Okina, find evidence of disintermediation during times of financial distress is important by itself, but considered in the context of a complete government deposit guarantee since late 1995 it suggests fundamental weakness in private financial institutions and less-than-firm pub-lic confidence in private financial institution deposits. As long as the deposit guarantee is in place, there is no legal difference between postal deposits and private-bank deposits, yet the public's reaction to private-bank deposits in times of financial distress suggests otherwise. The complete deposit guarantee was scheduled for removal on 1 April 2001. The removal date was moved back one year and the removal was phased-in over a two-year period. The complete guarantee on time deposits was removed 1 April 2002 and the complete guar-antee on transaction and other deposits is scheduled for removal 1 April 2003.

4.8. IS THERE A GOVERNMENT-BANK NONPERFORMING-LOAN PROBLEM?

Table 4.14 presents loan-loss reserves reported by government financial insti-tutions and by private banks for various years from 1987 to 1996. Government financial institutions did not report estimates of nonperforming loans during this period; however, one can infer the exposure of these institutions to non-performing loans from three considerations.

First, the ratio of loan-loss reserves to total loans for the government institu-tions is significantly lower than for private institutions, suggesting one of two explanations. Either the government institutions have done a better job in eval-uating and monitoring credit and thus can operate with a lower loan-loss reserve, or else there is significant exposure of government institutions to loan defaults because these loss ratios are set at unrealistically low levels. It is

Table 4.14. *Loan-loss reserve positions of government and private banks, 1987–1997*

Year	Export–Import Bank	Japan Development Bank	Hokkaido Yohoku	People's Finance Corporation	Small Business Finance Corporation	Environmental Sanitation
1987	0.30					
1988	0.30					
1989	0.33	0.30				0.53
1990	0.30	0.30				0.37
1991	0.30	0.30				0.31
1992	0.30	0.30	0.37	0.35	0.34	0.26
1993	0.30	0.30	0.44	0.09	0.17	0.23
1994	0.30	0.30	0.52	0.12	0.11	0.16
1995		0.30	0.51	0.03	0.02	0.04
1996						

Year	Shoko Chukin	Agricultural	Norin Chukin	Government Housing Loan Corporation	Okinawa Development Bank	Public Enterprise Finance Corporation	Domestic Banks
1987							0.7
1988							0.7
1989		0.5					0.7
1990		0.5					0.7
1991		0.5					0.7
1992	1.4	0.6				0.2	0.7
1993	1.6	0.4	16151.0	0.0	0.6	0.2	0.9
1994	1.6	0.3	49148.0	0.0	0.6	0.1	1.2
1995		0.0			0.0	0.1	1.6
1996							2.4

Source: Fiscal and Monetary Statistics, FILP Issue, Ministry of Finance.

unlikely that the mutual-support system and nontransparent reporting methods that have been used to misrepresent the level of nonperforming loans at private banks are absent in the government-financial-institution sector. Likewise, there is no reason to believe that borrowers from these institutions are any less immune to the economic and financial distress in Japan than are those of private banks. In fact, the quality of some of the borrowers in the second half of the 1990s has probably declined since these borrowers were unable to obtain credit at the private banks. And finally, there is no reason to assume that the Ministry of Finance has done a better job in monitoring the risk-taking of government financial institutions than it has the risk-taking of private banks.

Second, the loan-loss ratios for the government institutions have remained relatively constant or have even declined. Either the government institutions have been insulated from Japan's most serious economic crisis since 1950, or there is significant exposure of government institutions to loan default that is being ignored and unreported.

Third, those government institutions that have large amounts of loans outstanding to cyclically sensitive sectors of the economy or loans to export industries are likely to have experienced nonperforming-loan problems. In particular, loans to small businesses and to housing grew significantly in the second half of the 1990s. These loans are the ones most similar to private-bank loans and as such are not likely to be immune from the same problems experienced by private banks in the 1990s. The decline in land and real-estate prices in Japan, combined with negative growth in 1998 and hesitant recovery in 1999 and 2000, suggest that official estimates of nonperforming loans in Japan understate the magnitude of the problem. They do so because they fail to recognize the exposure of government financial institutions to nonperforming loans.

In fiscal 2000 and 2001 five government banks began to publish estimates of nonperforming loans based on the same framework as required by private banks. These are the Development Bank of Japan, Japan Bank for International Cooperation, Peoples' Finance Corporation, and the Small Business Finance Cooperation. Estimates of nonperforming loans range from about 3.5 to 7.5 percent. These estimates are lower than reported by private banks, whose estimates of nonperforming loans were about 6–8 percent in 2001, but still indicate a meaningful nonperforming loan problem. All government banks now report estimates of nonperforming loans. It will be instructive to see how these estimates develop over the coming years.

The above discussion is superficial and only raises the issue of a nonperforming loan problem in the FILP system, which government officials have not adequately disclosed. This is also an aspect of Japan's nonperforming loan problem that outsiders have seldom considered, primarily because the FILP and PSS receive so little outside attention. Doi and Hoshi (2002) documented a far larger nonperforming loan problem embedded in the FILP system. Based on publicly available information, they conclude the size of the nonperforming loan problem is large. According to their analysis, 75 percent of FILP loans are nonperforming representing 16 percent of GDP. This is large and even if Doi and Hoshi's estimate is overstated, combined with the suggestive evidence presented above, there is a very large and yet undisclosed nonperforming loan problem in the FILP system. Combined with the nonperforming loan problem in the private depository sector of the economy (10 or 12 percent of GDP), Japan's nonperforming loan problem, as of 2002, is immense by any standard.

4.9. CONCLUDING COMMENT

The interest-rate subsidy embedded in FILP-system loans was fairly large before 1975 and, for many sectors dependent on government-bank loans, the interest-rate subsidy was important as measured by a percentage of after-tax retained earnings. The subsidy, however, has declined over the past two decades and, along with the decline, the subsidy now represents a small percentage of after-tax retained earnings. The decline reflects the effects of financial liberalization on the banking system as banks have offered more competitive rates and have been forced to reduce and eventually eliminate compensating-balance requirements as a precondition for establishing a bank-borrower relationship.

The FILP system's effect on investment spending and hence on economic growth can be decomposed into three influences. First, an interest-rate effect (interest-rate subsidy increases investment spending); second, a quantitative effect (larger supply of funds increases investment spending); and third, a cowbell effect (government-bank loans stimulate private-bank lending to those sectors borrowing from government banks). The interest-rate-subsidy effect was the largest and most significant of the three before 1975, although it had only a relatively small quantitative impact on investment spending. The other two effects before 1975 were either insignificant or quantitatively small. All three effects are either insignificant or quantitatively minor after 1975.

The ratio of postal deposits to bank deposits is significantly influenced by the post office's branching network and the reliance on *teigaku* deposits. Although private banks have to some extent reduced the competitive advantage of the PSS's branching network, the presence of 24,500 post offices spread throughout Japan provides the PSS with a considerable advantage in the deposit market. Many of these post offices are in areas that cannot support a branch of a private bank. The influence of postal-deposit rates relative to bank rates also suggests that the PSS has a considerable advantage in that over 80 percent of its funds are obtained from *teigaku* accounts. Supporters of the PSS argue that this advantage exists only because private banks are unwilling to offer a similar deposit. As of 2001, about twenty private banks offered *teigaku*-type accounts, but it is unlikely that these deposits will represent a major source of funds for private banks, given their inherent interest-rate risk.

There were shifts of funds from banks to post offices in the early 1990s as the public became increasingly aware of the banks' problems and the growing volume of their nonperforming loans. In addition, there is evidence of a shift of funds in 1997–98 in Osaka and Tokyo. Some of the transfers in the early 1990s can be attributed to expected interest-rate declines; however, a case can be made that a shift in funds resulted from the financial distress in the private financial sector and the perception in the minds of many Japanese that postal deposits are a more secure asset. In addition, post offices encouraged such shifts by emphasizing that postal deposits had a complete government guarantee, in contrast to private-bank deposits that were guaranteed only by the Deposit Insurance Corporation. Although the most dramatic shifts persisted for only about a year, there has been a general and more gradual shift of funds to postal deposits reflected by the relatively high growth rate of postal deposits compared to deposits at private institutions. At a minimum, the existence of the PSS complicates Japan's efforts to establish a deposit-insurance system as the primary safety net for bank deposits.

The potential of a nonperforming-loan problem residing in the government banks is suggested by the very low reserves that government banks set aside for bad loans, compared to private banks. Private-bank reserves themselves were, in hindsight, unrealistically low, given the economic and financial conditions of the 1990s. The Ministry of Finance in the past has provided no information about potential nonperforming loans at the government banks. However, several government banks have begun to publish estimates of nonperforming loans as a foundation for offering FILP-agency bonds.

5

Reforming the Postal Savings System and the Fiscal Investment and Loan Program: Summing Up of the Issues, Reform, and Recommendations

5.1. INTRODUCTION

The PSS and the FILP are important features of Japanese postwar finance, and despite an official policy of financial liberalization for over two decades, they have continued to expand their roles in Japan's financial system. As of fiscal year-end 1999 (31 March 2000), postal deposits represented 34 percent of total household deposits and 18 percent of individual assets. Postal deposits accounted for 62 percent of FILP lending, and the FILP budget represented 10.9 percent of GNP. Postal life-insurance accounts for 30 percent of total life-insurance sales. Postal deposits as a percentage of total deposits, postal life insurance as a percentage of total life insurance, and the ratio of the FILP budget to GDP were larger in 2000 than at any time since the start of reindustrialization in 1950.

The PSS has possessed a wide range of advantages that account for its increasing market share of postal deposits to total deposits over time. Some of these advantages have been eliminated or reduced. Since 1987, the PSS no longer benefits from a tax system that permitted easy avoidance of taxes on interest income, and since 1994, postal-deposit rates have been set "close to" bank-deposit rates. Even the advantage of a wide-ranging network of post offices has been eroded to some degree as banks have expanded their branching networks, and the highly regarded *teigaku* deposit has been facing competition since banks started to offer a competitive *teigaku*-type deposit on a limited basis in 1999. Nonetheless, the PSS retains considerable advantage over private-bank time-deposits and, more important, it has aggressively positioned itself as a provider of financial services and has increasingly moved into providing payment services. The PSS is becoming part of the payments system because of its increasing relationships with private financial institutions through CD and ATM connections. Okina (2000) has documented the various payment and settlement services offered by the PSS that compete on a more favorable or at least on an equal basis with private financial institutions.

The PSS does not pay income taxes, is not required to hold reserves against deposits, is not required to pay deposit insurance, is not subject to regulation to the degree imposed on private financial institutions, enjoys the full faith and credit of the Japanese government for both principal and interest, and has the potential to cross-subsidize its deposit services. As a result, the PSS has been able to extend deposit services to areas of the country that are not economically viable for private banks and can offer *teigaku* deposits whose high-interest-rate risk renders them unfeasible for private banks to rely on as a major source of funds. The maturity differences of private-bank and PSS assets make it easier for the PSS to issue a *teigaku* deposit. Private banks operate with shorter-term assets and hence cannot easily offer a *teigaku* deposit, whereas the PSS invested funds in the Trust Fund Bureau before 1 April 2001 at fixed rates for seven years, thus reducing potential interest-rate risk. Long-term asset investments will continue after 31 March 2001. The extensive branching network of the PSS and its reliance on the *teigaku* time-deposit account have been the most significant advantages that the PSS has enjoyed over the private banks, and these advantages are likely to continue into the future. The PSS, however, is moving away from offering deposits to merely satisfy store-of-wealth objectives and toward integrating itself more broadly into Japan's payments system and becoming a "financial convenience store" (Okina, 2000). The more integrated the PSS becomes in the payments system, the more difficult it will be to reduce the role of government banking in Japan.

The PSS enjoys two other advantages that make reform politically difficult. First, the PSS has been viewed by the public as a safe haven for wealth during uncertain times when private banks have been distressed, such as the 1990s. This has been at a high price, however. The existence of the PSS complicates Japan's efforts to establish an explicit and limited deposit-insurance system to replace the implicit and general government guarantee of all deposits that characterized postwar finance. If the complete deposit guarantee established in late 1995 is entirely removed on 1 April 2003, as planned, the PSS will likely further enhance its reputation among the population as the only truly safe depository, which can only increase the competitive advantage of the PSS over private financial institutions. Second, the PSS has focused on serving the financial needs of individuals and households throughout the postwar period, while during much of the same period the private banks focused their attention primarily on the large business sector. It has only been since private banks lost market share in the late 1970s because of liberalization and a slower growth-path of the economy that they turned to the individual sector as a potential profit center. As a result, the PSS has widespread and deep support among

Japan's public, and its aggressive marketing of payment and settlement services only strengthens that support. The PSS effectively employs this public support in countering increasing complaints from the private banks that the PSS creates an uneven playing field. The PSS responds to the private-bank view by pointing out that private banks have the ability to extend their branching networks, can offer competitive deposits, and can service the household sector more aggressively. That is, the PSS argues that many of its advantages are the result of servicing a part of the Japanese financial system that has been neglected in the past by the larger private banks. Politicians also support the PSS. Establishing and maintaining post offices throughout Japan is an important part of the way politicians maintain and enhance their regional support, which partly explains why the LDP has been able to hold on to political power for such a long period. Politicians also support the PSS because it provides a major source of funds to the FILP system, and the FILP budget is part of the national budget, which in turn provides additional instruments to maintain and enhance political power.

As a result, the PSS had few critics, with the exception of private banks, some academics, outsiders with knowledge of the FILP system, and perhaps the Bank of Japan. Critics emphasize the incompatibility of a large government bank, even if operated as a "narrow" bank, with a modern liberated financial system and the effort to establish a more market-sensitive deposit-guarantee system.

The FILP is also highly popular in Japan and has few critics. FILP lending was important in rebuilding Japan's infrastructure and supporting regional development in the 1950s, and its continued lending to improve living conditions, especially housing, and its lending to small and medium-sized business has created broad-based support for the FILP. This is especially the case with respect to housing and small-business lending, since these areas were neglected by commercial banks until liberalization in the 1980s forced private banks to seek out new markets. The FILP enhanced its broad support during the last part of the 1990s, when FILP lending to small and medium-sized businesses and to housing mitigated some of the credit crunch in the private-banking system. FILP lending is thus widely supported by local governments, households, and business, as well as by the politicians who represent these groups. FILP lending, like post offices, is also an important element in enhancing and maintaining the regional power base of politicians.

Critics of FILP lending focus on two issues. First, the critics argue that business and housing loans are substitutes for private-bank lending and, as such, should be left to private banks in a more competitive and open financial system. Competition between government and private banks cannot, because of their inherently different structures, be equal. Second, although critics recognize that market failure justifies some degree of government financial intermediation, they also maintain that political influences and/or an industrial policy insensitive to market forces can rationalize loans to unproductive sectors and functions. The politicization of the FILP system, judged by the strong support it has received over the years from Japanese politicians and the general unwillingness to depart significantly from the old financial regime, suggests that a considerable part of the funds provided by the FILP may have supported unproductive spending.

Despite the popularity of the PSS and the FILP and the resistance to meaningful change during the last two decades of liberalization effort, the PSS and FILP were finally placed on the financial liberalization agenda in 1998. Four factors account for this change in attitude. First, anyone familiar with Japan's financial system knew that the PSS and FILP could not long remain outside of the liberalization agenda. They were simply too large and represented a key element of the old financial regime. The PSS and FILP, as they matured during the postwar period, were inconsistent with the type of financial regime envisaged by the 1996 Big Bang announcement, which remains the operating blueprint for financial liberalization. In particular, the large amount of household wealth held by the PSS limits money and capital market development making it more difficult for Japan to shift away from the bank-finance model.

Second, the financial and economic distress of the 1990s accelerated the agenda of including the PSS and FILP in the liberalization process. In particular, issues raised about the destabilizing influence of postal deposits, and about the relationship between the PSS and the deposit-insurance system that is scheduled to assume the bank safety-net responsibility after 31 March 2003, rationalized a more thorough review of the PSS. Although FILP lending in the late 1990s was viewed positively because it offset some of the credit-crunch conditions in the private-banking system, there was growing concern that much FILP lending lacked the degree of market sensitivity required by the environment facing Japan in the new century.

Third, concern over the rate of return on savings became acute in the 1990s, as evidence showed that Japan's population would begin to decline around 2010 and that the dependency ratio, defined as the percentage of the nonworking population to total population, would increase significantly. The policy implication is clear if Japan is to maintain its past standard of living. Japan needs to reform its economic and financial institutions to achieve a higher rate of return on invested savings, and in this regard, the FILP system is in need of reform. Despite the popularity of the PSS and FILP, and even granted that these institutions had a positive impact on Japan's postwar development, the Japanese economy can no longer afford the low-return projects often financed by FILP lending.

Fourth, a relatively recent problem arises from the increasing role of the PSS in the payment-and-settlement system and from the increasing formal relationships between the PSS and private financial institutions documented by Okina (2000). To the extent that the PSS is not part of the Bank of Japan's

Financial Network System and Data Telecommunications System of All Banks in Japan, Japan's settlement system is inefficient. At the same time, incorporation of the PSS into the formal settlement system will only strengthen the importance of postal deposits and make reform even more difficult in the future.

The remainder of this concluding chapter summarizes the discussion of the previous chapters, reviews the 1998 reforms, evaluates the reforms, and provides recommendations for further reform.

5.2. SUMMING UP OF THE EVIDENCE

Chapters 2, 3, and 4 reviewed the PSS and FILP as they existed prior to 1 April 2001, from three perspectives: first, their quantitative and qualitative role in the financial system; second, their theoretical role in the financial system; and third, various empirical issues regarding their influence on financial and economic activity. The flow-of-funds model in Chapter 3 also evaluated the impact on the financial system and economy of the 1998 reform that became effective on 1 April 2001.

The statistical information in Chapter 2 reveals the importance of the PSS and FILP in Japan's postwar financial system. It was during the postwar period that the Japanese approach to financial infrastructure reached maturity and served as a model for other Asian economies wishing to copy Japan's economic success. The PSS and FILP formed an important component of a regulated, administratively controlled, internationally isolated, and segmented financial system whose objective was to reduce risk and bankruptcy and to maintain a high rate of saving and investment. This approach began to unravel in the second half of the 1970s in response to new forces that required Japan to relax the complex set of constraints on financial transactions. The PSS and FILP, however, largely avoided reform in the 1970s and 1980s. In fact, the PSS and FILP expanded their role in the financial system during this period.

A formal model in Chapter 3 combines the PSS and the FILP into a government bank that collects deposits in competition with private-bank deposits and makes loans in competing and noncompeting bank-loan markets. The model suggests that the claimed positive effects of government-bank loans may be exaggerated. Only in the case of market failure or positive externalities can an argument be made that government banks positively contribute to economic growth. Of course, there may be other channels through which government banks contribute to economic growth that are not incorporated into the model; however, the fact that the model shows the ambiguity of the effect of government-bank loans on income is an important finding and, together with the growing conflicts between the PSS and FILP and a more liberated financial environment, suggests that reform is long overdue. The model suggests that the PSS and FILP may interfere with the conduct of monetary policy. It also provides a basis to compare the PSS and FILP before and after 1 April 2001, in order to determine the impact that separating the PSS from the government banks would have on the financial system and on the economy overall. The logic of the model suggests that in terms of funding government banks and the comparative statistic results, there is no meaningful change if postal deposits are used to purchase agency or FILP bonds instead of transferring the deposits to the Ministry of Finance. This may be too pessimistic, however. There are other aspects of the reforms to be considered before an overall judgment can be rendered.

The empirical results in Chapter 4 add further insight into the role of the PSS and FILP in Japan's flow of funds. The positive impact of government-bank loans on industrial investment spending in Japan appears to have been exaggerated. Even before 1975, when the interest-rate subsidy was large, the quantitative effect on industrial investment was small and, after 1975, for all practical purposes, nonexistent. The size of the interest-rate subsidy declined significantly after the 1970s as liberalization forced banks to dispense with compensating-balance requirements and narrowed the gap between private-bank and government-bank loans. This finding, however, does not imply that FILP lending for infrastructure or improved living conditions was not productive in the early part of Japan's reindustrialization process, nor does it suggest that all of current FILP lending is unproductive in those areas not serviced by the private-banking system. However, as the economy matured, opportunities for profitable lending to sectors or functions with positive externalities declined.

Estimates of the demand for postal deposits relative to private-bank deposits shows that postal deposits are sensitive to both convenience (number of branches), interest-rate spreads, and whether interest rates are increasing or decreasing. This suggests that post offices will continue to have a competitive advantage over private banks because of the large number of post offices and their reliance on the *teigaku* deposit. The *teigaku* deposit, however, might not be as advantageous as in the past since reliance on market rates of return on assets will make it more difficult to rely on *teigaku* deposits because of their considerable liquidity and interest-rate risk. The advantages enjoyed by the PSS, however, ultimately reside in the cross-subsidization that is enjoyed by the post office and is unavailable to the private banks.

The empirical results suggest that it is unlikely that postal deposits and, indirectly, the FILP interfere with the conduct of monetary policy in Japan. This is especially true since 1994, when postal-deposit rates were set close to bank-deposit rates. Although reliance on the *teigaku* deposit may still interfere with monetary policy, given the *teigaku*'s option feature, a general review of monetary policy since the 1970s, combined with the results from two empirical models of monetary policy, suggest that any quantitative effect, if any, is small. Bank of Japan policy has been successful on many occasions, and for those times when Bank of Japan policy has failed, the failure can easily be traced to factors independent of the PSS or the FILP. Thus, arguments for PSS and FILP reform cannot be reasonably based on accusations that these agencies interfere with monetary policy.

Finally, the empirical results suggest that the PSS may have played a destabilizing role in the 1990s when Japan faced its most serious economic and financial challenges in the postwar period. There is evidence of disintermediation from bank to postal deposits for Hokkaido, Hyogo, Osaka, and Tokyo prefectures and evidence that a nonperforming-loan problem may exist in the government banks that has not yet been revealed. These results provide further incentive for reform. Not only are the PSS and FILP incompatible with the goals of the Big Bang, but the PSS and FILP may have also contributed to Japan's financial distress. In particular, as Japan moves toward an explicit deposit-insurance system as the deposit-guarantee or safety net, the relationship between postal deposits and private-bank deposits needs to be carefully considered. The nonperforming-loan problem has been a dead weight on private banks, and the more the government banks are exposed to nonperforming loans, the more difficult it will be for the entire financial system to recover from the economic and financial distress of the 1990s, which can now be referred to as Japan's lost decade.

5.3. RECOMMENDATIONS FOR REFORM: ASSET MANAGEMENT COUNCIL FOR THE TRUST FUND BUREAU OF THE MINISTRY OF FINANCE

The PSS and FILP were not part of the Big Bang announcement of November 1996, and little discussion regarding either institution occurred during the flurry of legislation that was enacted in mid-1997, with the exception of some references to reforming government enterprise and corporation accounting. The PSS and FILP, however, were like an elephant in the room that no one wanted to discuss but which everyone knew was there. It was only a matter of time before some type of official dialogue would be initiated. The financial distress of the 1990s, deposit-insurance reform, and the need to modernize Japan's financial system in the face of major demographic changes ultimately placed the PSS and the FILP on the reform agenda.

The first reform was initiated by the Ministry of Finance in 1998 and was followed by a series of administrative decisions by the Ministry of Posts and Telecommunications (since 6 January 2001, the Ministry of Public Management, Home Affairs, Posts and Telecommunications). Indirectly, administrative decisions by the Ministry of Welfare (since 6 January 2001, the Ministry of Health, Labor, and Welfare) and the Postal Life Insurance Fund also contributed to the reform process.

The Asset Management Council of the Ministry of Finance's Trust Fund Bureau had been in existence for many years and in the past confined its activity to reviewing decisions by the government as to how to allocate funds in the Trust Fund Bureau. In late 1997, the Council adopted a more active role, expanded its membership to include individuals critical of the FILP system, and was charged in 1998 with developing recommendations to reform the FILP system. The Council produced a report in June 1998 that provided the basis for subsequent legislation to restructure the FILP system and, indirectly, the PSS.

There were two components of the Council's report. The first component summarized the role of the FILP system in Japan's financial system and economy during the postwar period. The system provided funds to those sectors that had little or no access to private funding and provided deposit services to households throughout Japan. The Council concluded that the FILP system was successful but noted that reform was needed in the new environment of liberalization. Thus, although some observers may have been critical of past FILP operations, the report adopted a forward-looking perspective instead of criticizing past FILP operations.

The second component of the report focused on the various problems of the FILP system. These were enumerated by the following five points. First, the allocation of postal funds to the Trust Fund Bureau and the size of the PSS and FILP were not compatible with a liberated financial market. The structure of government intermediation by its very nature is inconsistent with an open and competitive financial system, and allocating a large role to government inter-mediation ensures that liberalization will be a slow, incomplete, and difficult process. Second, in the past the FILP system focused on only long-term lending; however, short-term lending and short-term government bond purchases were becoming a larger part of FILP distribution of funds. These are portfolio operations that compete most directly with the private sector and are at variance with the original objectives of the FILP system. As a result, FILP was moving away from its original objective of contributing to the long-term development of the national economy. In this regard, the Council was especially concerned about the mitigation role of FILP lending during the credit-crunch conditions of the late 1990s. Third, postal-deposit rates were liberalized in 1994, but funds transferred to the Trust Fund Bureau continued to be distributed to government financial institutions and government enterprises at fixed rates. The unbalanced maturity between sources and uses of funds exposed the FILP system to serious interest-rate risk. Fourth, the Japan National Railroad (JNR) was privatized in 1988 with large deficits that had been financed by the government since 1988; however, no solution to resolving the JNR deficit had been developed. The Japan Forest Agency, separated from the FILP system in 1988, also had large deficits that had been financed by the government. Fifth, housing loans were becoming an increasingly important use of FILP funds (35.6 percent in 1998 compared to 13.8 percent in 1955). This use of funds competed directly with the private sector, and the Council recommended that more efficient means of subsidizing the housing sector than government-bank loans should be considered, such as tax credits.

The basic concern expressed by the Council focused on the size and non-market allocation of the FILP, characteristics that were incompatible with the goal of a competitive, free, and fair financial system envisaged in the original Big Bang proposal. The report did not focus on the changing demographic environment, but the implications of a declining and aging population on the need to develop efficient economic and financial institutions were apparent.

The Council recommended the following points for reforming the FILP system:

1. The entire set of subsidies contained in the FILP system needed to be evaluated in terms of cost-benefit analysis to determine whether any given subsidy should be continued.
2. The cost-benefit analysis needed to be disclosed to the public to render the process transparent.
3. The assets and liabilities of each government bank and enterprise needed to be disclosed on a mark-to-market basis.
4. Government banks needed to adopt the type of cash-flow analysis recommended by the US GAO and codified in the Credit Reform Act of 1990.
5. Lending rates offered by government banks needed to be market sensitive. In this regard, government banks and enterprises should either issue their own bonds (agency securities) or participate in FILP bonds issued by the Ministry of Finance to support lending activities, instead of relying on postal deposits, life-insurance funds, or pension funds. Agency securities could be issued with or without a general government guarantee, while bonds issued by the Ministry for purposes of supporting government banks and enterprises would represent general government debt.
7. Postal deposits, life insurance, and pension funds should no longer be provided to the Ministry of Finance.

5.4. LEGISLATIVE ACTION FOLLOWING THE JUNE 1998 COUNCIL REPORT

Shortly after the Council's report was submitted to the Ministry of Finance and published, the Fundamental Reform of the Central Government Industries and Agencies Law was enacted in June 1998 and became effective on 1 April 2001. Part of the law pertained to the FILP and PSS programs and focused on three issues. First, the FILP system needed to be reformed and rendered compatible with a liberalized market; second, postal savings, life insurance, and pension funds would no longer be transferred to the Ministry of Finance; and third, government banks and enterprises would be required to raise their funds in the open market.

The practical result of the 1998 legislation was the abolishment of the Trust Fund Bureau as a separate account within the Ministry of Finance, separation of the PSS from the Ministry of Finance, and establishment of the PSS as a separate public corporation, to take effect in 2003. Starting on 1 April 2001, entities previously financed by the FILP were to move toward a system of financing their activities through one or more of the following three methods: (1) FILP agency-type securities with a government guarantee; (2) FILP agency-type securities without a government guarantee; and (3) FILP bonds issued by the Ministry of Finance that are essentially general government bonds.

In early 2001, thirty-three entities previously financed by the FILP system (Trust Fund Bureau-dependent entities), including government banks, were scheduled to start a process that would eventually provide all of their own funding either through agency securities or FILP bonds. Of these, twenty were scheduled to issue securities without a guarantee during fiscal year 2001; however, entities that issue securities, with or without a government guarantee, were scheduled to obtain only a small part of their budgets from issuing these bonds. In fact, the amount of planned agency securities represent only 3.3 percent of the FILP budget for fiscal 2001. The majority of funding will be provided by the Ministry of Finance with funds obtained through the sale of FILP bonds or, in essence, government bonds with funds earmarked for government enterprises and government banks. Thus, in fiscal 2001, a large number of FILP entities, some of which are government banks, will be required to secure funding from the capital market, based either on their own assets (agency securities without a government guarantee) or on the full faith and credit of the Japanese government (agency securities with a government guarantee or FILP bonds). The other entities will eventually be privatized or directly funded through the national budget. Despite the willingness to consider privatization of FILP entities, it is most likely that entities previously funded by the FILP that cannot raise funds in the capital market will become part of the national budget.

In addition to moving toward a system of finance based on capital markets, in June 2001 all of the thirty-three FILP entities were required to provide more transparency with respect to the subsidies received from the government. They are now required to compute the present value of government support with the truncation date of future support specific to each entity.

5.5. EXAMPLE OF SUBSIDY COST ANALYSIS

A key element of the 1998 reform is to provide greater transparency in the government support of FILP entities. There are two reasons for greater transparency. First, enhanced transparency is part of the overall goal of making the financial system more transparent, efficient, and competitive, and second, enhanced transparency is required to give FILP entities the ability to raise funds in the open money and capital markets.

To illustrate, all eight government banks are required to compute the subsidy they obtain from the general budget to support their activities. The subsidy represents the difference between the government bank's borrowing cost (assuming that all funds are obtained through FILP bonds) and the interest rate they charge on loans, plus whatever is required to finance their overall operations. Each government bank is required to compute the subsidy it receives from the budget over a period of time, depending on the maturity of its loan portfolio, and to convert the subsidy into a present-value amount. The interest rate for computing present value is the long-term government bond rate. The Government Housing Loan Corporation, for example, will publish the present value of the subsidy received from the central government over a twenty-year period.

The other FILP entities, such as the Japan Highway Corporation and the Tokyo International Airport Corporation, compute a similar subsidy defined as the difference between their total cost of operation, including borrowing through FILP bonds, and their total revenue. Again, this subsidy is computed over a long period of time and is converted to present value using the long-term government bond rate.

The requirement to publish the present value of subsidies is not as dramatic as it sounds, because much of the information was already available; however, the new form of presentation will make the information more transparent and, hopefully, will initiate more open discussion as to the desirability of government support of the specific entity.

The thirty-three FILP entities listed in Table 5.1 are regarded as the most important in terms of FILP funding. These are also the entities that are encouraged to issue agency bonds to finance part, and ultimately all, of their operations. There is no timetable or requirement at this point that the FILP entities become entirely dependent on agency bonds. In fiscal 2001, twenty of the thirty-three entities issued agency bonds; however, the amounts were small.

5.6. ASSET MANAGEMENT FOR POSTAL SAVINGS, POSTAL LIFE-INSURANCE PREMIUMS, AND NATIONAL WELFARE AND PENSION PREMIUMS

The 1998 legislation severed the direct relationship between the PSS and the Trust Fund Bureau. New postal deposits will remain with the PSS and postal deposits previously loaned to FILP-financed entities will be returned to the PSS as they are repaid. This process is anticipated to take about seven years, after which the separation between the PSS and the Ministry of Finance will be complete.

Table 5.1 *Subsidy cost estimates (100 million yen), 1 April 2001 (thirty-three government FILP entities)*

Entities	Present value of the subsidy	Number of years
Government banks		
Government Housing Loan Corporation	−1,549	32
National Life Financial Corporation	436	31
Japan Financial Corporation for Small Business	887	21
Agriculture, Forestry and Fishery Finance Corporation	4,990	57
Japan Finance Corporation for Municipal Enterprises	93	30
Okinawa Development Finance Corporation	50	37
Development Bank of Japan	1,282	31
Japan Bank for International Cooperation	7,231	—
International Financial Account	889	27
Overseas Economic Cooperation Account	6,342	40
Government agencies and semi-government bodies		
Housing and Urban Development Cooperation	12,342	80
Pension Welfare Service Public Corporation	3,257	36
Japan Environment Corporation	365	24
Teito Rapid Transit Authority	−107	38
Japan Regional Development Corporation	787	—
Local city-development account	167	33
Industrial relocation account	257	22
Coal-mining regions redevelopment account	363	28
Japan Sewage Works Agency	747	29
Social Welfare and Medical Service Corporation	696	—
General account	649	25
Pension collateralized loan account	47	6
Promotion and Mutual Aid Corporation for Private Schools of Japan	49	21
Japan Scholarship Foundation	1,049	26
Japan Green Resources Corporation	13,743	—
Large-scale forest road account	2,203	37
Water-reservoir forest account	10,142	80
Agricultural land redevelopment account	1,398	25
Japan Highway Public Corporation	34,615	51
Metropolitan Expressway Public Corporation	3,712	36
Hanshin Expressway Public Corporation	2,709	46
Honshu-Shikoku Bridge Authority	6,306	54
Japan Railway Construction Public Corporation	20	32
New Tokyo International Airport Authority	−620	23
Corporation for Advanced Transport and Technology	33	17
Water Resource Development Public Corporation	2,354	37
Metal Mining Agency of Japan	6	15
Japan National Oil Corporation	18,242	21

Table 5.1 *(Cont.)*

Entities	Present value of the subsidy	Number of years
Special Firms		
Shoko Chukin Bank	532	21
Kansai International Airport Corporation	22	35
Central Japan International Airport Corporation	−112	33
Organization for Promoting Urban Development	13	16
Electric Power Development Ltd.	−1,523	12

Source: Ministry of Finance, Fiscal Council, June 2001.

The Ministry of Posts and Telecommunications in June 2000 announced a management strategy that planned to allocate 80 percent of available funds to government bonds and other "safe" assets and the remaining 20 percent to assets with varying degrees of risk. The Ministry of Posts and Telecommunications since 1987 had managed a percentage of postal deposits that grew to about 20 percent of postal funds by 2000, transferring the other 80 percent to the Trust Fund Bureau. As of 31 March 2000, the portfolio managed by the Ministry was 58.9 trillion yen and consisted of government bonds (47.3 percent), local government bonds (15.9 percent), public institution bonds (4.5 percent), private bonds and bank debentures (6.2 percent), and foreign bonds (7.9 percent). The remaining 18.1 percent was invested with private financial institutions. It is unlikely that the new PSS will manage the entire portfolio of postal funds differently.

The June 1998 legislation also required the Postal Life Insurance Fund to develop a portfolio-management strategy, since postal life-insurance premiums were previously contributed to the FILP. Like deposits to the PSS, however, part of the insurance premiums were retained for self-management, though the percentage of self-managed funds was about twice as large as the percentage for the PSS. The Postal Life Insurance Fund's allocation of self-managed funds as of 31 March 2000, was the following: 57 percent to securities, most of which were central and local government bonds; 26 percent as loans to local governments and government agencies; 10 percent to Trust Banks; and the remainder to miscellaneous items, such as bank deposits. Like the new, independent PSS, the Postal Life Insurance Fund will not likely change its allocations.

The Ministry of Welfare (or Ministry of Health, Labor, and Welfare since January 2001) will now be responsible for managing national pension and welfare premium payments instead of transferring part of these funds to the Trust Fund Bureau. Its investment strategy will incorporate a larger share of equities and long-term investments than the PSS or the Postal Life Insurance Fund have in the past.

5.7. IS THIS REAL REFORM?

One could view the June 1998 legislation and the subsequent administrative decisions regarding portfolio management in a cynical manner. In fact, the formal model in Chapter 3 demonstrates that there is essentially no difference between the old and new FILP systems as long as those institutions that formerly provided funds to the FILP system now purchase the bonds used to raise funds to support entities previously financed by the FILP. This view may be too cynical.

The positive perspective emphasizes subtleties in the 1998 legislation and subsequent administrative decisions that set the stage for fundamental change. The importance of this point can be illustrated by considering what happened in the late 1970s in the government bond market, when what appeared to be at the time an innocuous policy to accommodate banks and security companies became a major force for broad liberalization in Japan's financial system. The authorization of a secondary government bond market in the late 1970s, while not considered a major change at the time, ultimately became a driving force for general interest-rate liberalization. The secondary bond market was established to provide banks and securities companies with more incentive to purchase government debt being issued in large quantities to finance the central government deficit. Likewise, the June 1998 and subsequent reforms of the PSS and FILP may have the same potential for substantial change in the future.

The new system has four elements of reform that potentially go far beyond the institutional separation of the PSS from the Ministry of Finance. First, the new system will be more transparent, and because entities previously financed by the FILP will henceforth obtain funds from the capital market directly or indirectly, their lending decisions and monitoring will be more market sensitive. Second, even though the initial offering of agency-type securities is small for any one entity, agency-type securities will still be market sensitive and will provide feedback information for future reforms. The feedback information will assist policymakers in deciding whether entities should rely on their own agency securities or should participate in FILP bonds. The possibility that entities are unsuccessful in raising even a small part of their own funding may force the more difficult decision of whether to make an entity part of the national budget, as opposed to funding it with FILP bonds, or even considering abolishment of the entity. The increased market sensitivity of funding will place a greater burden on each entity to justify its existence. Even a small amount of agency-type security funding can accomplish this task, much like requiring banks to obtain part of their capital by subordinate debt issues on a periodic basis. Third, the PSS system's uses of funds will become more market sensitive. In the past, the PSS provided funds that were loaned at fixed rates of interest. In the new PSS, funds will be allocated to assets with rates determined by the market. This may make it more difficult than in the past to offer the type of time-deposits that have been so important in sustaining the growth of the PSS. Fourth, and most important, the separation of the PSS from the FILP sets the stage for a more conducive political economy environment to encourage further reform of both the PSS and the FILP. The combined PSS and FILP represented a major economic and political entity in Japan simply because of their size. The institutional interests of each were close because one depended on the other. Separating the two weakens their mutual relationship and provides an opportunity to evaluate each; moreover, once divided, each provides less inertia for reform.

At this point, it is difficult to project the outcome of the reform process initiated in 1998. There is more than enough evidence to support the cynical view that nothing has changed in essence; however, the reforms do have the potential for fundamental change in the FILP system. The reforms, however, have left unsettled the future of the PSS. As of early 2001, the PSS was in some regards a narrow bank, since 80 percent of its assets are to be allocated to government bonds and other safe assets. At the same time, 20 percent of a large base of postal deposits represents a major influence in the financial system that is directly under government control. Even though PSS uses of funds will be more market sensitive than in the past, the allocation of over 232 trillion yen of deposits as of 2000 represents a major force that is simply incompatible with a liberated financial system. The new system perpetuates a framework that provides a ready market for government debt, either to finance the general budget or to finance entities previously dependent on the FILP system.

The PSS continues to represent a major competitive force in the deposit market. Although the PSS may be required to be more market sensitive in pricing the allocation of its funds, other subsidy elements continue to provide an uneven playing field between the PSS and the private banks that will interfere with the liberalization process.

The PSS complicates Japan's deposit-guarantee system and may become a destabilizing element once the complete government deposit guarantee established in late 1995 is removed on 1 April 2003 (Cargill, 2002).

5.8. PRACTICAL AND SECOND-BEST SOLUTIONS

Resolution of the problems of government financial intermediation in Japan must incorporate economic, institutional, and political dimensions because the PSS and the FILP have become embedded in virtually all aspects of Japanese economics and politics. Resolution that does not focus on all three dimensions will be counterproductive. Thus, although an efficiency argument can be made that Japan would be better served by a reduction in government financial intermediation and privatization of the PSS, the argument fails to consider the important institutional and political dimension of government financial intermediation. Government intermediation finance is longstanding and has been an important institutional feature of Japan for over a hundred years; as such, it is resistant to major change over short periods of time. Institutions, either as material manifestations, like a government bank, or as ways of thinking, like dependence on government, must be considered in evaluating any potential reform of the PSS and the FILP. The importance of these institutions not only makes them resistant to major adjustment but at the same time increases their political support. Ultimately, political institutions must formulate and execute financial reform.

There is an even more fundamental reason why the reform of government financial intermediation needs to proceed in an evolutionary manner consistent with its past role in Japanese finance, history, and culture. The system is so large that any major adjustment would generate significant and uncertain effects. Japan faces many problems in the next few decades, such as a rapidly aging population, declining population growth, and increasing levels of debt relative to GDP. In this context, prudence suggests a less-than-revolutionary resolution of the problems of government financial intermediation.

With this in mind, we offer suggestions for a practical or second-best resolution of the various problems identified in this book. The suggestions represent a middle ground between the ideal market-oriented reform and a continuation of the status quo.

5.8.1. *Government Banks and Enterprises*

Each government bank and enterprise should be evaluated in terms of a cost–benefit framework with methods commonly employed to evaluate public projects. This evaluation must incorporate consistent and market-oriented accounting procedures to generate realistic financial statements. Both cost–benefit and financial statements need to be made public and generated with the objective of transparency. A process was being developed for fiscal 2000 to disclose the future taxpayer burden of funds provided to selected government entities. In addition, the requirement that some entities previously funded by the FILP raise funds in the capital market based on their own assets provides further transparency regarding their economic basis.

The outcome of this evaluation and of a more transparent presentation of the activities of each government bank and enterprise should provide a basis for further institutional reform that places each entity into one of three categories: the entity should be abolished; the entity should raise a significant part of its funding in the capital market; or the functions of the entity should be supported in a different manner.

The most difficult decision is the elimination of an entity and its function. However, cost–benefit evaluation may suggest that there is insufficient justification for the continued operation of certain specific government banks or enterprises. This decision would set into motion a timetable and discussion to terminate an agency's activities and to release its resources to the private sector. On the other hand, the evaluation may suggest that sufficient market failure exists to justify government support of the activities of a specific bank or enterprise. In this case, these entities would issue their own agency securities, but even without a government guarantee they would receive a subsidy much as agency securities do in the United States. The subsidy in the form of lower interest than equivalent private debt exists because the issuing entity is part of the government, and unlike most private enterprises, can resort to the government to avoid defaulting on its debt. Those entities that cannot raise a major part of their funding in the capital market should be targeted for further reform. Although it would be convenient simply to allow them to participate in FILP bond issues by the Ministry of Finance, the fact that they cannot raise capital on their own provides important market-feedback as to the desirability of their continued operation. In this case, alternative forms of government support may be more efficient, such as using tax credits to support specific activities.

The intent of the evaluation and cost–benefit analysis is to require self-funding with government sponsorship except in clear cases where dependence on government bonds is justified. Resort to FILP-bond finance, however, should not be automatic, and the inability to rely on agency securities should initiate policy discussions as to alternative methods of supporting the specific activity. Again, this process needs to be transparent in the hope of constraining the political log-rolling that is sure to accompany any such evaluation. Even if such a process is adopted, it would be difficult to carry it out politically and would take several years at best. This can be accomplished, however. Japan has already reached a turning point with respect to bank failures and has accepted the fact that the "convoy" system is no longer operable. The same attitudinal change can occur with respect to government banks and enterprises, though this will be more difficult since regulatory authorities had no choice but to accept bank failures during the 1990s. The FILP entities are not in a short-term crisis situation, so there is no sense of urgency to reform these institutions.

5.8.2. *PSS*

The first step is to make the PSS a separate agency independent of the post office and the Ministry of Public Management, Home Affairs, Posts, and Telecommunications (formerly the Ministry of Posts and Telecommunications). Oversight responsibility could be assigned to the Financial Services Agency, which became operational in the first part of 2001 and is the result of a merger of the Financial Supervisory Agency and the Financial Reconstruction Commission. Instead of permitting the PSS discretion in the allocation of funds, the government should require that postal deposits be invested only in government bonds, thus making it difficult for the PSS to offer deposits significantly more competitive than those offered by private banks. Thus, this proposal separates the postal-deposit function from the Ministry and transforms it into a narrow government bank. The new agency will be required to reimburse the postal system for office space and related expenses, since the existing post-office branch network will still be utilized. The enabling legislation needs to make it clear that under no circumstance is the new agency permitted to function as anything but a narrow bank. The new agency, however, will have the authority to contract with private banks, securities companies, insurance companies, and other financial institutions to offer financial products on their behalf to depositors. These activities will not result in changes in the agency's balance sheet but will generate revenue based on the fees charged for serving as a representative of the private entities. In this way, the benefits of the post-office network of branches can be utilized to bring an improved mix of financial products to all areas of Japan. In this regard, the PSS should be required to provide information on urban versus rural costs of operation, which at the time of this writing has not been available. This information is needed to help policymakers understand the cost of providing postal deposits, postal life insurance, and postal services throughout Japan.

The second and more difficult step is the ultimate privatization of the PSS. The narrow-bank proposal is only a transition stage. A large postal-savings system is inconsistent with financial liberalization and, irrespective of what provisions are in place, the PSS has the potential to adversely influence the financial system, especially during periods of financial distress. The government can easily offer substitutes for postal deposits in the form of government savings bonds and bonds with put options. Even if the government decides to privatize the PSS, many complex issues need to be settled. For example, how will services be provided to some rural areas that clearly require a cost of operation higher than any private entity would undertake? Or how will the deposits of the PSS be distributed to ensure that they have no adverse impact on the competitive structure of private financial institutions?

The life-insurance function of the PSS should also be privatized, with policies sold at auction to the private sector within the near future. Postal life insurance accounts for about 30 percent of the Japanese life-insurance market. This large share restrains competition and limits the economies of scale that private insurance companies can achieve by combining life insurance with other insurance and financial services.

5.9. **KOIZUMI, PRIVATIZATION OF THE PSS, AND REFORM OF FILP**

The dynamics of PSS reform changed in April 2001 when Junichiro Koizumi won an unexpected victory over former Prime Minister Hashimoto at the local level to replace the unpopular Prime Minister Mori. At the time Prime Minister Mori resigned, he had a 6-percent approval rating. Prime Minister Koizumi assumed the leadership role with one of the highest approval ratings in postwar Japan (80 percent). His popularity was reaffirmed in the July 2001 elections for the Upper House of Representatives, where the LDP won a clear majority. Koizumi, although he comes from the ranks of the traditional LDP, has shown a willingness to advocate far more radical policies than has the status quo LDP in dealing with Japan's decade-long economic malaise. In particular, he has advocated the privatization of the PSS. This is the first time a major political figure has openly criticized the PSS—and, by implication, the entities that relied on postal and life-insurance deposits—and called for privatization. If successful, privatization would represent the most significant structural change in Japan's financial system since the early 1950s.

In June 2000, Koizumi formed a Council to Reform the Postal Business, whose task was to make recommendations on the future of postal deposits, postal life insurance, and postal services. The Council was chaired by Naoki Tanaka (21st Century Research Institute) and includes as members Keimei Wakasugi (University of Tokyo), Kazuhito Ikeo (Keio University), Yuri Okina (Japan Research Institute), and Kazuharu Kiyono (Waseda University). The Council report released September 2002 covered postal services, postal deposits, and postal life insurance issues. While reviewing a number of issues and outlining possible reforms, the Council's report had little impact on the reform effort and as of late 2002, the PSS and FILP will not be reformed beyond what had already taken place.

The consensus for reform of the PSS and FILP was formed in the late 1990s, and the 1998 reform set into motion a process that has the potential to achieve important changes; however, the process lacked strong political support. The political support provided by Koizumi was a positive turn of events and increases the probability that Japan may be in a position to reduce the role of government financial intermediation.

The willingness of Koizumi to confront the problems of government financial intermediation were revealed in a 27 November 2001 announcement by Minister Nobuteru Ishihara, who was appointed by Koizumi as a special cabinet Minister of Government Reform, shortly after becoming Prime Minister. Ishihara announced his first set of recommendations regarding FILP on 27 November 2001, which were endorsed by Koizumi. The recommendations are subject to approval of the Diet, which will start debating the recommendations in December 2001. The recommendations represent a significant change in the structure of government financial intermediation.

Seven government agencies (Japan Highway Corporation, Metropolitan Expressway Public Corporation, Hanshin Expressway Public Corporation, Honshu-Shikoku Bridge Authority, Government Housing Loan Corporation, Urban Development Corporation, Japan National Oil Corporation) were the focus of the 27 November 2001 report. These agencies represent a large part of the FILP budget.

The announcement called for the abolishment of the first four listed agencies: The Japan Highway Corporation, Metropolitan Expressway Public Corporation, Hanshin Expressway Public Corporation, and the Honshu-Shikoku Bridge Authority. The agencies would be replaced by a transitional agency charged with the objective of privatizing the agency's functions where possible. In addition, the budgets of each agency should be restricted in the transitional phase and the functions of each agency should be financed by a more rational foundation than to date. A five-year timetable is implied.

The announcement also recommended the abolishment of the Government Housing Loan Corporation within five years. Lending should be immediately reduced in an incremental manner to zero in five years. A new agency should be established charged with establishing a secondary mortgage market. It is unclear whether the new agency would be private or public, but most likely, the agency would be a government sponsored private agency. The new agency might also continue to make direct loans; however, this depends on whether private banks become more active in making mortgage loans.

The Urban Development Corporation should be abolished by fiscal 2005 and immediately prohibited from purchasing new land and/or building new government housing. Existing government property will remain with the government, but rental servicing will be placed in the private sector. A new agency should be established to encourage private sector involvement in urban development.

The Japan National Oil Corporation, which provides funds for oil development overseas, should be abolished. The government should continue to subsidise oil exploration, but at less than 50 percent of Japan National Oil Corporation levels and not through government banks, but funded through the budget of the central government.

These are bold recommendations. If enacted, they would not only affect a significant part of the FILP system, but more important, set a precedent for further reform of the FILP system and ultimately, the PSS. Unfortunately, Japan was again in recession in late 2001 making it politically difficult to make fundamental reforms in a set of institutions, which many argue have provided stability in the past.

The announcements by Koizumi to privatize and reform parts of the FILP system have restricted development of the agency security market. As of late 2002, there is no secondary market and the spread between government bonds and agency bonds has widened somewhat due to uncertainty over the future of the FILP system, especially the Government Housing Loan Corporation. The agency–government security differential ranges from 20 to 100 basis points.

As of late 2002, Koizumi had not achieved the announced reforms of the PSS and FILP. There is no serious discussion to privatize the PSS and the overwhelming majority of FILP entities appear to have little to fear of being shut down or forced to reply on the private capital market for funding. The PSS will become a public corporation 1 April 2003 largely unchanged from the PSS as it existed after the 1 April 2001 institutional changes. This underscores the point made in this study. The PSS and FILP have been, and continue to be, main features of Japan's financial structure and as such, are resistant to change.

5.10. CONCLUDING COMMENT

The PSS and FILP are not compatible with the modern financial system outlined in the 1996 Big Bang proposal. These institutions perpetuate inefficiency in the flow of funds and, in the case of postal deposits, complicate efforts to establish a government deposit-guarantee system consistent with a modern financial regulation and supervision framework. This is not to deny any role for government financial intermediation when there are clear cases of market failure. However, the tendency for government intermediation to go far beyond the market-failure level is great, and the more mature the economy, the more the potential for inefficient government intermediation because it becomes more difficult to find clear cases of market failure.

Japan still has a window of opportunity to deal with the PSS and FILP, but time is running out. Continued economic and financial distress as of late 2002 combined with projected demographic changes compound the inefficiencies embedded in the PSS and FILP. Despite Koizumi's popularity, he has been unable to make much progress in reforming the PSS and FILP beyond what was started in 1998. The potential for disintermediation remains high. The government has postponed the removal of the complete deposit guarantee for transaction-type deposits again until 1 April 2003. There was indication that even the 1 April 2003 removal date might not end the complete deposit guarantee on transaction-type deposits. In any event, as the government deposit guarantee is lowered, even if not on all deposits, and deposit insurance becomes the primary safety net, the PSS possess a serious source of instability.

Despite the need for reform, the PSS and FILP will resist change for the simple reason they have considerable economic and political strength and continue to increase that strength. The PSS and FILP may have been justified by past conditions, but they are increasingly at odds with the emerging, new environment. FILP entities need to be required to raise funds in the open money and capital markets without, or with only limited, government guarantees, and the government needs to remove itself from the business of collecting deposits. It is unlikely that the goals of the 1996 Big Bang will be achieved unless the PSS and FILP are reformed and their respective roles in the financial system are either eliminated or reduced.

References

Alexander, Arthur J. (2000). "Where Will Japan's Maturing Postal Savings Go?" *Japan Economic Institute Report (Part A and B)*, 14 April.

Anderson, Stephen J. (1990). "The Political Economy of Japanese Saving: How Postal Savings and Public Pensions Support High Rates of Household Savings in Japan." *Journal of Japanese Studies* **16**: 61–92.

Blomstrom, Magnus, Bryon Ganges, and Sumner La Croix (2001). *Japan's New Economy*. Oxford, England: Oxford University Press.

Borio, C. E. V., N. Kennedy, and S. D. Prowse (1994). "Exploring Aggregate Asset Price Fluctuations Across Countries." *BIS Economic Papers*, No. 40 (April).

Calder, Kent E. (1990). "Linking Welfare and the Developmental State: Postal Savings in Japan." *Journal of Japanese Studies* **16**: 31–59.

Cargill, Thomas F. (1986). "Japanese Monetary Policy, Flow of Funds and Domestic Financial Liberalization." *Economic Review* (Federal Reserve Bank of San Francisco) (Summer): 21–32.

—— (1990). "Financial Reform, Inflation, and Monetary Policy in Japan: Lessons for U.S. Policy." In Joint Economic Committee of the U.S. Congress, 101st Cong., 2nd Sess., *Japan's Economic Challenge*. Washington, DC: US Government Printing Office.

—— (1993). "Deposit Guarantees, Nonperforming Loans, and the Postal Savings System in Japan." *FDICIA: An Appraisal*. Chicago: Federal Reserve Bank of Chicago.

—— (1999). "Korea and Japan: The End of the 'Japanese Financial Regime.'" In G. Kaufman, ed., *Bank Crisis, Causes, Analysis and Prevention*. Stamford, CT: JAI Press.

—— (2001). "Monetary Policy, Deflation, and Economic History: Lessons for the Bank of Japan." In *Monetary and Economic Studies* (Bank of Japan). (February): 113–134.

—— (2002). "Japan Passes Again on Fundamental Financial Reform." *FRBSF Economic Letter*, Federal Reserve Bank of San Francisco, Number 2002-28, September 27.

—— and Michael M. Hutchison (1988). "The Bank of Japan's Response to Macroeconomic and Financial Change." In H. Cheng, ed., *Monetary Policy in Pacific Basin Countries*. Boston: Kluwer Academic Publishers.

—— and Naoyuki Yoshino (2001). "Modernising Japan's postal savings system." *The Financial Regulator* **6** (June): 42–47.

——, ——, and Takatoshi Ito (1996). "Deposit Guarantees in Japan: Aftermath of the Bubble and Burst of the Bubble Economy." *Contemporary Economic Policy* **14**: 41–52.

——, ——, and —— (1997). *Political Economy of Japanese Monetary Policy*. Cambridge, MA: MIT Press.

——, —— and —— (1998). "The Bank Crisis in Japan." In Gerard Caprio Jr., William C. Hunter, George G. Kaufman, and Danny M. Leipziger, eds, *Preventing Bank Crises: Lessons from Recent Global Bank Failures*. Washington, DC: World Bank.

——, ——, and —— (2000). *Financial Policy and Central Banking in Japan*. Cambridge, MA: MIT Press.

—— and Shoichi Royama (1988). *The Transition of Finance in Japan and the United States: A Comparative Perspective*. Stanford, CA: Hoover Institution Press.

Cargill, Thomas F. and Shoichi Royama (1992). "The Evolution of Japanese Banking and Finance." In George G. Kaufman, ed., *Banking Structures in Major Countries*. Boston: Kluwer Academic Publishers.

—— and Naoyuki Yoshino (1998). "Too Big for Its Boots." *The Financial Regulator* **3**: 39–42.

——, ——, (2000). "The Postal Savings System, Fiscal Investment and Loan Program, and the Modernization of Japan's Financial System." In Takeo Hoshi and Hugh Patrick, eds, *The Japanese Financial System: Restructuring for the Future*. Boston: Kluwer Academic Publishers.

——, ——, (2001). "Modernising Japan's Postal Savings System." *The Financial Regulator* 6:42–47.

Chadha, B., M. Lutz, G. Lipworth, D. Mihaljek, K. Okamura, R. Wescott, and E. Prasad (1996). "IMF Staff Country Report No. 96/114, October 1960." In International Monetary Fund, *Japan—Selected Issues*. Washington, DC: International Monetary Fund.

Doi, Takero and Takeo Hoshi (2002). "Pay for the FILP." Forthcoming in *Structural Impediments to Growth in Japan*. Magnus Blomstrom, Jennifer Corbett, Fumio Hayashi, and Anil Kashyap (eds). Chicago: University of Chicago Press.

Durbin, J. and G. Watson (1971). "Testing for Serial Correlation in Least Squares Regression—III." *Biometrika* 58: 1–42.

Economist (1997). "Banking in Emerging Markets" 12 April.

—— (1998). "Japan's Other Debt Crisis." 12 December.

Elixman, Dieter (1992). "Current Status of Postal Banking: The Case of Europe." Presented at the Korea Information Society Development Institute Conference (June).

Feldman, Robert Alan (1986). *Japanese Financial Markets: Deficits, Dilemmas, and Deregulation*. Cambridge, MA: MIT Press.

—— (1996). "The Golden Goose and the Silver Fox." *Japanese Economic/Market Analysis*. Tokyo: Salomon Brothers, 12 June.

Hoshi, Takeo and Anil Kashyap (2001). *Corporate Financing and Governance in Japan*. Cambridge, MA: The MIT Press.

—— and Hugh Patrick, eds (2000). *The Japanese Financial System: Restructuring for the Future*. Boston: Kluwer Academic Publishers.

Hutchison, Michael M. and Kathleen McDill (1999). "Are All Banking Crises Alike? The Japanese Experience in International Perspective." *Journal of the Japanese and International Economies* (December).

Kamada, Koichiro (1993). "The Real Value of Postal Savings Certificates." *Monetary and Economic Studies* (Bank of Japan) 11 (November): 59–96.

Kanabayashi, Masayoshi (1997). "Postal Savings May Prove Popular Throughout Asia." *Wall Street Journal*, 18 April, B7B.

Kuwayama, Patricia (2000). "Postal Banking in the United States and Japan: A Comparative Analysis." *Monetary and Economic Studies* (Bank of Japan) **18**: 73–104.

Lee, Chung H. (1992). "The Government, Financial System, and Large Private Enterprises in the Economic Development of South Korea." *World Development* 20 (1992): 187–97.

Lincoln, Edward J. (2001). *Arthritic Japan: Explaining the Slow Pace of Economic Reform*. Washington, DC: Brookings Institution Press.

Lindgren, Carl-Johan, Gillian Garcia, and Matthew I. Saal (1996). *Bank Soundness and Macroeconomic Policy*. Washington, DC: International Monetary Fund.

Mikitani, Ryoichi and Adam S. Posen, eds (2000). *Japan's Financial Crisis and Its Parallels to U.S. Experience*. Washington, DC: Institute for International Economics.

Ministry of Finance, Financial Bureau. *FILP Report 2000*.

Nakajima, Zenta and Hiroo Taguchi (1995). "Toward a More Stable Financial Framework: Long-Term Alternatives—An Overview of Recent Bank Disruption World Wide." In Kuniho Sawamoto, Zenta Nakajima, and Hiroo Taguchi eds, *Financial Stability in a Changing Environment*. New York: St. Martin's Press.

Nakata, Masao (2001). "Changes in the Inducement Effect of Investment by Government Financial Institutions." Paper presented at the Japan Finance Association, Tokyo, Spring (in Japanese).

Ogura, Seiritso and Naoyuki Yoshino (1988). "Tax System and the Fiscal Investment and Loan Program." In R. Komiya, M. Okuno, and K. Suzumura, eds, *Industrial Policy of Japan*. New York: Academic Press.

O'Hara, Maureen and David Easley (1979). "The Postal Savings System in the Depression." *Journal of Economic History* **34**(3): 741–753.

Okina, Yuri (2000). "Recent Developments Surrounding Japan's Postal Savings Business and Its Future Position in the Financial System." *Japan Research Review* (July) (in Japanese).

Patrick, Hugh T. (1967). "Japan 1868–1914." In Rondo Cameron, ed., *Banking in the Early Stages of Industrialization: A Study in Comparative Economic History*. New York: Oxford University Press.

Rhodes, James R. and Naoyuki Yoshino (1999). "Window Guidance by the Bank of Japan: Was Lending Controller?" *Contemporary Economic Policy* **17** (April): 166–176.

Sakakibara, Eisuke (1991). "The Japanese Politico-Economic System and the Public Sector." In Samuel Kernell, ed., *Parallel Politics*. Washington, DC: Brookings Institution Press.

Strom, Stephanie (1997). "Crusader Takes On the Postal Piggy Bank." *New York Times*, 18 November 1997.

—— (2001). "In Japan, People's Choice Isn't the Party's." *New York Times*, 23 April, p. A4.

Suzuki, Yoshio (1980). *Money and Banking in Contemporary Japan*. New Haven: Yale University Press.

——, ed. (1987). *The Japanese Financial System*. Oxford: Clarendon Press.

Takayama, Noriyuki (1998). *The Morning After in Japan: Its Declining Population, Too Generous Pensions and a Weakened Economy*. Tokyo: Marauzen Co.

Takeda, Masahiko (1985). "A Theory of Loan Determination in Japan." *Monetary and Economic Studies* (Bank of Japan) **3**: 71–114.

Trust Fund Management Council (1998). *Major Reform of the FILP System*. First summary published November 27, 1997, and full report published June 1998. Tokyo: Trust Fund Management Council (in Japanese).

Ueda, Kazuo (2000). "Causes of the Japanese Banking Instability in the 1990s." In Takeo Hoshi and Hugh Patrick, eds, *The Japanese Financial System: Restructuring for the Future*. Boston: Kluwer Academic Publishers.

United Nations (1993). Domestic Resources Mobilization Through Postal Savings: Experiences of Selected Asian Countries. New York: United Nations.

Wada, Ryoko (2000). "Panel Data Analysis of Japan's Households' Asset Allocation." In K. Matsuura, Y. Yoshino, and Y. Yonezawa eds, *Changing Financial Market*. Tokyo: Nihon Hyoron-sha (in Japanese). Ms. Ryoko Wada was previously Ryoko Sano in Yoshino and Sano (1997).

Yoshino, Naoyuki (1987). "Sources of Fiscal Investment and Loan Program and Its Impact on the Financial Market." In Shiro Yabushita and Kazumi Asako, eds, *The Japanese Economy and Fiscal Policy*. Tokyo: Toyo Keizai Publishing (in Japanese).

—— (1993). "The Role of Post Office Savings and the Fiscal Investment and Loan Program of Japan." In *Domestic Resources Mobilization Through Postal Savings: Experiences of Selected Asian Countries*. New York: United Nations.

Yoshino, Naoyuki (1996). "The Historic Role of Policy-Oriented Financing in Japan's Economic Development, as it Relates to the Current Issues within Transitional Economics." EXIM Japan Symposium 1996 Report. The Export–Import Bank of Japan (in Japanese).

—— (1998). "Various Tools of Housing Support Program by the Government." *House and Loan Monthly Magazine* (Government Housing Loan Corporation) No. 557 (June): 22–25 (in Japanese).

—— and Masao Nakata (1997). "Effect of FILP Lending to Promote Investment." Paper presented at the Nippon Finance Gakkai, Tokyo, in 1997. Keio Economic Society Discussion Paper, No. 9901 (in Japanese).

——, ——, Ryoko Sano, and Thomas F. Cargill (2001). "The Role of FILP in Promoting Investment." Keio Economic Society Discussion Paper Series No. 20–2 (in Japanese).

——, and Ryoko Sano (1997). "Panel Data Analysis of Japan's Households' Financial Assets." Presented at Kinyu Gakkai (Finance Association of Japan), Hokkaido, 1997. In Matsura, Yoshino, and Shijyo, eds, *Henkakuki no Kinyu-Shiho Shijyo* (Changing Period of Financial Market) (in Japanese).

——, and Seiji Yoshimora (1995). "Changes in the BOJ's Monetary Policy Reaction and Money Supply Control." *Kiryo Keizai Kenkyu* (Journal of the Japan Finance Association), No. 8 (in Japanese).

——, —— (1997). "Changes in the Monetary Policy Instrument and the Money Supply Behavior." In Kazumi Asako, Shin-ichi Fukuda, and Naoyuki Yoshino, eds, *Economic Analysis of Contemporary Macroeconomy: Turning Point of the Japanese Economy*. Tokyo: University of Tokyo Press.

Index